20—

SWEAT OF THE SUN, TEARS OF THE MOON

SWEAT OF THE SUN, TEARS OF THE MOON

◆◆◆◆

A Chronicle of an Incan Treasure

PETER LOURIE

ATHENEUM
NEW YORK 1991
COLLIER MACMILLAN CANADA TORONTO
MAXWELL MACMILLAN INTERNATIONAL
NEW YORK OXFORD SINGAPORE SYDNEY

Special thanks to my grandfather, Franklin Clement, and to Jeannette Haien, Frank MacShane, Stephen Koch, Eric Ashworth, Moritz Thomsen, David Means, Nancy and Bob Stout, Donold Lourie, Steve and Barbara DeClerque, and of course Suzanna and Melissa.

Atheneum
Macmillan Publishing Company
866 Third Avenue, New York, NY 10022

Collier Macmillan Canada, Inc.
1200 Eglinton Avenue East, Suite 200
Don Mills, Ontario M3C 3N1

Library of Congress Cataloging-in-Publication Data
Lourie, Peter.
   Sweat of the sun, tears of the moon : a chronicle of an Incan treasure / Peter Lourie.
      p.   cm.
   ISBN 0-689-12111-3
      1. Treasure-trove—Ecuador. 2. Incas. I. Title.
G525.L86   1991
986.6—dc20   90-48963   CIP

Macmillan books are available at special discounts for bulk purchases for sales promotions, premiums, fund-raising, or educational use. For details, contact:
Special Sales Director
Macmillan Publishing Company
866 Third Avenue
New York, NY 10022

10 9 8 7 6 5 4 3 2 1

PRINTED IN THE UNITED STATES OF AMERICA

IN MEMORY OF EUGENE BRUNNER

CONTENTS

◆◆◆◆◆

PART ONE

◆◆◆◆◆

SWEAT OF THE SUN

There is no getting away from a treasure that
once fastens upon your mind.

—JOSEPH CONRAD, *Nostromo*

CHAPTER 1

♦♦♦♦♦

In 1982 I journeyed to the Ecuadorian cloud forest where the Incas hid seven hundred tons of gold from the plundering conquistadors. I climbed to the treasure lake in the Llanganati Cordillera in the Andes even when it seemed impossible to touch the gold with my own hands, which were not the same hands as those of the treasure hunters I came to know over the years—men who never doubt they will be the first to fondle that ancient metal.

Yet I'm certain the gold is still there in those bewitching mountains, and someone will soon discover it. The history convinces me, the treasure hunters themselves convinced me, and I want to believe. I yearn for the mystery of this treasure tale.

Perhaps the Inca hoard lies buried beneath tons of rock under the lake, as the great treasure hunter, Brunner, told me before he died—an artificial lake pinpointed at 14,500 feet on his topographic map—the very lake on which I camped in the fog and endless cold for days of freezing rain. Yet I myself stood on the brink of that Inca lake and learned that gold is also a longing in the heart. This story is my treasure.

♦♦♦

I first came to Ecuador to study monkeys. Having worked one high school summer in East Africa with a primatologist in Tanzania and then with the Leakeys in Kenya, for years I had dreamed of becoming a physical anthropologist. Someday I hoped to find a treasure of prehistoric bones or travel to unexplored jungles in search of new species.

A primate specialist at Harvard told me that Ecuador and Paraguay had never even been surveyed. He suggested I focus on one of these two "virgin" countries—to make a preliminary survey of monkeys before entering graduate school. I could establish an academic focus while seeing parts of the Amazon rain forest few scientists had ever visited.

So I studied Spanish for a month in Cuernavaca, Mexico, then flew to Quito, Ecuador, 9,500 feet above sea level, the world's second highest capital after La Paz, Bolivia.

In this brilliant mountain city I rented an apartment in an old mansion in the colonial quarter, and made weekly forays into the Amazon basin, east of the Andes. For the entire summer I rode old buses, pickups, dump trucks, and vans along dirt tracks, arriving before dawn or late at night in tiny villages where I slept in a hammock with a mosquito net in the back room of some *cantina*. The next day, bleary-eyed and deflated from humidity and lack of sleep, I would hire a guide to take me into the jungle to find monkeys.

But primates are difficult to see in the rain forest.

Incredibly, my Indian guides could smell monkeys from a long way off, and with their hunter-sensitive ears, they could hear the chatter of distant troops, when I could hear nothing but the sound of my own loud breathing. "*Vámonos!*" they shouted, and together, lunatics, we'd race through dense bush chasing invisible noises, shadows in high branches.

Weeks passed. My field work in Ecuador grew tedious, and I felt I was failing. I wondered if I would make a good scientist. I never once spotted a night monkey. And generally I grew frustrated; my whole "survey" relied too heavily on information gathered by word of mouth, research requiring no empirical talent. I took data from the Indians, and the missionaries told me what the monkeys looked like, but I saw up close only the few dead squirrel monkeys the Indians had skinned and boiled before we ravenously ate them with plantains, spitting out bones on either side of our hammocks in the tropical darkness of our river camp.

Meanwhile, I'd fallen in love with the country—especially the mountains. Ecuador itself is enchanted, with its florid lowlands, bleak Andean passes, active volcanoes. And I wanted desperately to stay on here, to explore the higher terrain where the nights were cool and I could think clearly in the dry blue air. My Spanish had grown nearly fluent, and I'd made a few good friends, mostly expatriates. But after three months of hard travel with few results, I had to admit this kind of anthropological field work didn't interest me anymore. Yet it was for this very "field work" that I'd decided to become an anthropologist!

Already accepted to graduate school, reluctantly I planned to leave Ecuador. I felt like a man who a month before his wedding realizes he's about to marry the wrong woman but can't bring himself to call it off.

Then I heard the story of Inca treasure; it came along like a windfall, a reprieve, and easily I let myself be snatched from five monkish doctoral years in some university library. I had no girlfriend in the States. I was twenty-seven. It seemed a perfect time not to go home. In a lawless place like Ecuador, a raw magic and a tale of gold drew me into the mountains the way a yarn spinner enchants an audience. So I let go of my Ph.D. plans and fell, however capriciously, under the wonderful spell of treasure hunters.

◆◆◆

It was on a weekend side trip to the coastal city of Guayaquil that I first heard about the lost Inca gold.

It was hot and hazy the day I landed in Ecuador's port city. I'd come down from Quito to meet the father of someone I'd known in high school. I was told he was a real "explorer." Not knowing what an explorer looked like these days, I called from Quito, and Andrés Fernández-Salvador said I could spend the night. So I flew the forty minutes from the cool capital to the sweltering Pacific coast.

In the back yard of a single-story, modern brick ranch house in the wealthy suburb of Urdesa, Andrés was running wind sprints by his pool. A vital man in his fifties, he had the toned, cared-for physique of a thirty-year-old athlete. His hair was cropped Marine-style, his face vigorous, sturdy, and competent-looking. He looked like a man you could trust. Yet when he stopped running, and laughed the moment he saw me, it was with such force that his laughter suggested a certain feverish quality. He was breathing heavily, his hands on his thighs, his back bent, and his eyes on the grass when he asked gruffly in English, "So, do you want a beer?"

"Thank you," I said. "Sure is hot."

A laugh shot from Andy's mouth like a bullet. "Such is life in the tropics," he said, a favorite expression he would deliver often in later conversations.

We sat on the terrace by the pool and talked under the open haze of the sun. A young sienna-skinned Indian boy with hesitant eyes brought cold beer. Andy began speaking of his love for the tropics, and I had a feeling he had come down off the Andes to escape something. For he told me he grew up in the sierra, and came from a very pure Spanish family in Riobamba, but he'd spent much of his youth on his father's cattle ranch in the Oriente, Ecuador's Amazon region. It was there that he'd fallen in love with the jungle.

"I love jungles. How about you?" he said, his eyes half closed from the sweat running off his forehead.

"Not much," I replied. "I get lazy in the heat."

"Most people do." Watching the timid boy slowly pour our

beer, Andy said too loudly, "But I love all jungles, low and high, and I love it here on the coast because the people are *tranquilo*."

I immediately decided I liked Andy. He was exuberant in spite of the heat.

Later that evening, however, after we'd gotten to know each other better, whenever Andy spoke of the Andes, its sad people, plaintive guitars and flutes, his eyes grew hard. The pace of his words quickened, and I could tell he was yearning for something from the past.

When he first mentioned gold in the sierra his eyes flamed.

"You don't know the story of the Inca treasure?"

"No, I don't," I said.

Andy jumped up, said in a raspy voice, "Just a minute." And disappeared.

When he came back into the living room, holding a document in his hands, he explained it was a two-hundred-page transcript telling what he knew about the treasure. Someone who'd wanted him to write a book had recorded his story. A strange smile ran across his face as he handed the book to me.

"We need something a little stronger, I think." Andy opened a bottle of scotch and poured two glasses.

"I'm not really a scotch drinker," I said, but when Andy scowled I quickly said, "except in the tropics."

"That manuscript might interest you," he said, leaning back into his chair and sipping whiskey. "Someday when I get more time, I'll use this to write a treasure book. That gold is up there, all right."

He pointed to the manuscript resting on my lap. "What a story that will make, Peter. What a story, indeed."

I could hardly wait to open his "book," but he talked until dawn. So it was much later, in his guest room, that I raced through those pages, until, at ten A.M., I started rereading slowly the entire text.

I couldn't sleep. I wondered why he hadn't completed his

manuscript, or published it the way it was, filled with stories about his difficult journeys into an uninhabited, mountainous cloud forest where the great Inca treasure of Quito had been hidden in 1534. Later I found out that he planned to publish his material only after he'd taken the gold out.

That day, at lunch, the more Andy spoke, the more I needed to hear about the mountains themselves, what they looked like, and how it felt to be lost in them for weeks in the fog.

"Ecuadorians believe they're bewitched," Andy told me. "So many men have gone crazy looking for Atahualpa's hoard in the Llanganati Mountains."

"Atahualpa? Llanganati?" Exotic names, I thought. Indian names.

"Yes, Peter, the history is long, but history is crucial to my story . . . so, if you don't like history . . ."

"Please, I want to hear it all, from the beginning," I said.

Andy looked pleased. "Okay," he said. "Atahualpa was the Inca King. This treasure would have been his ransom money, but one of his generals hid the gold in the Llanganati Cordillera when Pizarro murdered the King. The Llanganati is a wild chain of mountains between the Amazon and the higher peaks of the Andes. No one lives there. No one can live there for long. A perfect place for a treasure. I've searched for thirty years in those horrible mountains."

Andy's eyes fixed on the aquamarine glaze of the pool. He seemed to shake off a slight stupor as he turned to look at me.

"But the treasure's still out there!" Andy shook his fist in the air; his face wrinkled as he smiled. "And I'm going to be the first to find it."

It was then, in the extreme need of his voice, in the convincing phrase "first to find it," that I knew, in one of those instant yet precise and absolute changes of heart, that I could not return to the States, as I had planned to do that very week, to enter graduate school in anthropology. Hearing Andy's story made me wish only to join him in his quest, to fling all previous intentions to the wind. Uncertain how I'd earn a living if I stayed in Ecuador, nevertheless I decided to remain here at all costs—to hear the whole of Andy's tale, to meet other treasure hunters, to delve into this beguiling story about gold and silver, the precious metals of the Incas.

I canceled my flight to Quito and stayed a whole week in Guayaquil. Finally I'd found a reason not to go home.

That night, when I sat down to write the university to tell them I would not matriculate in the fall, I thought only that I was doing the right thing. I wrote terse sentences boldly on the page. But when I had finished the letter and placed it irretrievably in the mail, I began to wonder what had come over me. Could I really survive here? Get a work visa? Keep my apartment in Quito? What was I doing? Was this a sensible substitute for anthropology? Or an illusion of some sort? And what made me so hungry to hear this particular story? Did I really think I could make a good treasure hunter? Or become so rich I could even buy a jet to fly home to New York?

◆◆◆

The next morning I drove with Andy in his Chevrolet pickup the two hours inland to his cattle ranch. The road was dusty, the sky a platinum haze. Ecuador's port was having one of its perennial droughts and the heat shimmered mirage-like off dilapidated wood shacks, rows of matchboxes with corrugated iron roofs. The bleached hills in the distance were bald and brittle as sandstone. A few scraggly trees stuck out of the earth like bent wire. It must have been 110 degrees outside, and just looking at it made me wish I were back in the open-lunged, cool Andes of Quito.

Cars were expensive in Ecuador because of the huge taxes on imports; Andy said his Chevrolet was worth about twenty thousand dollars. But money was not a problem for him; his father, years ago, had founded Güitig, Ecuador's only successful mineral water company. Andy now ran the business on the coast.

He talked a lot that morning; I asked so many questions. His face was striated like weathered rock. Around his eyes and mouth, the deep lines moved as he spoke.

"I don't want the money, Peter."

I asked, "Is that really true?"

"I have to unravel a mystery. Do you understand? A mystery no one else can solve." Andy spoke English with the slightest Spanish accent. He'd been educated in the States.

"It is the greatest treasure in the New World. More than seven hundred tons of worked Inca gold and silver. My life is devoted to the search."

"But what do the Llanganatis look like?" I asked, gazing out at the scorched hills beyond the Guayaquil floodplain.

Andy struck back at my question with a certain vindictiveness, an oddly gruff timbre to his voice, and I wondered if I'd opened some old wound.

"Fog. Snow. You can't imagine how difficult that terrain is. Jungle at such an elevation, my God. Not normal jungle like we have around here; but a tangle of stunted mountain vegetation. . . . I'm close, very close to taking this treasure out of there. Like a jaguar, I move around the gold waiting for the right moment to strike."

The pickup raced through the heat, our cabin air-conditioned, removed from the slums around us. The cool air from the large vents gave the parched outside world a fake appearance, like an Arabian desert movie set. The only people out on the burning pavement moved phlegmatically on the street, Coca-Cola bottles in their hands. We passed a mangy dog lurking in the shade of a slat hut. We went by so fast, I wasn't even sure I'd seen him.

Andy talked briskly, unraveling the history of the treasure, weaving his own tapestry of fact and experience, as if, should he stop for a moment to discuss something other than the gold, all would be lost. And my ears drank in the history as I had once consumed books about Leakey's work at Olduvai Gorge.

◆◆◆

"The treasure was assembled as a King's ransom," began Andy.

Atahualpa was the Lord Inca when Pizarro conquered the empire in 1532. Atahualpa's great-great-grandfather had prophesied that white men with beards would someday come to destroy the Inca empire.

A sixteenth-century historian wrote about the state of Inca society before Pizarro attacked: "A curious, mysterious fear had seized upon all Peru, when one unusually bright night the new moon appeared with a halo of three large rings; the first one was the colour of blood, the second a greenish black, and the third seemed to be made of smoke."

On his deathbed Atahualpa's father, Inca Huayna Capac, asked his son to bury his heart in his beloved Quito, the northern capital of his realm, and to carry his body to the royal tombs in Cuzco, the official Inca capital farther south. He decreed that his favorite son Atahualpa should rule the province of Quito. And before he died he reconfirmed the prophecy that after the twelfth Inca King, the empire would fall. He himself was the twelfth King.

When Pizarro landed on the coast of Ecuador for the first time in 1527, Huayna Capac died of smallpox. The disease may have spread from Spanish colonies already established in Central America. Thousands of Indians were dying.

About the death of the last great Inca King at the height of his empire's greatness, the historian Garcilaso de la Vega, part Inca himself, wrote:

The mourning for Huayna Capac's death was such that the lamentations and shrieks rose to the skies, causing the birds to fall to the ground. In Quito it is said they wept for him for a whole moon, and his body was escorted to Cuzco by many chieftains, the roads lined with men and women weeping and shrieking.

Thousands of wives, pages, and servants sacrificed themselves to lie in his tomb with him.

If the Sun God ever called for him, the dead Inca ruler would return to earth. Living again, he would need his earthly possessions, so all the treasure the Inca ruler had amassed in his lifetime was buried with him against his return.

When Pizarro returned to Peru a second time in 1532, many coastal villages had vanished, made into ghost towns from the spreading smallpox. Atahualpa, the new King, heard of the arriving bearded white men and knew they were the invaders of the prophecy.

◆◆◆

If an alien smallpox had begun to weaken the empire, five years of civil war had all but destroyed it from within, even before Pizarro conquered it.

Huayna Capac had many sons by many wives, but he loved Atahualpa best, for this son had accompanied his father on numerous military campaigns in the north. Before Huayna Capac died he gave Atahualpa the northern province with its provincial capital in Quito, while the rightful heir to the kingdom, Huáscar (Atahualpa's half-brother), would rule the Cuzco area to the south. The generals of the Inca army, which had spent recent years conquering tribes in the north, also favored Atahualpa, with whom they'd fought side by side. So the empire began to divide between northern and southern rulers. According to the conquistador and Spanish chronicler Pedro de Cieza de León, Huáscar was clement and pious while his brother was ruthless and vengeful: "Atahualpa was a man of greater determination and endeavor"; he "made up his mind to rule, and to accomplish this, he broke the law which the Incas had established in this matter which was that only the eldest son of the Inca . . . could be Lord Inca."

Alerted to a growing insurrection in the north, Huáscar sent Atoc, his finest general, with forty thousand men, to supress the rebel forces.

Atahualpa moved south to meet Huáscar's army. Near Ambato, just west of the Llanganati Mountains, Atahualpa's men captured and killed Atoc and made a drinking cup out of his skull. A conquistador later described the skull, with its dried skin and hair. The closed teeth held a silver spout. A golden bowl was fixed to the top of the head, and the *chicha* (a fermented corn drink) was poured into the bowl and ran down through the silver tube into the mouth of the drinker.

With his victory at Ambato, Atahualpa's army moved south toward Ecuador's town of Cuenca in the sierra. Here the rebel half-brother assumed the royal fringe and title of Lord Inca, in a ceremony traditionally held only in Cuzco.

Atahualpa left Rumiñahui—a trusted officer and also a half-brother ("Remember this name, Peter," said Andy. "A very important figure in my story.")—in charge of the northern province of Quito while he himself proceeded to the famous hot springs in Cajamarca in modern-day Peru to celebrate his victory.

Assured of taking Cuzco now, Atahualpa, who had heard of Pizarro's recent landing on the coast, was not at all worried about the newcomers. This was, after all, the greatest civilization the Andes had ever known, a civilization which had blossomed only ninety years before and which now stretched 3,250 miles from present-day Chile to Colombia.

Atahualpa was aware of the progress of white strangers inland, but they were fewer than two hundred men and so he let them come while his spies kept him posted about their every move.

◆◆◆

"Are you following all this?" Andy asked.

I said, "I think so." But it wasn't until weeks later, after hearing the history told many times and after studying all the books, that I memorized the facts, which gave the mystery the resonance of legitimacy.

I remember wanting to take notes as Andy spoke, but it would have been a useless endeavor because the history came in torrents, and I let it rain on me until even my bones got drenched.

One hundred and seventy Spaniards looked down from the mountains to the flat valley of Cajamarca. After their long trek from the sea, the town below must have been a fantastic sight. The houses in the village were sun-hardened clay with thatched roofs, and across the valley Atahualpa's victorious army, eighty thousand strong, stretched out in tents.

"That must have been a beautiful thing to see," said Andy, shaking his head in awe.

The Europeans descended on Friday, November 15, 1532, into the town of Cajamarca. A small party of Spaniards then rode into the hills to the hot springs, where the Inca King was bathing, to invite Atahualpa to a peaceful conference with Pizarro. But Atahualpa delayed.

All night the campfires of the Incan army shimmered like stars on the distant hillside while the Spaniards planned a surprise attack.

(Here Andy broke the flow again to say, "Those brave conquistadors wet their pants with fear waiting that night, outnumbered four hundred to one!")

Next day, the Inca celebrated victory over Cuzco. Late in the afternoon Atahualpa agreed to come to Pizarro. But he wanted to convert the meeting into another display of victorious celebration. With great pomp, with six thousand unarmed warriors, the Inca King entered the square, and, seeing it empty, he yelled out, "Where are they?" At which point a Spanish friar emerged from a nearby building, advanced through the unarmed Indian troops and, through an interpreter, spoke to the Inca about the Christian religion. He showed the Bible.

The Inca threw the Bible onto the ground. Horrified, the friar retreated screaming. Pizarro, who had watched the exchange from his hiding place, gave the war cry of "Santiago!" And the Spaniards attacked.

After two hours of slaughter, thousands of Indians lay dead. Many had suffocated in the mad rush and panic. A village wall had been knocked over in a wild attempt to escape the flash of Spanish swords.

"That proud Inca so easily captured! And not one Spaniard died! No Indian raised a hand against the Europeans," Andy said, his eyes glistening with pain.

Perhaps due to the confusions of a long civil war, or because of the Inca's own underestimation of the cunning of the intruders, the empire had been conquered at the very moment the new King hoped to unify it under his own command.

Andy, talking rapidly, drove extremely fast. We ripped through endless slums on the periphery of the city, then, finally, out into irrigated fields, pastures dotted with cattle, a few horses.

"Peter, you have to know the history to understand the story of this treasure. Be patient. I'm coming to the best part. About where the gold was hidden. And what a place it is!"

I watched Andy's face as he drove, his thin lips and stony eyes. He seemed in a trance, though he drove well, and I had no desire to make him stop telling his tale. I felt a kind of safe euphoria just listening to him, as we hurdled through the parched world in our air-controlled American truck. "Here," I thought, "this man is a treasure himself," and the few doubts I'd had deciding to stay in Ecuador were quickly buried beneath the layers of his narrative.

But no sooner did I feel secure when suddenly Andy braked hard and we came to a full stop in front of a shack, a few men grouped around a table among many bottles of beer. They sat surveying us.

"Let's have a beer. My throat's so dry," Andy said as he jumped out into the dust and slammed his door. I got out with him but for a moment I was afraid of the men watching us. Two of them looked mean. One leered and then, I thought, scowled at me. I'm sure they were drunk because when they laughed, their laughter burst into the air like birds escaping cages.

Andy and I sat at one of the wood tables away from the men. Andy yelled *"Dos cervezas rápido"* to the owner, who, I hadn't noticed, was sitting in the shade of a nearby palm tree.

When the beer came and Andy kept talking, I couldn't relax. The story of the treasure, the history behind it, this sudden heat after the cool truck, and the men watching us, all made me dizzy. The scene seemed unreal. I was unable to drink; I had no taste for beer.

But then Andy's animation, unfazed by the heat, eclipsed my fear. All the tension in my body focused on the details of the complex story of the Inca's ransom, and the rest of the world vanished. Andy was telling his tale the way a great magician performs. He was in love with embellishment. And I delighted in the performance itself.

"Pizarro and his men imprisoned Atahualpa in the Temple of the Sun, where the Incas had worshiped the highest god of their religion," he went on. With reduced royal pomp, the Inca Emperor continued to rule his empire from captivity. History says even in prison he ate from golden dishes. When he spat, one of his servant women held out her hand. And everything he touched was kept in a special box that later was burned because no mortal was allowed to touch what this divine descendant of the Sun had touched.

"But now the Lord Inca himself was forced to wear the common clothes Pizarro had ordered him to put on."

Noticing that the Spaniards were obsessed with gold and silver, Atahualpa offered, in exchange for his freedom, to fill his prison room with gold up to a mark on the wall as high as he could reach on tiptoe. He offered Pizarro gold jars, pots, tiles, jewelry, sun disks. The room was seventeen by twenty-two feet; the mark was said to reach eight feet from the floor. He claimed also that he would fill a smaller room twice over with silver if Pizarro would let him go free. And he promised to do all this in two months.

Pizarro, of course, agreed and drew up a contract. The Inca then gave orders to couriers sent to all parts of the empire to bring his ransom.

During the next weeks as the treasure began to trickle in, Atahualpa ordered his generals to hold their positions and not attempt a rescue.

Amassing the gold and silver, and transporting it to Cajamarca took time, however, and the Inca only increased the Spaniard's lust for gold by describing the great treasures in the Temples of the Sun in Cuzco and Pachacamac in the desert of northern Peru.

Pizarro dispatched his half-brother, Hernando, to Pachacamac and another small group of men to Cuzco, where the Spaniards did indeed find huge gold artifacts. The Temple in Cuzco, the official Inca capital, was then sacked and destroyed.

By May 1533 the Spaniards had collected 1,326,539 pesos of worked gold. At $350 an ounce this would roughly equal $200 million. Francisco Pizarro alone guarded the ransom, and then he began to melt it all down into ingots. For four months thousands and thousands of tons of Inca objects were fed into the furnaces at Cajamarca.

Although Hernando Pizarro brought some art objects to Spain for the King, on February 30, 1535, Charles V ordered that all the remaining gold and silver from Peru should be melted down in the royal mints of Seville, Toledo, and Segovia. Between Pizarro's Peruvian and the King's Spanish furnaces, not one object of Inca art survived.

The historian William Prescott in 1847 described the objects which were melted down:

These articles consisted of goblets, ewers, salvers, vases of every shape and size, ornaments and utensils for the temples of the royal palaces, tiles and plates for the decoration of the public edifices, curious imitations of different plants and animals. Among the plants, the most beautiful was the Indian corn, in which the golden ear was sheathed in its broad leaves of silver, from which hung a rich tassel of threads of the same precious metal. A fountain was also much admired, which sent up a sparkling jet of gold, while birds and animals of the same material played in the waters at its base. The delicacy of the workmanship of some of these, and the beauty and ingenuity of the design, attracted the admiration of better judges than the rude Conquerors of Peru.

"Peter." Andy, who had been chanting history while gazing at the stream of cars and trucks passing on the road, turned his severe eyes to mine and said:

"You have to understand the Inca mind. The people had no free choice. Only the nobles were educated. The masses paid their dues by working land they didn't own. They were assigned marriage partners. Everyone took his turn in the mines."

Prescott wrote, "It was the object of the Incas to infuse into their subjects a spirit of passive obedience and tranquility—a perfect acquiescence in the established order of things."

Avarice, ambition, and social mobility were not a part of the society which provided for all. Change was anathema. Everything was done for the community, not the individual. Hard work and industry were key to the success of the system, which functioned for nearly a century, until Pizarro came and the construct of the social whole was shattered by the greed of a materialistic culture.

"You see, Peter, gold and silver were symbols of harmony in Inca society. Metals were mined in honor of gods. The Sun was honored with gold. His sister-wife, the Moon, was praised with silver. Thunder and Lightning were the Sun's ministers, and the Stars were the Moon's attendants."

Andy reached out and grabbed my wrist.

"These metals the Spaniards desired—they were aesthetically pleasing to the Incas, who had no such thing as currency." Andy's fingers gripped tightly and hurt.

"Gold was a quality of the Sun. Sweat of the Sun. And silver was Tears of the Moon. A beautiful idea, yes?"

"Very."

Andy pulled his hand back, his face radiating perplexed joy, but then dropped his head like a bull about to make his last charge at a bullfighter. Fixing purposeful eyes on his empty bottle, he began again.

I could still feel the wire of his fingers around my wrist long after he'd taken his hand away, and I wondered if Andy told his tale to everyone he met, or if I had been singled out for a reason. It was not a story you could tell quickly, and the narration seemed to exhaust him.

◆◆◆

As descendant of the Sun, the Lord Inca laid claim to all gold and silver in the realm, which he used to build and adorn his palaces and possessions. Wherever the Incas brought their empire, there they established Inca religion and erected Temples to the Sun and Moon. But the gold and silver had true meaning to the Inca rulers only after the metal had been fashioned into ceremonial articles in honor of Inca gods.

In the days following the conquest, Indian goldsmiths had the unhappy task of melting down what they themselves had fashioned. All day and night, driven by the greedy Spaniards, they worked to decimate the crafted symbols of their culture.

The King in Spain received one-fifth of the booty, the "royal fifth." In his edition of the writings of Cieza de León, the Spanish soldier and chronicler of the conquest, Victor von Hagen, himself a historian, has written that Cieza as a young boy in Seville witnessed the arrival of the first ship from the New World carrying Atahualpa's ransom:

"I remember the rich pieces of gold that I saw in Seville, brought from Cajamarca, where the treasure that Atahualpa promised the Spaniards was collected." His [Cieza's] imagination naturally was fired by the glitter of the gold and the swaggering, commanding presence of Hernando Pizarro, who only a few years before had been no more than a human cipher in the harsh lands of Extremadura. Now he was dressed in velvets with glittering ear-ornaments and with small Negro pages to do his bidding. . . .

Back in Peru, Governor Francisco Pizarro himself kept the golden throne on which Atahualpa had traveled.

Andy's narrative was broken as he stood up, his face tight. He held one hand delicately in the air while the other men watched him in silence.

"That throne, Peter, weighed 183 pounds, of *pure gold*." Andy paused as if about to lecture to a classroom, but then, thank goodness, sat down. He could not contain his fervor, which thrilled and frightened me simultaneously.

Cajamarca was a gold-rush town, crazy with greed. Prices of food and goods among the Spaniards had skyrocketed. Men paid debts with sacred golden objects, sometimes without even knowing how much they weighed.

Although Pizarro had drawn up a document absolving the Inca from his promise to fill the room with gold, Atahualpa had by this time suspected the Spaniards would kill him rather than let him go. He had established a rapport with Hernando, and when his only Spanish friend left Peru to accompany the first ransom-laden ship to Spain, Atahualpa wept openly.

The Inca captive was desperate now. He saw a comet in the sky—one like his father had seen before his death.

He was confident of one thing, however: His best general, Rumiñahui, still held Quito.

Among the Spaniards a rumor began that Rumiñahui was preparing to attack.

Pizarro's partner, Diego de Almagro, who had just arrived from Panama, wanted to march immediately on Cuzco for the gold he had not yet got. But in order to leave Cajamarca, Almagro believed the Inca leader must be killed.

A few conquistadors were against killing the Inca King. A small reconnaissance party traveled northward to investigate the rumors of Rumiñahui's hostile forces.

Back in Cajamarca a debate began about when to kill Atahualpa. After a farcical trial, Francisco Pizarro, for reasons of expediency and fear, gave orders to burn the Inca, who had been absurdly charged with crimes of polygamy, usurpation of the Inca crown, idolatry, and, finally, conspiracy against the Spaniards.

With Atahualpa at the stake, the Europeans chanted prayers, and the Spanish friar is said to have converted the Inca to Christianity just before he died. Atahualpa may have chosen finally to take the vows because the Spaniards had offered strangulation as a Christian instead of burning as a heathen. And the Inca knew that death by fire meant the Sun could never call him back to another life on earth; if, on the other hand, he was strangled, he might return for revenge.

When he was brought out in the dusk of July 26, 1533, into the same square where he'd been captured eight months before, his subjects fell down, prostrate, as if in a drunken stupor. With characteristic courage and austere countenance, and likely with the faith too that his Sun God would somehow bring him back to earth, Atahualpa was garroted at the stake.

Then dowsed in fire, part of his clothing and flesh burned,

he was left there for the night so the people would know their emperor had been killed. He was buried as a Christian, but the Indians exhumed his body and reburied him in the mountains with his maternal ancestors.

Meanwhile, the Spanish reconnaissance party returned from the north to report they'd found no hostile activity.

Espinosa, then governor of Panama, wrote, "the greed of Spaniards of all classes is so great as to be insatiable: the more the native chiefs give, the more the Spaniards try to persuade their own captains and governors to kill or torture them to give more . . ."

◆◆◆

Andy leapt out of his seat, threw some money on the table, said, "Let's go!" and was making for the truck. The story had made him moody, restless. I'd lost all sense of time. Nearly two hours had passed since we sat down. I quickly followed Andy to the truck. The men at the tables, I could see, were surprised at the abruptness of our departure. We drove off with pebbles flying from under the tires.

Speeding down the road again, the air cooling the cabin, Andy said:

"The Llanganati treasure is the biggest and final portion of the Inca King's ransom, and it was on its way from Quito to Cajamarca when Rumiñahui learned of Atahualpa's murder.

"When the general discovered his leader's death, he took the treasure into the Llanganati Mountains. Only eighty miles southeast of Quito, the Inca general hid that gold in the most ghastly, godawful region of the Andes—that strange cloud-forested mountain range between the higher volcanoes and the jungle basin. Peter, the general knew the area well because it was his own province of Píllaro."

Andy's fist punched the steering wheel as the pickup hit

ninety miles an hour. And then he was silent all the way to his ranch.

◆◆◆

We reached his land by a muddy road. It was a large mass of land, some cleared for cattle and some still overgrown with dense secondary growth. We drove through huge mud puddles I feared the pickup could not pass. Andy just plowed right through, splattering our windows with the mud. He showed me where he wanted to build a polo field and a weekend house for his new girlfriend, a young Peruvian travel agent from a wealthy Lima family. (Andy had been married and divorced twice, and months later I heard one rumor that whenever he came to Quito, mothers of pretty daughters barred their doors and locked their windows. So I suppose I admired him also because he was a ladies' man, for I too wanted to be like him when I reached fifty, still vibrant, daring, alive.) The carefree way he talked about his "weekend house," though, made it sound more like a pipe dream.

He told me when he first bought this land he had come out here for days on end to guard his new jungle. With machete and shotgun, he'd wait in the bushes to chase off the squatters who had lived here for years and would not move. "I understood their feelings, believe me, but it was *my* land now. I gave them plenty of time and warning. At times, it got pretty rough with those fellows. They were fighting for their lives."

Andy respected those men, even if he disagreed with them and would have killed them if they had crossed him. In those days, Andy told me, he would land his private airplane on the dirt road which passed the farm.

All kinds of mutts barked at us, and several barefoot children stared as we approached a flimsy wooden structure where the caretaker lived with his family. Dust clouded the air. Andy got out of the truck and a quiet cautious man of forty, a machete over his shoulder, walked out to greet him.

I liked seeing Andy be kind to this fellow. His caring for the man brought a grin to the caretaker's sun-dried face. Even his wife came out smiling.

Andy could have been my father, my adopted father. From the moment I'd met him, I was drawn to his patrician magnetism. I felt safe in his presence, and he seemed to adopt me, too, if you could judge by the bulk of information he'd already imparted. He wasn't giving me the *Reader's Digest* version of this treasure story. But through detail, step by step, he brought me along, as if I were a prime student, or perhaps the son he'd always wanted.

"Stay in the car while I talk to my man," he said gently. "I won't be a minute; just some business."

That minute turned into hours. When Andy came back he apologized. We drove around a little and then headed back to Guayaquil. So much of the day was spent driving, but as far as I could tell we might have been on the other side of the moon. I had never in my life thought so much about treasure and related things.

"We're having big trouble with the herd," he said. Some of his animals had developed an odd disease that was killing off a large part of his stock. So he'd engineered a serum in his company lab in Guayaquil, which seemed to be curing at least some of the cattle but for no obvious medical reason.

Andy smiled, "And you know something, Peter? I myself am taking the same serum—to preserve my youth!"

I couldn't help laughing because this captured perfectly my idea of Andy's personality, the risk, the emphasis on youth, the gamble, the magic of the serum.

"So what's in this magic formula?" I asked, but he would not discuss the details.

"Let's just say that it comes from the cartilage of horses."

"Andy!" I practically shouted, "that's what my father's taking, too!" Almost completely blind now, my own father had a circulatory disease, something very rare, some recessive family gene, and he too had resorted to injections of cartilage.

Andy did not look surprised. He said, "Well, then you see—the discovery is being made all over the world."

This seemed to me then more than coincidence: Andy and my father both about the same age, both taking some medically unproven yet strangely effective essence of cartilage (in my father's case it was cartilage from sharks). How many men in the world were taking cartilage? The coincidence drew me even closer to Andy, wiped away occasional doubts, and I began to feel as if fate had kept me in the country after all.

There were other parallels between my father and Andy, too. Like the Ecuadorian, my father was also a businessman with similar entrepreneurial inclinations. He had founded his own computer software company and there was a time a number of years ago, I think, when he had seriously thought about investing in South America. But when he went blind, he got out of business altogether. I had the strong feeling, after I spent time with Andy, that he and my father would like each other. And now I could just picture them discussing in vigorous conversation the youthful cartilage racing through their veins.

"Your father sounds like a wise man," Andy said as we passed slow banana trucks in the deepening dusk. The road was tediously straight; Andy intent; the cigarette ember in his hand the only visible sign he was holding the wheel.

"But you haven't finished the treasure story," I said.

"So, my story interests you?"

"Tell me all of it. Please. Where exactly is the gold?"

After a silence, in which perhaps the storyteller geared himself up to his task (or was he only listening to the eager panting of my heart?), he began in a gentle cadence, his tone tightening as his tale evolved.

"The mystery of the treasure, Peter, is made so very strange because of its actual hiding place: the Llanganatis. What mountains! Do you know what a cloud forest looks like? No?"

"It's a high jungle in the clouds, no?"

"No. Not the jungle you imagine from your Tarzan movies. Clouds, yes. But thick, wet, cold, stunted vegetation like a million claws of weasels. First, you walk for days and days from Píllaro, the last town you see. Then, once you get over the *páramo*, the high, boggy moors of the Andes, you descend into that cloud jungle, into the cold fog. Jungle the likes of which you have never seen. *The beard of the world!*

"You have to cut your way with machetes, and some days you can not go more than a hundred yards. You carry every ounce of food you will eat. And if you're lucky you might shoot the hairy, white-lipped tapir, the *danta*, which looks like a small mountain horse. But you can never count on getting food inside the Llanganati Mountains, never.

"The Pastaza, the Río Verde, and the Río Grande, these rivers surround Cerro Hermoso ..."

"What's Cerro Hermoso?"

"The mountain that hides the treasure. Fifteen thousand feet high. And those rivers are lined with jungles so thick and knitted you go crazy trying to pass through them. So many times I have followed the *danta* trails on my hands and knees, like a beast. The Indians of Píllaro call the tapir the builder of highways in the mountains. Oh, the Incas knew where to hide that gold, all right."

"Andy?"

"Yes." Andy was irritated by another interruption.

"I must know more about how the gold got buried in those mountains. I still don't know."

"There's a lot you don't know yet. So . . ."

Dusk dissolved into darkness; the pickup appeared to drive itself. The green glow from the dashboard made Andy's hands on the wheel seem radioactive, like clumps of disembodied energy.

"After hearing of his half-brother's murder (You remember that Huayna Capac was father to both these men, don't you?), Rumiñahui amassed the treasure of Quito, by far the largest that had been on its way to ransom the Lord Inca. He proclaimed himself ruler and took the gold first to Quito, then to Píllaro. Píllaro, he knew from birth, was close to the Llanganatis, which could foil any treasure hunter."

◆◆◆

The reason for killing the Inca was the Spaniards' desire to get out of Cajamarca and to plunder the rest of the empire before all the gold was hidden from them.

Moving north from Cajamarca after Atahualpa's murder, Sebastián de Benalcázar, one of Pizarro's most ruthless commanders, hoped Quito would hold as much gold and silver as Cuzco had. Pizarro himself had gone south toward the capital. But news of the murder of the Inca Emperor had spread, and the conquistadors knew they would have to hurry.

After a long battle, unable to fight successfully against Benalcázar's superior weaponry and horses, Rumiñahui retreated to Quito, burned the city and took all the treasure to Píllaro: a village hidden in the deep Andes east of the big volcanoes that run like a dinosaur's spine from Quito southward.

The first official Spanish chronicler of the conquest, Fernández de Oviedo y Valdés, wrote in the sixteenth century:

Hearing of the death of Atahualpa and of the departure of the governor of Cajamarca [Pizarro] for Cuzco, many Indians came and stormed the town and they left no stone unturned.

They exhumed Atahualpa's body and carried it off to no one knows where. It is known with great certainty that Captain Rumiñahui (who, history has said, with certain other people stole the treasure of Atahualpa) left with twelve or fifteen thousand warriors and he carried away sixty thousand loads of gold ... to where he thought it best to hide. He succeeded because no one has found more than little quantities of that sixty thousand "cargas." Even Captain Benalcázar couldn't find it, despite the fact that he killed and burned alive many important Indians in and around the city of Quito ... demanding to know if more of Atahualpa's gold remained, more than what had already been given to the Christians. In response, the Indians took a peck or more of maize and they made a pile from which they took out one grain only and they said: "This grain is what Atahualpa has given you from his treasures and what remains is the other," signaling with their fingers the pile of maize, signifying that what was still out there was without number or comparison.

Pedro Pizarro, Francisco's cousin who was also present at the Conquest, wrote his journals after returning to Spain and described how a treasure was safely buried after Atahualpa's murder. Gold and silver were carried by porters and accompanied by an armed guard. When the treasure caravan reached the appoximate area where it would be hidden, most of the men were sent away. Fifty to a hundred remained behind under the direction of a select group of Inca nobles. These men then moved the treasure in stages to the chosen burial ground. After it was hidden, the nobles led the men to a distant place and hanged them. Later the nobles themselves committed suicide.

Benalcázar tortured and killed as he moved over the Andean spine into Quito. He and his men must have passed by thousands of Indians who had carried the famous treasure. Oviedo wrote:

The Spaniards arrived at a village which is eight leagues from Riobamba and there the Indians told them that twelve leagues further on, near a river [the Patate, which passes through Píllaro] there were fifty thousand men with trenches and defense walls because the Christians had to pass through there. . . .

The Indians yelled out to the frightened Spaniards. They taunted them, "We have the treasure and you will never get it." And they laughed through their teeth at the conquistadors.

We passed an occasional *cantina* beside the now-empty road where men were drinking in clusters around candles on small tables under jacaranda trees. The few houses with electric lights seemed like useless beacons of humanity in a sea of nothing out there. Most of the land around us was dark and secret and yet for me this night felt more full of promise than any star-lit evening.

"For revenge!" Andy's words startled me. "Those Indians drove the conquistadors mad with gold lust. They invented tales of imaginary treasures, I'm sure. They knew how to goad the white men, their awful weak spot."

In his original belief that Quito would be another Cuzco, Benalcázar arrived in the northern capital disappointed and murderous. He then pursued Rumiñahui to Píllaro, where the Inca general had dug himself in. Rumiñahui escaped, but the resistance movement he'd organized fell apart. And later he was captured and brought to Quito.

Benalcázar continued to torture and burn Inca chiefs who would not tell him where the great treasure of Atahualpa's Quito had been buried.

Rumiñahui was finally executed in the plaza of Quito. An

Ecuadorian wrote, "Benalcázar continues to pursue the treasure
... in the mysterious LLANGANA [workshop or mines] of
the invincible ATI-Rumiñahui, who was left burning alive in
the recently founded plaza de Quito. He died without ever
revealing his invulnerable secret to the murderers of the
Inca."

◆◆◆

"So why not use a helicopter?" Into the darkness I lobbed
the question I'd wanted to ask for the last hour. "If the terrain of the Llanganatis is so bad, why not just drop in from
the sky?"

At first, no response from Andy. Then: "You think it's that
simple, do you?"

I opened my window slightly. The air outside had cooled
considerably, and there was a sudden tension between Andy and
me. I waited for him to answer my question, which finally he did,
but he took his time and his tone reprimanded:

"Well, it isn't simple. I'm telling you. Weather is too risky up
there. Sometime I will tell you what happened to me when I did
take a helicopter into the Llanganati Mountains and crashed
and lived with no food for a month, and with dysentery! Not
simple, no.

"A helicopter—for food drops?—forget it! You can count on
absolutely *nothing* in those mountains; and Rumiñahui, the sly
one, he knew it. The icy fog rolls in for months at a time. No,
no, no, I'm telling you. The only way to be certain of feeding your expedition is to supply it by land, and it's no easy
trick, sir."

Andy turned on the cabin light to search for his cigarettes on
the seat between us, and I saw the wrinkles from the corners of
his squinting eyes flare like gulls' footprints in sand. Even his lips
strained to evoke the hardships of thirty years going to those

mountains. I felt ashamed. I hadn't meant to sound glib, but wasn't Andy overreacting to a simple question?

I wondered what Andy really thought of me. Why was he telling me so much?

After he lit a cigarette he turned off the light, but the image of his hard face hung firmly in the air between us like the lingering image of an austere portrait of some Renaissance priest.

From the darkness came the words, "Valverde. Valverde is the key to the story."

"Who, Andy?"

"The treasure will never make any sense to you until I tell Valverde's story, the only Spaniard ever to have seen the gold. Valverde held it in his hands!"

Half a minute passed, then another half minute. Andy had stopped in midstream. He seemed to pull back on the reins of his tale, which, until now, had fairly cantered along. I wondered if I'd offended him. I couldn't tell what made him so moody.

I had to ask: "Well, who is Valverde?"

"I'm sorry." Andy laughed sardonically as he swept his hand along the windshield. "It'll have to wait, my boy. As you see— we're home."

Which was true. Somehow camouflaged by the spell of Andy's voice, Guayaquil's slums had imperceptibly engulfed us. Bright saffron street lamps and red and blue neon signs advertising Coca-Cola and Fanta pained my eyes. The city seemed a leviathan of commercial advertising, of fragments and flashes of industrial color. Cooler now than in the morning, the air was nevertheless fetid, smelling of urine, and the zoo smell was the big city's smell of defeat. The buildings brought me rudely back from a fairy tale which, until right now, had not seemed like a fairy tale at all, but rather like the real world of adventure.

We opened our windows wide, and the music from *cantina* jukeboxes, loud and brassy, blasted the tropical *salsa* of so many Latin coastal cities into our privacy until there was no privacy.

And worst of all, Andy seemed to deliberately hold me at arm's length. A bitterness had seeped into his voice, or so I imagined. Perhaps I had wished for, and therefore only imagined, his fatherly acceptance. But, then, why would a treasure hunter tell so much to a near stranger?

A few hours before, after we had left his ranch, I confessed to him about leaving anthropology behind in order to stay in Ecuador to pursue the treasure tale. I told him that the last time I was in the jungle, I stayed for a week with a missionary my age, who had grown up with the Indians and learned to hunt with a blowgun and walk in the jungle with his bare feet; that he had taken me with the Indians on a long hunting trip downriver and I was so sick for days I lay in my hammock while he and his friends went out to shoot wild pig and macaw and even monkeys to eat; that this missionary had told me one night in the darkness as we lay in our hammocks with the loud sound of frogs around us and the cool air coming up from the Río Aguarico, that he did not think I was much of a scientist; and that when I quickly and defensively asked why not, he said it was because I didn't have the curiosity of a scientist.

I now told Andy, "When I got back to my apartment in Quito, I realized the missionary was right." And that's when I decided I might not really have what it took to be a physical anthropologist—a certain dedication, an insatiable curiosity for bones and animals. On my last trip to the jungle I discovered that I'd rather lie in my hammock feeling vaguely sick, lethargic, and sorry for myself than go out and search for invisible monkeys.

"So your treasure story comes to me with perfect timing," I said.

I told Andy all this with the racing eagerness to have him

understand, to get his blessing, to sanction my decision to remain in Ecuador; but he listened with a stone face. He showed
little sympathy. He said, "Well, it was wise you got out when
you did."

I realize now that Andy had no desire to give me solace. He
sought only to instigate with his treasure talk, to create a need to
know more and then only to half satisfy that need. He was my
agent provocateur.

He dangled his stories before me like flies before a trout in
springtime. And then Valverde was indeed the hook, the bait, the
final key bit of history that drove me crazy to get into those
fog-freezing mountains myself.

CHAPTER 2

◆◆◆◆◆

Andy drove through every red light, not a policeman around to stop him. He even speeded up when the lights turned yellow, then red.

I clutched the door handle as we careened through downtown Guayaquil. This fiercely lawless side of Andy thrilled me. Compared to the long soporific bus rides to the Amazon and the deadly weeks of not finding a single troop of monkeys, this recklessness was anything but dull.

"The law in Ecuador is different." Andy laughed. "It's flexible."

I said, "I love Ecuador. This is my new home." I was thinking about staying here forever. I loved the rawness of the land. Since arriving in Ecuador, especially at the higher elevations, Quito for instance, where the air was so dry and cool, I'd felt childish again.

Most of Ecuador has remained exactly as it was a hundred years before—unspoiled and full of cowboy flare. The country, the size of Arizona, has a population roughly equivalent to that of New York City. Colombia to the north and Peru in the west and south cup the tiny nation against the Pacific, and the equator runs through Ecuador, giving it its name.

A geographically diverse nation, the Cordillera of the Andes splits east from west, running up the country like a dragon's spine. Actually the Andean Cordillera is really two spines—the Eastern and Western Cordilleras—with a valley between, where

Quito and the other sierran cities lie on a north-south axis. Deserts line the southern Pacific coast while dense jungles flourish east of the Andes. Twenty-two of the nation's volcanoes rise higher than Mount Rainier in Washington State.

Ecuador itself is a treasure: Potatoes had been grown here before anywhere else; Ecuadorian avocados were the first introduced to the European diet; the country claimed the discovery of rubber, platinum, and quinine; and Darwin drew upon notes made in Ecuador's Galápagos Islands for the theory of evolution.

A country rich in resources, Ecuador nevertheless has a poor population. A small group of elite Ecuadorians own all the land, industry, and business.

Andy was a prominent member of this elite, which made me feel safe. If I should get into any trouble, I knew Andy would help me get out of jail quickly. Or so I thought.

A block from his house, Andy asked, "Have you any idea what the treasure's worth?"

I said, "No, I suppose I don't. I'm no good at converting seven hundred and fifty tons of gold into anything."

"Eight billion dollars."

The motor purred in his driveway. Andy stretched for the overhead light switch and leaned forward to slide a slim leather briefcase out from under the seat.

"Read that!" He threw me a few Xeroxed pages from some book, held together with a large paper clip.

"It's in English, no less. That, Peter, is the entire *Guide* of Valverde. It will tell you where the gold is buried, almost."

"Valverde?" That name again.

Andy took the key from the ignition and walked to the front door of his house and said, "Just read it."

As we walked through the silent vestibule, through an empty hall and into the tomb-still living room, the extreme quiet of the house created the illusion of some secret activity, as if the house, aroused by our footsteps, might eavesdrop on our conversation.

Andy turned on the lights and called out to his servants, but no one answered. We sat in armchairs and I could hear the rustle of the dry palms out back.

Andy's voice was subdued now; we'd come a long way in one day. He said, "A few years after Pizarro captured the Inca empire, a poor Spanish soldier named Valverde married an Indian girl in Latacunga, that town just south of Quito on the Pan American Highway. You know the town? Yes? Good.

"Her father was a chief in the nearby village of Píllaro and one day he told his son-in-law about the treasure." Andy's eyes narrowed and his voice dropped so low I strained to hear him.

The Spaniard became very rich, making numerous trips into the nearby Llanganati Mountains for gold. Years later when Valverde returned to Spain, on his deathbed he composed a written guide for the King explaining how to reach the treasure in Ecuador. That text is the *Derrotero* [Path] *de Valverde*. (Andy told me that a copy of the original guide was still in the Archivo General de Indias in Seville, Spain.)

The King immediately sent the *Guide* with a royal warrant to the magistrate of Latacunga and Ambato ordering him to look for the gold. The magistrate himself, accompanied by a friar, Father Longo, formed an expedition which followed the landmarks mentioned in the *Guide* until one night in the rugged mountains Father Longo mysteriously disappeared.

"The man just vanished," said Andy, "into thin air!" Andy's eyes sprang wide open.

Valverde's *Guide* had appeared accurate. Actual landmarks matched the descriptions Valverde had written out for the King, but after searching for three days, the expedition returned without the friar and without the treasure.

"Three hundred years later the British botanist Richard Spruce, while traveling through Ecuador from 1857 to 1863, uncovered this story in the Latacunga archives. He found the *Guide* itself,

the royal warrant of the King's expedition, and a map of the
Llanganati region drawn in 1800 by a Spanish botanist and miner
named Atanasio Guzmán."

Spruce, who had been hired by the British government to
collect quinine seeds in Ecuador to send to India to establish
quinine plantations, never completed a book about his South
American wanderings. His colleague, Alfred Russel Wallace,
however, the man who devised the theory of evolution six years
before Darwin, compiled Spruce's writings and published them in
1908 as *Notes of a Botanist on the Amazon and Andes*. The last
chapter, entitled "Hidden Treasure," includes Spruce's translation of the Valverde *Guide* and his speculation on the treasure's
location.

"That very document you hold in your hand, Peter. Spruce
found that. You realize, of course, that Spruce and Wallace were
not stupid men with dreamy minds. They were the scientists of
their day."

There is no evidence that Spruce himself ever really searched
for the gold. But his editor, Wallace, was fascinated by the Inca
story and interjected commentary in the treasure chapter, inciting
the reader to take up the search. Like Spruce, he was convinced
of the treasure's existence. Wallace wrote:

> I am convinced that the "Route" of Valverde is a genuine and
> thoroughly trustworthy document, and that by closely following
> the directions therein given, it may still be possible for an
> explorer of means and energy, with the assistance of local
> authorities, to solve the interesting problem of the Treasure of
> the Incas . . .

"A small version of Guzmán's map of the area," Andy said at
the moment I was thinking him an ideal "explorer of means and
energy," "accompanies the chapter on hidden treasure." The

larger original, Andy assured me, was still in the British Museum in London.

"About Guzmán, I'm afraid we know very little." From Guayaquil, Spruce wrote in 1863 that from the writings of Humboldt, the German naturalist and South American explorer, he had come to know more about Guzmán. When Humboldt met Guzmán, he was a pharmacist in Quito, and he later had the same profession in Latacunga and Píllaro.

Guzmán apparently lived for years in Píllaro in the late eighteenth century and made many trips into the Llanganati Mountains. He discovered several silver and copper mines which had been worked in Inca times. He and a few partners began to work those mines, but because of disputes among them and because of the slow acquisition of wealth, the mines were abandoned. Familiar with local legends, the miners must have been acutely aware that a great hoard of gold had been hidden nearby.

"But Guzmán was a sleepwalker, and one night he fell into a canyon, in 1807 or so," Andy said in a loud whisper. "Since Spruce discovered Valverde's *Guide* in the 1860's in the archives of a small Andean town, hundreds of people have looked for Atahualpa's hoard. After thirty years, Peter, I can tell you with absolute certainty that his *Guide* is accurate—to a point."

Andy's face drooped with fatigue. His sturdy jaw seemed doubly thick tonight; his eyes closed from time to time. He no longer looked that young. The long drive and the ceaseless talk had drained him.

Intoning a quotation from the *Guide*, he shut his eyes and pointed his face to the ceiling, his voice deep and gravelly: "thou shalt perceive the three Cerros Llanganati, in the form of a triangle, on whose declivity there is a lake, made by hand, into which the ancients threw the gold they had prepared for the ransom of the Inca [Atahualpa] when they heard of his death." Andy had memorized the *Guide* long ago.

"So, read Valverde, Peter. I will lie down for a while. But it is from that document that I have discovered the treasure mountain, Cerro Hermoso, the Beautiful Mountain, sacred to the Indians. But I tell you it is not so beautiful; it is very ... different up there, like nothing else in this world."

And on such a strange note Andy vanished. So I quickly turned to the *Guide*, studied it, became easily entranced by the arcane sound of the sentences. This document was better than a treasure map, perhaps more suggestive because of its verbal ambiguities. As with pornography, words, more than pictures, take the imagination further into the realm of possibility. And this was true with the *Guide*.

Valverde's *Guide* brought to mind the map in H. Rider Haggard's *King Solomon's Mines*, that classic treasure tale I read when I was a boy, the very book that first launched me in the direction of archaeology and prehistory, the book that taught me the wonderful relationship between adventure and searching for the past, for nostalgia, whether it was buried treasure or ruined civilizations or one-million-year-old human-ape bones.

And I began to think also that Andy was not too different from the hunter-narrator of Haggard's book, Quartermain, a middle-aged, equitable man of larger-than-life stature, who leads Captain Good, Sir Henry Curtis, and a Zulu chief through a desert into the Solomon Mountains of Africa in search of Sir Henry's lost brother.

Quartermain takes with him a copy of a three-hundred-year-old map, the only guide in existence to Solomon's diamond mines. The book is pure naive action and adventure and the story line moves linearly.

As I read Valverde, I wondered if by undertaking my investigation into this treasure story I too would undergo what the men in that book went through: near death in a desert, starvation in the mountains, journeys into uncharted land, a fight with a tribe, outnumbered just as Pizarro had been outnumbered when he took the Inca captive.

I hoped my adventure would end as simply, and as painlessly, as Quartermain's or Pizarro's. For in those early days of my involvement with treasure, I was on the side of Pizarro. Later, I grew to hate Pizarro and did not want to be associated in any way with the illegitimate former pig farmer from Spain's bleak region of Extremadura.

◆◆◆

For the next few days, Andy came alive at night, but slept most of the day. He seemed to live on a permanent graveyard shift, rising around one or two in the afternoon, breakfasting on coffee, reading the daily paper, talking to me for a few hours, then disappearing at dusk to God knows where, until he'd return just as the sun's oven reheated the city, the slums and pavement conducting heat like metal, and the new light slanting sharply through my window blinds as I lay awake hearing Andy drunkenly throw himself onto his bed. Then silence in the house, a distant dog barking.

On the fifth night he took me with him into the city and I learned more about Andy then, but each day I had a block of time in which to read, waiting, anxiously storing questions about the treasure, until the afternoons when he would emerge from sleep, rubbing his eyes at me as if he'd forgotten who I was. But this was his sober time, when, spurred by caffeine, he was willing to talk.

Before he disappeared into the balmy nights he would dig around in his chaotic closets to find Inca history books for me, and when he came into the bright living room on the fourth day of my visit he had a copy of Spruce, which he lay gently on the table. His voice was hoarse, his fingers shaky, eyes burning.

"There's the Valverde source," he said.

I opened the book and here was the *Guide*, the one he had Xeroxed and given me already. I wondered if he had forgotten.

Andy ate toast and sipped coffee, the Guayaquil daily newspaper untouched on the table. Hoping to spark his memory and jolt him out of a strange sudden malaise—I hated to see him in low spirits—I read aloud those great opening lines from Valverde, some of the same lines he had chanted on our first night together:

Placed in the town of Píllaro, ask for the farm of Moya, and sleep (the first night) a good distance above it; and ask there for the mountain of Guapa, from whose top, if the day be fine, look to the east, so that thy back be towards the town of Ambato, and from thence thou shalt perceive the three Cerros Llanganati, in the form of a triangle, on whose declivity there is a lake, made by hand, into which the ancients threw the gold they had prepared for the ransom of the Inca [Atahualpa] when they heard of his death.

I would gladly have reread the whole *Guide* if Andy had not broken in on the word "death." Here he could not refrain from commenting, but spoke quietly.

"Goddamn, they knew where to hide it, didn't they." Andy's head moved slowly back and forth as if he were puzzling out a problem, as if perhaps he was more baffled than he wanted to say. There was a powerful blank look in his leached eyes.

"Someone I haven't mentioned yet, someone you should know about—a man you must meet if he's still alive."

"Who?"

"A treasure hunter. A German-Swiss fellow by the name of Eugene Brunner. He and I were partners once. No longer."

Andy held his coffee cup beneath his lips, the steam rising into his eyes, his forehead furrowed. And I wondered if these deep creases came from the thought of this man Brunner, or was it the natural grimace of a man with a terrible hangover about to take his first sip of hot coffee? He looked so distraught.

"I've not seen him in many years. But Brunner is the true expert on these mountains. He says he's found the old Inca mines, and he roams alone for months in those haunted peaks. A strange fellow."

"But how do I contact him? Where is he now? How old is he?"

This whole treasure story was an endless puzzle to me. I was hungry to find the pieces, to know more of the other treasure hunters. But just when I thought I'd learned the names of the main characters in the saga, another one appeared.

Until now, also, when I thought of Atahualpa, I associated the Inca gold with only one living man, and that was Andy himself. In fact, it seemed slightly sacrilegious that, after thirty years looking for Atahualpa's gold, Andy should not be the only expert. How many experts can a treasure have? I wondered.

"Just one minute." Andy called for more coffee, frowning at the Indian boy, who was slow in bringing it.

It was Brunner's theory, Andy explained, that Cerro Hermoso was an important mining area in pre-Inca days. And certain passages from the historians validated such a theory.

The Indians did in fact use the high mountains for their furnaces. They harnessed the trade winds blowing up from the Amazon in the east. The historian Garcilaso wrote in 1617:

> It was also necessary to temper the wind, for if it was very strong it wasted the charcoal and made the metal cold, and if it was gentle there was not sufficient force to flux the metal. They, therefore, went up the hills at night, and put it on the high or low declivities, according to whether the wind was high or not, so as to adapt the exposure, according as it was more or less open. It was a beautiful sight in those times to see ten to fifteen thousand little furnaces burning on the hill sides. There they made their first melting.

"The importance of Brunner's work, Peter, is that these smelting areas are mentioned in Valverde's *Guide*, and the little square lake that Brunner discovered on the slopes of Cerro Hermoso, this was also a smelting pit. In fact, it's the very lake Valverde calls the treasure lake. Brunner made the connection; Brunner's done valuable work up there . . . Of course, he's had access."

"Access to what, Andy?"

"Documents, maps. It's a long story."

"But why won't you tell me the whole thing right now?"

"I've got to go out. I'll tell you later." More bait.

Andy was ready for his nighttime activities, leaving me hanging midair. Our afternoon talk was over, and it left me frustrated and angry. I said, "Please, tell me now," but he disappeared into his bedroom to dress for the night, and I remembered I was his guest; he'd welcomed my extended stay, and it would accomplish nothing to get angry with my host.

Just before he went he said, "But you must find Brunner, somehow. If he's still alive."

"But why wouldn't he be living?"

"Haven't heard from him in years."

Andy left the house, and I walked around the city until dark, smoldering with the frustration of a story so unfinished. Some dispute must have passed between these two veteran treasure hunters, but what? Getting Andy to speak about Brunner was not easy. Brunner was some sort of key to this puzzle and I vowed to myself I'd find him.

At two P.M. the next day, when I asked more about Brunner, Andy described him as an odd, even crazy man who once had stayed for 127 days alone in the Llanganatis, often with no food. Brunner saw the sun three times, and for a month—even in that good season (November and December)—he had only five days when the weather was clear enough for exploration. For weeks he stayed in his tent.

"The old German has gone more times to the Llanganatis than any man alive. He does nothing else but look for treasure. Last I heard he was on the coast searching for emeralds." Andy's tone mixed respect with (what was it?) disdain? a glint of rivalry?

"In the morning you might wake to sunshine, a crystal blue sky, ha!, then you get dressed and put your boots on and when you go outside suddenly you can't see from here to the back yard of my house. Brunner knows all about how bad it gets."

One aspect of the treasure story I never tired of were the reports of bad weather in the mountains—how the moist air from the Amazon condenses with the Andean cold, creating constant precipitation. I never got bored with Andy's meteorological descriptions because there was something in what Andy had lived through up there in that rarefied fog and desolate landscape that I also wanted to experience: the wonder, the fear, the mystery of that place—and also perhaps a test of manhood. Finally I had no choice but to ask the question, until now suppressed.

"Andy?"

He'd gone into a familiar trance: "You climb and descend all day long . . ." I tried to break in, but couldn't.

"Fog socks you in for weeks. A frozen vapor."

"Andy," I said a little louder.

"Jagged peaks, miserable wet and cold, the mountains stacked against you, and you begin to wonder why the hell you came to this terrible place . . ." Caliban was telling a secret. "But then you catch a clear day. It comes along like a gift of God and the craggy black mountains enchant you and there's no escaping, Euphoria boils in your veins like molten blood."

"Andy, please, I have something to ask you."

A vicious afternoon sun shot through the palms outside the glass doors and glazed the bright surface of the pool.

Andy turned to look at me as if he already knew.

"Yes?" He half smiled.

"Andy. Can I go into those mountains with you?"

Even as I asked, I wondered if it was the right thing. Nothing in this world scared me more than the Llanganatis. But now I was begging to subject my fragile body to those harsh cold crags.

No other request could have brought such a full sincere smile to Andy's rugged face.

"I had a feeling you might ask that," he said as if he'd expected it all along. As if I'd just joined a secret society. "You're in luck."

Good God, I thought, What am I doing? Has he been waiting for me to ask permission? Am I so predictable?

Andy's eyes were radiant.

"I'm funding an expedition this year. My son-in-law, Diego, will lead the party. He went with me a few times before. Why not go with him? He owns a little bar in Quito. Go see him when you get back. Diego needs a companion these days."

"But what about you? Aren't you going?" My courage sank; I wanted Andy there, for safety.

"I can't this year. Trouble at the office. But Diego will take you to Cerro Hermoso and the lake. In two months, November or so. Both of you can go when the weather gets better."

I couldn't help wondering if there was another reason for him not going, some secret he wasn't telling.

But Andy was genuinely warm toward me now. He assured me I would be rewarded with an experience he could never adequately paint in words, "To feel the fog on your skin, the mist and freezing rain and the gnarled plants hemming you in. To know the story of the treasure, you have to be there. That place will speak to you."

There was a pride in Andy's voice, and if I hadn't been so scared, I might have felt content to be a good son in a happy father's eyes. He said he'd take me out that night on the town to celebrate my going. I tried to picture myself in those mountains, but couldn't.

"I wish you'd go, too," I said one last time.

Andy's response was: "Come out back for a minute, Peter."

He led me into his yard. "Now let's see just how strong you are."

Still beaming, Andy fell to the grass. "Come on," he said, and I lay down, too. He wanted to arm wrestle.

Two seconds after he clasped my hand, he pinned my fist to the earth as surely as a carpenter drives home a nail.

"Okay, left hand," I said, a little confused, my arm sore, frustrated. With the other arm it took him perhaps twenty seconds before he beat me. Back home with my friends in New York after much drinking I'd been a regular champion with my left arm. Unbeatable no more. Yet I thought it fitting that a man like Andy should beat me.

We sat up; the palms rustled above us, an exotic sound, and he said:

"Do you know what Brunner calls that ancient lake on Cerro Hermoso? Can you guess?" Andy was ready to laugh.

"Lake Valverde?"

"No. He calls it Lake Brunner. Ha. That tells you what a man Brunner is. Ha ha."

Andy sprang to his feet, brushing grass from his pants.

"Want to see nightlife in Guayaquil? Eh?"

"Yes, sir!" I saluted. Andy slapped me on the back, then shook my hand, a hardy grip. My fear traveled underground as I wondered about tonight.

"One hour from now. After we dress."

In the guest room I sat on my bed and thought, What am I doing this for? Why was I going to those mountains. Last week I'd never heard of the Llanganatis or the treasure, and now I'd risk anything to go. I must be crazy.

I found a piece of paper and composed a letter to my parents, asking for a loan of five hundred dollars. I did not immediately tell them why I was staying, but let them infer it was for monkey research. But I did write my twin brother the truth and all the details about the trip I hoped to make in a few months. If anything went wrong I wanted him to know what I was doing. For although he lived in Seattle and we had not seen each other in a long time, because we were born only three minutes apart, we were, without ever having to say it to each other, very close friends. I told him I'd have to find a job, get a work visa; my tourist visa was about to expire.

Frankly, during that week I was not very cautious or reflective or wise or nearly skeptical enough or particularly conscious of my actions. Andy's story was not fiction, not *King Solomon's Mines* or *Treasure Island*. Yet I might have been a character in some book, the way I was behaving. The past five days had the distilled, accelerated quality of fiction and I felt uncontrollably whirled up into a hidden plot.

I needed time to make it real, here in this wonderfully lawless country. How could I leave now? I had to meet Diego, hear his story, go to the mountains; then find Brunner if he was alive.

And there was of course a distinct if remote possibility of returning home a hero and a multibillionaire—of glimpsing those golden birds and Inca corn stalks of beaten silver. Of feasting my eyes on moon disks or the famous fountain that sprayed a sparkling jet of gold.

CHAPTER 3

◆◆◆◆◆

Andy was nothing like my father, not really. He was shorter and stockier, he drank more than my father, and he was more athletic and grandiose. He seemed to have done everything in the world a man could do, from treasure hunting to polo playing. He'd been a great athlete at the University of Southern California, where he broke two of Jesse Owen's track records. In World War Two, he fought for the United States; later, he trained an elite group from the Los Angeles police force.

He had a hero's past, but he didn't brag about these things; they came out in the conversation almost accidentally. Sometimes I would pressure him for specifics, but he rarely wanted to dwell on himself, especially on those things that might make him seem too important.

Andy's modesty came not so much from self-confidence, but rather from some wound I never did figure out. Through a cool exterior, I noticed a grief scraping at Andy's insides. He simply did not believe in his own accomplishments. Perhaps that's why he drank as he did.

Even so, he was my idea of a perfect treasure hunter; he was my tutor. He was shameless when it came to drawing me into his story. He was like one of those impassioned salesmen who win customers through sheer exuberance, a fearless indoctrinator. I loved his blind passion for treasure and I loved the courage he must have shown on dangerous expeditions into the mountains. And I'm not at all sure I would have asked to go into the Llanganatis if I'd known he would not go with me this year, for it was Andy himself who made the treasure attractive, and I had no guarantee that Diego, or any other treasure hunter, would be as flamboyant.

As for Andy's self-doubt, nothing obliterated those occasional signs of self-abnegation as did talk of Atahualpa's hoard and all things related. The times I liked him best were when he was so fired up about all his journeys that no amount of booze could deter or deflect his story, which had a rocket's momentum.

◆◆◆

He wasn't ready to go out until eleven that night.

As we drove through deserted streets, he explained that, after Atahualpa's murder in 1533, the conquistadors of Peru and Ecuador were rolling in gold and silver. Fortunes were won and lost in a single day as the soldiers threw dice. One man, Leguizano, had received for his booty a golden image of the Sun from the temple at Cuzco. "But he lost it in one night of gaming, and afterward, a saying began in Peru, *Juega el Sol antes que amanezca.*

"He plays away the Sun before sunrise," Andy translated as he parked the truck, and we went to an outdoor café for beer. When we got back to the truck a young black girl, drunk and sloppy and reeking of perfume, was sitting inside, waiting. Andy opened the door and told her to get out. She put her arms around his neck and kissed him. He said, *"Fuera, niña!"* and called her by name, but she pleaded to go with us. He finally pushed her out, gently but firmly, and left her crying as we drove off.

"Who's that?" I asked.

Andy laughed. "Just a friend."

I would be merely an observor of Andy's nightly rounds, and I vowed not to criticize what I did not understand. Next, he led me into a Guayaquil casino.

As we got out of a tiny elevator, Andy grinned and said, "Watch me lose five thousand dollars. To lose, ah. Now that's the best feeling in the world."

"You mean you don't want to win?" I asked.

"Watch." We each bought a drink, then Andy went to the tables.

I'd been once to the outer rooms at the Monte Carlo casino and like any other tourist I'd levered a few slot machines. The inner rooms at Monte Carlo were not for light gamblers. This casino was like those inner rooms, sanctum sanctorum, so I kept silent.

We sat at a roulette table where I felt odd being the only one not playing. I felt like a spy. Each chip had a value of two hundred dollars. I was holding half of the five thousand in chips in my hand while Andy played two chips a spin. From one to six in the morning, Andy won five thousand dollars without so much as a smile or a grimace. At first he lost, then luck went his way and it seemed he'd never lose again.

While the city slept its tropical stupor, Andy played as indifferently to his luck as if he were taking a stroll down the Pacific boardwalk only a few miles away.

The table was lined with carnival faces. A midget in a red hat stood behind Andy with an intent expression. A hulkish bouncer lurked gloomily in the shadows shifting his eyes around the room, giving his lackeys silent imperceptible signals. Like those of heroin addicts, many of the gaunt faces that hovered palely over the green felt table blinked bloodshot eyes, agonizing over the outcome of chance.

The owner of the casino sat across from Andy as if to do battle. Andy whispered challengingly, "Watch every move he makes, Peter." He was going to play against the house.

Suddenly a fight broke out in the back room. Haggard,

stone-eyed, with thin white hair and a thoroughly disgusted look on his face, the owner turned his head to the noise. Bouncers and dealers all rose in unison like soldiers and ran.

A brawl was a moment of glory here. Men swarmed all over a little drunk and hustled him out, not without a few solid punches, a gratuitous kick to the face.

At five A.M. Andy had been winning every spin. He drew a crowd. The owner had had to relinquish his seat, he was losing so badly. Perhaps this was all a show on the owner's part, a way of encouraging business. Andy looked like a hero. An individual could beat the house. Tonight. But what about tomorrow? People like Andy came every night.

Andy's soldier-of-fortune veneer never shattered. He was a twentieth-century conquistador playing away the Sun and winning it back again.

Across the table a man's head twitched, his bird's eyes blinked. He lost to Andy once, his eyes fluttered; he lost again, face strained. Sweating, he wiped his forehead.

Andy kept winning. I held the chips. I had to find space in my pockets. Then I ran out of space and began to put them on the floor where I guarded them carefully. I separated three thousand dollars' worth of chips and kept them hidden, thinking Andy would forget about them. My instinct had been to protect him in case luck turned against him. But a half hour later, when he needed more chips, he said suddenly, "So give me the rest of the chips." And I knew he had absolute control over his game, no matter how many whiskeys he'd had, which was many more than I had counted.

The man across the table wiped his chest, his arms. He started to take off his shirt but the bouncer lightly touched his wrist, and he forgot about the perspiration. Soon, dazed and beaten, he left.

Three Germans engulfed Andy, their faces cunning, pragmatic, amiable. One spoke English to me, asked me where I was from, "Your country of origin?", but I didn't bother answering because he wasn't really talking to me; his eyes never left the table. He had an odd emaciated bloodless leer. He seemed to be calculating the odds, waiting to pounce on the table and take Andy's money away from him. They all envied and detested Andy, who owned a large company and could afford to take so many chances.

A rich Chinese woman ("That one there has a million dollars on her tonight," said Andy) who'd lost whatever mysterious beauty she might have had in youth, flirted with the conquistador between spins. Like the black woman in his truck earlier, this woman too had a history with Andy. She had a lovely and gentle way of lifting her fingers into the air when she lost, and smiling so openly when she won.

At six, with the sun brightening outside, two of the Germans, Andy, and I took the elevator to the café for breakfast. Andy paid, of course. No one else put down money. No one thanked him. All was taken for granted. We ate in silence, like dining on cakes and coffee at a wake.

At seven A.M. the respectable suburb where Andy lived was bathed in sober light. We pulled into his driveway just as I was asking why he gambled. I couldn't understand how anyone liked to risk losing so much in one night.

"No, no, no, you don't understand at all, do you?" He glared at me, the vigor gone out of his eyes.

"No, I don't." What I didn't say was what I feared: that perhaps I hadn't the courage to risk so much. I really wanted to understand Andy's gambling. I'd gambled by staying in Ecuador, but to be a true treasure hunter I would have to gamble even more.

"Jesus, Peter. It's much better to lose. Better if I had lost to-night. Of course I was *trying* to win, but to lose when you try to win—that's the best feeling in the world. You can't understand that. No, you'll never understand." He looked bored with me and went to bed without another word.

I understood one thing: Gambling and treasure hunting were

linked somehow. I understood the connection in my head, but not in my wallet. But, I wondered, did you have to be rich to be a good treasure hunter?

◆◆◆

The next evening at dusk, the day before I left Guayaquil for Quito, while Andy was still sleeping, I called an acquaintance I'd met years before when he was an AFS student in a tiny Adirondack town in upstate New York, of all places, where our family had a summer house on a private lake.

Oscar Lalama was a gentle, very dark boy whose father was a colonel in the Ecuadorian Air Force and (in the military government) president of the national telephone company.

Oscar's older brother, who was a pilot, took us flying in his little Cessna over the many channels that twist like a thousand muddy brown snakes between the Guayaquil harbor and the open Pacific.

I sat in the front with Oscar's brother, a short, thin, reserved man of twenty-nine, not quite as dark-skinned as Oscar, who sat behind us. The sky was growing dimmer by the second, and for me it was thrilling to be in a foreign country, with people I knew only casually, high up in an oyster sky, with the land and the city and the water below us turning a uniformly darker grey.

We flew over many ships of different sizes. Their lights were off and we could barely discern their phantom shapes tucked against remote islets in the myriad of river bends below. Oscar said they were smugglers. Guayaquil, he said, was one of South America's busiest contraband ports.

Over the rasp of the engine, Oscar's brother told me that the police couldn't stop them. There were just too many and the area was too vast to control. I wondered if it was dangerous to fly over them as we were doing, again and again, in our flight to the southwest of the city.

When we landed in darkness I asked Oscar's brother if he

knew of the Llanganatis from the air. *"Cierto,* sure," he told me; every Ecuadorian pilot knew that region, the worst in the country. The Air Force had lost three jets there in the last several months, he said. And the Quito-to-Cuenca flight was notoriously hazardous—doomed, he said. It was a gamble to fly the direct route. Last April a plane had left Quito and was lost over those mountains. No one ever found it. But there were stories that some Indians had come out with the rings and money of the dead.

"When veteran travelers want to go from Quito to Cuenca," Oscar said with a straight face, "they fly first to Guayaquil then from there to Cuenca, in order to avoid passing over the Llanganatis."

There was a lot of superstition about that eastern side of the Andes, Oscar's brother told me as he locked up the Cessna for the night and secured the wings with ground ropes. Something like the Bermuda triangle. Pilots know that over those mountains the compass goes haywire.

He told me, *"Allá, la brújula baila; sí, baila la brújula!"* Out there the compass dances, dances the compass, he said.

I was struck by the beauty and precision of the Spanish phrase. It communicated something the English could not. The word *"brujo"* means witchdoctor and a *"bruja"* is a witch. So the word for compass, *"brújula,"* derives from the same Latin root for sorcery. And *"baila,"* from *"bailar"*—to dance—was such a festive word, a popular word always at the edge of the coastal people's tongues. Everything in that heat *baila,* dances. To tell me that in the Llanganatis, where I wanted to go with Diego, *"baila la brújula"*—the compass dances—this struck a chilling chord inside me: such a uniquely Latin American phrase, mixing magic, a mechanical device, and dancing.

Also, the way Oscar's brother, that reserved and rational pilot in the air, so quickly acknowledged, without the slightest hesitation, the magic and mystery of that part of Ecuador, surprised me, made me feel how palpable was my imminent adventure.

I learned later, too, of the extreme rivalry between coastal and mountainous Ecuador. The Quiteños, the *serranos*, refer to coastal Ecuadorians pejoratively as *"los monos,"* the monkeys, and the coastal people view the Andes with much skepticism. The Llanganatis are perhaps the quintessential symbol on the coast for forbidden mountain areas.

Before I left Oscar and his brother, they both asked, "But why would you want to go east of the Andes; that is such taboo country. Jívaros live there." Savages, they said.

When I got home that night around ten, Andy was waiting for me. It was my last evening with him, and I think he wanted to stay home and just talk treasure talk. This was the night Andy came very close to telling where the gold was hidden on Cerro Hermoso; he was also candid about his motivations for becoming a treasure hunter.

We sat on his back porch. We didn't drink at all. It was slightly cooler than it'd been all week. The parched palms rustled in a Pacific breeze as Andy showed me pictures of past expeditions. Thirty, forty serious men stood on the side of desolate fuzzy-looking hills in the *páramo* near Píllaro. The photos seemed ancient, coffee-stained. The men looked as hardworked and ragged as lumberjacks in the Yukon a hundred years back. But these pictures had been taken only twenty, ten, even five years ago. They were like paleontological specimens, fossils, and once again I tried with difficulty to picture myself in those mountains.

I'd never done anything like this before. I'd traveled with a scientist through the forests on the coast of Tanzania, done a lot of hiking in the Adirondacks when I was a child, walked through southern Spain, but had never risked my life, certainly not at fourteen thousand feet in fog and snow and cloud forest jungle, and with no one around to help if I got into trouble. The coward in me hoped Diego would say no to my joining him. Then I'd be safe; I could go home to New York City, move safely to Vermont, perhaps, grow vegetables, start a small farm, marry, and find a teaching job.

Andy's eyes that night were austere as slate.

"To go into the Llanganatis," he said, "is to go back in time."

The Indians in the photos were the sons and grandsons and great-great-grandsons of Llanganati guides and porters. Life for the mountain Indian, Andy told me, hadn't changed since Inca— even pre-Inca—times.

"There's something else, Peter. You must know that a few people say the gold is already in Scotland."

"What?" What was he telling me? "Scotland?"

"Part of it, they say, was taken out in the nineteenth century and shipped from Lambayeque on the coast of Peru. It's only a rumor, however, and I don't believe this for a goddamn minute because I know where it is, but I don't want to find it just yet, no, not just now anyway."

Andy had first heard of the treasure as a boy. His father showed him a copy of the Valverde *Guide* in Richard Spruce's *Notes of a Botanist*.

In the two-hundred-page transcript I'd read when I first came to his house, Andy had said:

"Call it a daring desire to believe in the unknown, or an extrasensory perception of some kind, or simply a subconscious need to get away from reality. I don't care what you call it. But from that moment my mind was fixed on that treasure and it still is."

On November 31, 1952, Andy made his first expedition. The porters took him in the wrong direction, and he got lost. The Valverde *Guide* seemed useless.

"Valverde said:

Following now on foot in the same direction, thou shalt come on a great black lake [Yanacocha] the which leave on thy left hand, and beyond it seek to descend along the hill-side in such

a way that thou mayest reach a ravine, down which comes a
waterfall. . . ."

On Andy's second expedition he still thought the Valverde
Guide might be mistaken, so he left the Black Lake (Yanacocha)
on his right and not, as Valverde instructed, on the left. The trip
was a bust.

In 1954 he flew over the area and went in again. It rained so
hard the water flowed up to his hips. One night there was no
place to sleep at all.

When they had left Píllaro, one of the carriers' wives followed
them for seven hours, crying aloud. Finally Andy stopped and
went up to her and said they were headed for the Llanganatis.
The very word made her scream and fall to her knees begging
them not to go; she said they wouldn't come home alive, and she
grabbed Andy's leg and would not let go.

Andy assured her they would send word; her husband would be
safe. Finally she turned and limped out of sight, sobbing the whole
way. A gust of wind caught up that horrible grief, and Andy
remembered the terrible feeling of doom it cast over the expedition.

"Her husband, the carrier, had seemed at first the most
intelligent of the group, but first impressions deceive. He grew
lethargic as we proceeded and the days passed; something had
definitely come over him—like a trance. He changed more than
anyone I've ever seen change up there.

"The rain, the storm, the thunder, we all had to put up with it,
all of us did. Yet that man seemed to be affected by the bad
weather more than the rest of us. Maybe he just had a weak spirit,
I don't know."

Andy picked the Indian up at times and pushed him, prodded
him to keep moving. Finally the expedition turned back because of
weather. They came to a gorge where each man had to jump a
distance of fifteen feet at a forty-five-degree angle. They had to

jump or die; no other way around. The rain had flooded everything from sight.

Andy's friend, Guido Boschetti, jumped first. Andy was next,
and after he made the jump, he waited on a little ledge below and
caught the rest as each came across, one by one. It was a big
group, and the hours were passing. The rain wouldn't let up. But
the Indian who had gone a little screwy threw his machete across
the gorge without alerting anyone and the men on the other side
had to duck to avoid the whirling blade. Then, without tying the
safety rope around his waist as the others had done, the man
jumped haphazardly. He didn't seem to care.

The Indian fell against Andy, then toppled backwards. He
started to pull Andy over with him into the gorge, and as they
both began to fall, Andy pushed the crazy man away in order to
save his own life.

"I watched him drop five hundred feet into the rushing river
below. I could see him grab a branch, which broke in the river.
He disappeared clutching that branch like a life vest. We went
below and searched until dark, diving into freezing water. Then,
exhausted, we slept like dead men."

The next day there was rain and thunder and lightning bolts
which shot down as often as seventy-two per minute—Andy
counted them with his watch as the men huddled together. And
they all prayed.

What made the carrier's death even more strange was that
when the group got back to Guayaquil, Andy and his friends
discovered that their wives had been to a fortune-teller who had
predicted that one man would die but that it wouldn't be the
leader. The leader, she'd said, would be solicited when he got
back to buy a foreign lottery ticket, and, if he bought it, he
would win.

A week later in Guayaquil Andy was speaking of this incident
to his friends, telling the story of the Indian's strange death, when
the doorbell rang, and he jokingly said, "Now this is probably the

lottery man." His wife got up to answer the door: a Panamanian was selling tickets to the Quito lottery. The party in the room went dead quiet; then Andy laughed and bought six tickets. Two months later, he won two thousand dollars.

A year later the dead man's body was found intact between two huge rocks. The cold had preserved him just as on the day he died: no decomposition whatsoever.

◆◆◆

At this point in one of Andy's soliloquies I broke in to ask about the *Guide*, the whole ending of which seemed crucial yet mysterious. I wished he'd explain it in terms of his own expeditions into the mountains. I opened the Spruce text and read part of the *Guide* aloud:

Go forward and look for the signs of another sleeping-place, which, I assure thee, thou canst not fail to see in the fragments of pottery and other marks, because the Indians are continually passing along there. Go on thy way, and thou shalt see a mountain which is all of margasitas (pyrites), the which leave on thy left hand, and I warn thee that thou must go round it in this fashion ⌒ . On this side thou wilt find a pajonál (pasture) in a small plain, which having crossed thou wilt come on a cañon between two hills, which is the Way of the Inca. From thence as thou goest along thou shalt see the entrance of the socabón (tunnel), which is in the form of a church porch. Having come through the cañon and gone a good distance beyond, thou wilt perceive a cascade which descends from an offshoot of the Cerro Llanganati and runs into a quaking-bog on the right hand; and without passing the stream in the said bog there is much gold, so that putting in thy hand what thou shalt gather at the bottom is grains of gold. To ascend the mountain, leave the bog and go along to the right, and pass above the cascade, going round the offshoot of the mountain. And if by chance the mouth of the socabón be closed with certain herbs which they call "Salvaje," remove them, and thou wilt find the entrance. And on the left-hand side of the mountain thou mayest see the "Guayra" (for thus the ancients called the furnace where they founded metals), which is nailed with golden nails. And to reach the third mountain, if thou canst not pass in front of the socabón, it is the same thing to pass behind it, for the water of the lake falls into it.

If thou lose thyself in the forest, seek the river, follow it on the right bank; lower down take to the beach, and thou wilt reach the cañon in such sort that, although thou seek to pass it, thou wilt not find where; climb, therefore, the mountain on the right hand, and in this manner thou canst by no means miss thy way.

"So," I asked, "did you follow Valverde's route all the way to the end?"

After several more expeditions, Andy explained, he was still unable to find Valverde's path after passing the Black Lake. Descending a gorge, reaching a river, Valverde had said to look for a "deep dry ravine" which was to lead into the "Way of the Inca." But Andy couldn't find it. This was the same problem all expeditions were having. They got lost at the Margasitas Mountain, which the Spaniard indicated to pass in this manner ☾ .

On one trek into that area, Andy's Indians abandoned him, leaving four men with only a bag of candles, seven potatoes, and a can of peaches. They managed to shoot four rabbits but, after the animals were washed, there was no meat found on them. They were nothing but hair and bones. Even the animals starved out there. The men ate them anyway. Knowing that food was scarce in the mountains, they ran the whole way back to Píllaro, afraid to be caught up there in bad weather. It took four days to get out. When they did, they were nearly frozen and starved.

"But, Andy, how could you keep going, if you got so few results?"

Even after all these failed expeditions, Andy felt he was the only one who could solve the perfect puzzle. "I love that terrain," Andy said, and in this one sentence he said so much. There were times he couldn't go more than a mile in a day, and other times no more than yards. "The jungle's so thick, we walked through the branches of trees." Andy's face filled with delight at this idea.

"But it wasn't just the terrain, was it? What about the gold itself? Did you always think you'd find it?"

Sure, he'd find it, he said, but originally it was the idea of discovering treasure and unraveling a mystery, not just the gold itself, but the discovery of an unknown truth which was being hidden just out of sight. The very thing he wished to pinpoint was so elusive, more mercurial the more he delved into the story. That paradox was what hooked him, he said. It wasn't the money; he had plenty.

"Also, the gold became my personal enemy. I refused to become the treasure's slave, so I decided to drop out of the picture for a while and take a break after giving it my all for four years."

From 1956 to 1962, Andy didn't make any trips to the Llanganatis. On the recommendation of his father, however, he talked to his father's friend, a famous British explorer living west of the Andes in a small village. Commander George Dyott, best known for his search for Colonel Fawcett in Brazil's Matto Grosso in 1928, told Andy he had some "special information" regarding Atahualpa's treasure—an interesting story about a British sea captain, named Barth Blake, who was supposed to have accidentally found the treasure but died before he had a chance to take it out.

"For Dyott, too, this treasure was one of the only real mysteries in the world. Dyott loved mysteries."

"So tell me the story," I pleaded because I could tell Andy was slowing down at this important place. Once again, for some reason, he was holding back; he wasn't telling me everything, and it was frustrating to hear only pieces of certain stories. I felt a surprising rage welling up inside me.

"Aw, come on, Andy. I have to know ..."

"Patience, Peter, patience," he said severely.

I noticed, too, at certain times he would actually skip important details. For instance, he didn't tell me what the nature of this "special information" was, or how Dyott had obtained it, or how Barth Blake fitted into the story.

Also, Dyott, Andy, and "that crazy German, Brunner," all three had apparently made some sort of secret contract in the 1960's. In any event, Andy's meeting with Dyott was impetus enough for Andy to begin searching again for the gold. Six idle years had gone by.

At one point Andy did tell me the story of the helicopter crash. Armed with the Blake story, whatever that was, and Dyott's "special information," inflamed again about the gold, Andy, an Air Force pilot, and an old prospector took off in a small helicopter from Baños on February 8, 1963. When they got over Cerro Hermoso, heavy winds buffeted them about. They spotted an island in the middle of a river but, as they tried to land, the rear rotor hit against a cliff and the helicopter plunged twenty feet into a quaking bog on the island.

They quickly put wood blocks under the machine to keep it from sinking in the muck and tried to take off again, but sparks from the engine flared at some dry grass around them, and a brush fire broke out. The pilot grabbed the fire extinguisher and put out the flames, but the chopper was charred and immobile.

Andy had planned merely to make a quick run over the area of Cerro Hermoso where he expected to find the *"socabón,"* or tunnel, of Valverde's *Guide*. After the short helicopter ride, he had planned to make a trek into this same area. When they crashed, all plans changed.

They had been using one of a few helicopters the United States had given Ecuador after that particular model had been rejected as unsafe in America. It had taken only twenty minutes to fly to where they now were stuck without a radio and without provisions. All they could do was hope for a rescue party.

Three days later they heard a plane searching back and forth just above the low clouds. The fog was thick as steam, the temperature nearly freezing. The plane flew away.

The helicopter pilot came down with pneumonia. And they knew it would take at least three weeks for someone to find them on the ground, so Andy decided that the only solution was to climb out of the valley they'd crashed in. But the walls up Cerro Hermoso at this point were nearly vertical.

Weak from lack of food, struggling like a cripple, Andy climbed three thousand feet but finally returned the next day to the helicopter, nearly collapsing.

He had, however, found a cave which he believed then, and still believes, was the *"socabón"* which Valverde described as a major landmark not far from the treasure.

Four more terrible days passed, when suddenly a noise like the distant buzz of a chainsaw ran up the canyon. They thought they were dreaming.

At seven-thirty in the morning a small shiny object moved very slowly through the air toward them. It was a Helio Courier, a small light plane designed to fly at low speeds without stalling. A man's voice came through the walkie-talkie in the helicopter. It was a pilot from the Summer Institute of Linguistics, a missionary group. The pilot returned in a few days; the plane dropped food, medicine, and insect repellent.

"I saw him in a Quito hotel years later. I heard him telling my story, about these crazy Ecuadorians. So I ducked out; I didn't want to be known as one of those crazy lost stupid Ecuadorians screaming up at him from beside our maimed helicopter. I never saw him again, but thank God he was flying up that canyon that day. I still don't know what he was doing out there, unless he was looking for converts. Ha ha."

The pilot made numerous trips with supplies and food. Later he dropped a rear rotor replacement which the Air Force had had to send to Miami to collect. "None of us was mechanically inclined, but we managed to put the rotor on. Then we discovered we needed batteries. So we waited more days. The whole time we expected a rescue party any minute. No one came.

"I didn't tell the others, but things were more desperate than we thought. I had an aerial photo of the region taken years before during the rainy season, which was due in a few weeks. No island showed on the photo, just rushing water!"

The missionary returned finally after weeks of bad weather. He called down asking how many people were on the ground. Andy told him three. The pilot hadn't remembered, as if something else was occupying his mind. Suddenly three Bibles and the necessary batteries rained down on the survivors.

The young captain of the helicopter was a religious man, and he prayed hard, but the gold prospector from Píllaro was a "natural man" and would have loved to stay there forever away from cities and civilization. This man didn't touch the Bible.

The fog and clouds never ceased, but one day the gray sky split in two, and there was a huge hole of clear blue air above them. It had been foggy all afternoon. The three desperate men jumped into the helicopter and ... "We were flying into oblivion."

The copter climbed and climbed and then they saw lights in the distance, the sky growing darker and darker, but they followed the lights of trucks which were driving to Puyo, where they finally landed at the Air Force base.

"We got so drunk, we slept the whole next day." A colonel showed them telegrams from little Oriente outposts. "We have seen the helicopter falling in flames." Another read: "We discovered remains of copter in jungle. Two men are crazy and naked in a tree."

A week later the same helicopter, this American reject, crashed during an Air Force demonstration. Fortunately, the pilot lived.

"I sent another expedition in to verify if the cave I'd found was indeed the *"socabón."* I wanted to see if water fell into it as the *Guide* says it must. My men discovered that, yes, water was feeding it. This tunnel then is on the northwest face of the Cerro. If you look closely at this topographic map you can see where I spent nearly a month on the island."

Maps and photos and old copies of Llanganati texts were spread around us in Guayaquil like a child's game.

"In 1965 this man Brunner I was telling you about and another man named Moerner had gone into that same region and came out very excited. Brunner had taken pictures; he'd found a pit, what might have once been a square pool, small, where the Incas had thrown the gold. But it was empty, no water, no gold. Very strange. It rains there all the time, but this little trench had not a drop of water. Very curious indeed.

"Next to the empty pit they found a very small square lake, and a wall with a gate which when you cross it you come into the trench itself. They also found a cave next to the square lake. It was on a forty-five-degree angle."

Andy agreed that the treasure was there in that very spot, somewhere near the lake Brunner found in 1965. Lake Brunner.

"No one has yet dug inside the bottom of the square lake. No one has gone more than fifteen feet into the cave because you need special equipment, pitons and ropes."

I asked, was Diego going now for this very purpose?

Andy smiled, said, "Perhaps."

Something in the way a treasure hunter puts information—as if he has discovered new clues only yesterday and all we have to do now is put them to the test—makes it all sound so simple. I wanted to be a part of Andy's experiments because after thirty years, I reasoned, an experiment is no longer just a wild guessing game; in time and through trial and error it becomes a hypothesis—almost a theory.

◆◆◆

Next morning Andy, for a change, was up early drinking coffee, bright-eyed and reading the morning paper.

"What kind of man is Diego?" I asked.

Andy looked out the window.

"For two or three years I consciously intensified his feelings toward the same goal as mine. When I first told him about the treasure, Diego snatched the idea and instantly made the quest his own."

Andy's voice seemed sad. The fumes from his black coffee curled into the air. He kept gazing out at the pool and the palm trees. And I remember feeling jealous of Diego's friendship with Andy. Obviously it had run very deep.

But perhaps, he said, he'd given Diego a false sense of the treasure's importance.

"You see, Peter, there are practical things to attend to in this life of ours, no? Family, for one, and making money. That's why I am unable to go with you this year. It's not only a life made of some fantastic search for gold, though God knows how important this is, too."

Andy regretted not inculcating Diego with a better sense of his responsibilities.

Those ideas, "responsibility," "family," "making money," seemed strange coming from Andy's mouth. This was the formal side of Andy I'd not seen. With these concepts he seemed to be going back on all his previous lawless enthusiasm, and his new caution about treasure hunting had the sober effect of making me cautious toward him. I wanted to pull away from him a little. He was sounding more like my real father. I had stayed in Ecuador to avoid responsibility. I wanted adventure, not family.

Andy said, "I had thought then that to find a friend was as good as finding a treasure. The fact that he was my son-in-law made no difference. We were excellent friends. And when you have a friend, then why not go find a treasure with your friend?"

Hearing this, I hoped Diego would be such a friend to me, too.

Andy paused, drank the rest of his coffee, and said very quietly, "But this will be the last expedition I fund for Diego . . . he is not well."

"What's wrong with him? Is he sick?" The idea that he might be too sick to go into the mountains in November surprised and depressed me.

"You will see when you meet him."

"What do you mean, Andy?"

Silence.

♦♦♦

Driving to the airport, Andy tossed off his temporary gloom and came alive again, almost, I feared, happy that I was leaving:

"You must talk to Brunner! You must! That is, if he is not dead by now. He's the greatest aficionado of the Llanganatis. Last summer they said he was looking for the ancient emerald mines of the Inca here on the coast, and I don't think he's been seen for months. If he was back in Quito, I would have heard about it. But he is the key, you know. He has all the information, more than anyone. You better pray he isn't dead if you want stories."

"But," I tried again, "what exactly was your relationship to Brunner?"

Andy talked freely now. He seemed to be loosening on the subject of the German, and I was sorry I was leaving.

"Brunner knew Dyott, too. The three of us made a contract years ago. Brunner had so much more spare time than any of us. Dyott had the new information about Blake. I had some money, and Brunner could spend months in those mountains every year.

He's made more trips than anyone except perhaps for Luis Andrade, who has made something like sixty, I think . . ."

"Another one?" I couldn't believe this. Another important lead to follow! Suddenly a new name, like a scarf pulled from a magician's sleeve.

"Luis who? Is he in Quito, too?"

"Andrade, yes, I think he still lives in Quito. Another crazy old man. They're all crazy. But Andrade gave up. I hear now all he does is sit in the Plaza de la Independencia and feed pigeons.

"But Brunner! He is still searching and he's the only one with access to the Blake maps. Sometimes Brunner, even though he's sixty-five years old now, will stay for months on end never coming out at all. Alone! Wandering the terrain. He's not at all like me, no. *His life depends on that gold.*" Andy's tone, filled only with respect, was so strongly envious. He spoke with none of his previous rivalry or condescension. Full of awe for this other treasure hunter, Andy made me long to find the German.

"If no one's seen him in Quito for months," I said, "then how will I locate him?"

Andy said he used to live somewhere in the old quarter of town, the colonial section which Benalcázar had burned while looking for the treasure. Unlike the old days, when they were partners with Dyott, Andy didn't even have Brunner's telephone number anymore.

"Time changes," Andy said nostalgically.

In a few more hours I'd be in the capital. After dropping my bag at my apartment, I'd go straight to Diego's bar. Perhaps he might know where I could find Brunner.

"Brunner came out with a story years ago, I remember," Andy said before we shook hands and I boarded my plane for Quito. "He'd heard of a book in the Leipzig library about a man who had walked into the Llanganatis, into the third Cordillera, and was captured behind the Black Mountain by some Indians he called Sabelas, who sucked blood from cuts in their arms. The man discovered a lost city with walls of gold, he said. And a year later he escaped . . . This is the story Brunner told me, anyway. I'm not sure I believe it, of course, but this treasure is Brunner's baby. If you don't find him, you will never hear the most incredible collection of facts and nonfacts of anyone alive, all strung together into Brunner's own truth. He's a perfect tale spinner."

PART TWO

◆◆◆◆◆

QUITO

CHAPTER 4

♦♦♦♦♦

Rusted DC-3's and eviscerated turbojets (one with its wings plucked out) lined the Quito runway like maimed insects. In half-cocked positions of neglect, wreckages of obsolete airplanes sat, paralyzed, where they had once crashed and were abandoned.

Quitenian air was dry, crisp, thin, fragile, and timeless. Knowing I was here to stay made me fall in love again with this tragic, beautiful fossil of a city.

From taxis and buses and tiny hidden *cantinas*, the flute music of the sierra wove its plaintive message, antithesis of Guayaquil's brassy *salsa* and *cumbias* which had blared all night long in the downtown streets. Here in the Andes, people were quiet. They wore reticent faces and dark ponchos and heavy layers of mountain clothing. Even when they smiled, their spirits seemed wrapped in sadness.

But when I landed and got a taxi home, I felt the rushing energy and joy of someone who has resolved a nagging question. Tonight would be cold and I would sleep soundly.

Isolationists even in the brightness of noon, Quiteños would rather gaze at the ground or the horizon than let their eyes meet yours directly. People here had a fragile outlook; confrontation was anathema. During a typical Quito night, the mists off the volcanoes roamed the empty streets like phantoms. Everyone was asleep by nine-thirty.

There was a kind of frigid northern European quality, too, about Quito, which I liked better than the coast because I felt more at home here, less vulnerable as a tourist, more secure with my new treasure story, perhaps.

Two degrees south of the Equator, nearly two miles above sea level, Quito, "City of Eternal Spring," is aligned on a north–south axis, its million residents spread out across the slopes of Pichincha, a sixteen-thousand-foot volcano, often covered in ice.

Paradoxes abounded in the magic city. When the nights were rainy, they were cold winter British nights. But when they were clear, the stars were like specks of glass in a coal sky. In the mornings, usually sunny, the air was thin and cool. The temperature plummeted during the night to forty degrees, yet many streets were lined with tropical palms. Cactus grew in my garden. And it was common to hear the saying: "Every day in Quito we have all four seasons, señor," because a perfectly sunny day could turn to cloud and hail, then clear up again and grow hot and dry as a desert.

The equatorial sun passed through a noon sky of perfect blue sea, but the clarity seemed deceptive somehow, like a two-way mirror. While the sun laughed, the severe faces of the Indians in the streets were taut, distressed. Their stocky sierran torsos forever buckled over from heavy loads of thatch, avocado, potato.

Mountainous Ecuador was a country of burden, a sad country in singing Andean light.

As from so many apartment windows in Quito, my view was magnificent. Early in the morning I could see no fewer than three snow-capped volcanoes. High on the slopes of Pichincha towering over the city were the ranches, green terraces, and checkered fields of corn, eucalyptus groves, and cow pastures. Some days in the still afternoons I spotted vertical trails of smoke rising from the mountain, silently pinning the sky. I heard some fascinating legends, too. Somewhere on the other side of the volcano, Inca gold was hidden when the Indians heard the Spaniards were coming to rape Quito's treasure. Gold that had never been found.

My little apartment in a large house was on the border between the new city and the old colonial quarter to the south. Modern Quito with its hastily constructed concrete buildings engulfed the airport and stretched northward where more and more construction continued to gobble up the countryside.

Since an exportable quantity of oil had been discovered in the country's Amazon region in the early 1970's, money had poured in to support an ever-expanding urban middle class. Ecuador was second only to Venezuela in Latin American oil production. For a select few, Ecuador was a nation of immense opportunity. If you were a foreigner with money or an Ecuadorian with *palanca* (translated equally as pull, leverage, connections), you could begin any number of profitable new businesses here, unencumbered by competition or legal restriction.

Yet the majority of the people had next to nothing. The average yearly income was five hundred dollars. The great rift between the rich and the poor retained its colonial significance. Established families owned huge sprawling estates handed down from the conquistadors. And rather than splitting these up, the government was offering 125 acres in the Amazon for aspiring homesteaders. In the sierra the peasants lived in mud and thatch huts or corrugated iron and wood-slat conglomerations, tending small divided plots on the great estates.

Outside the city, most of Ecuador's roads were dirt, one-lane tracks, often too muddy to pass. Leaving the city was like entering U.S. Indian Territory circa 1861: Anything could happen out there.

Conditions in much of the Andes continued to border on the feudal. Only a few decades ago, a system called *huasipungo* had operated where serfdom was legal on large haciendas. Landowners could buy and sell Indian peasants. Although the system was no longer practiced outright, its oppressive effects were far from over.

Living in modern Quito, however, one easily got the illusion that Ecuador was leaping into the twenty-first century. Because of the oil boom, car factories, beer and soft-drink plants, match and plastic companies encased the extreme northern and southern sides of the city like industrial bookends. Quitenian salesmen and accountants in immaculate suits, brandishing slim Samsonite briefcases, hurried purposefully through the streets. On Amazonas, the main avenue of the new city, secretaries with eye shadow, and bank clerks with darting metropolis eyes and oil-sleek hair, reminded a traveler of more sophisticated places like Buenos Aires or San José, Costa Rica.

Yet for all its cosmopolitan aspirations, Quitenian drivers were perhaps the best barometer of this country's degree of civilization. I once saw a car go past a police officer who had motioned it to stop. Ignoring the officer, the driver stepped on the accelerator and, after nearly running him down, drove against the traffic on a one-way street at fifty miles an hour. The officer, stern-faced, squinting, punctilious, feigned a stately mental notation of the car's identity (it had no plates), then continued to direct the chaotic traffic with his stiff-armed, white-gloved gesticulations. Perhaps the police officer had accepted the car's inviolable status: It was a Mercedes-Benz. After all, this was the same lawless country I witnessed when Andy drove through red lights in Guayaquil.

Lawless on the coast, even more lawless in the Andes. At the site of any accident on any street here, there were always people fleeing. If the police caught a particularly reckless or drunk driver, they inevitably demanded bribes, and threatened a jail term. It was unfair, unjust, but this random police corruption and Latin American bureaucracy added a wonderful gambling flavor to my days in Quito. Just to live here seemed a kind of risk. You never quite knew for sure whether you or some friend might spend the night in jail.

◆◆◆

Diego's bar, the Wonder Bar North, was located in the modern section of town, just off Amazonas in a new corner building, up one flight of steps. From the outside, it was indistinct except for the stained-glass windows and a medium-sized sign that blew in the wind.

Every day whenever I got the chance, I passed by the Wonder Bar, but the door was always locked; no lights inside, not even late at night when I walked the ghostly streets because I could not sleep.

Where had he gone? I wondered.

Then one evening I found the door open, the lights on, soft music, and Diego, alone behind an empty bar.

Diego had a Byronic face, droopy eyelids, a furrowed and anxious brow. About the same height as his father-in-law, five foot five or so, this treasure hunter lacked the mercenary, soldier-of-fortune flare. Diego's complexion was dark and brooding; he looked part Indian. Yet he seemed to smile too much or laugh when a laugh wasn't appropriate.

In the room beyond the bar, shiny French cutlery and Italian porcelain dishes sat neatly atop peach-colored table-cloths. The chairs were made of wicker. A burning candle was on each table. There was an air of delicate expectancy, as if a party were soon to begin. Diego was leaning over some game at the counter.

I introduced myself. I was very nervous. Diego said he had not talked to Andy in weeks. He had no idea who I was.

"But Andy said I should come see you. Didn't he say anything about me?"

"No."

My God, I thought, why hadn't Andy called him? Once I'd left Guayaquil, had he forgotten all about me?

Diego was not exactly sober when I first met him, either. Perhaps I should have taken this as a warning. But I was blinded by a kind of desperation to ingratiate myself so he would take me to the mountains. Here I was, beginning all over again, explaining myself.

Diego had been away from the city for a couple of weeks, he said. When I'd walked in he was casting the *I Ching* and drinking brandy from a highball glass. He rolled five pennies on the bar as if they were dice. I wanted a drink, but he didn't offer one right away. He spoke to me in English. He too had been to college in the States.

His question to the *I Ching* was: "Will I find treasure in December?" The answer came out. Diego's interpretation was something about a corporate ladder: One must proceed from A to B to C in order to find success.

Diego heaved a big sigh, disappointed.

Disco music whispered through miniature speakers at the far end of the room. Diego stood on the other side of the bar and poured me a brandy. I told him I didn't have much money. He said it didn't matter; he wanted to drink with someone.

The only light in the bar was the one over the counter. A fire roared for no one in the next room. Diego smelled of cologne and I couldn't help the feeling that any moment some woman would return from somewhere. But no one came.

The second question to the *I Ching* was: "Should I trust Barth Blake?"

All I knew about Blake was that he was the man who'd found the treasure "by the merest chance" in the late 1800's and had drawn some secret maps which had come into Andy's and Brunner's possession by way of the explorer named Dyott. Diego must have seen these maps, too. I was anxious to ask him, but held quiet for the moment.

The answer to this last question involved something vague about "nourishment." Neither Diego nor I understood, so he put it away and we talked.

Diego, I discovered quickly, was much friendlier than he looked. Once he knew I was serious about the treasure, he couldn't help me enough. And he basked in the attention I gave him.

The night passed as if between old friends. I could hardly believe my good fortune. I told Diego about my talks with Andy and my desire to go on his next expedition. Diego said, "Fine. You and I will go in December, then. But you should have the proper equipment. It's no picnic in there, you know. I can help you with that, too."

I liked Diego partly because he was close to my own age. But he was not the same kind of treasure hunter as Andy. Diego was more self-satirical. He seemed to pull back from his sentences, as an actor might when he is learning his part in a comedy, to watch himself perform the part of treasure hunter.

It was now three o'clock in the morning.

Through the early hours, the fire was stoked and Diego talked—the wonderful endless talk of treasure hunters.

If Andy had hinted at some psychic wound, Diego's wounds were right on the surface, festering. At one point he chugged a whole glass of brandy and then let out such a howl of sadness and hurt I thought he was making a joke.

"You cannot know the pain I am in," he said, suddenly very somber. Later I found out that Diego's wife had recently left him and now he wanted her back. He seemed like a man badly in need of friends.

◆◆◆

Rather than being cautious, however, I was just the opposite. After a week of partying with him, I would do anything, drink, dance to any hour of the night or morning in the elite discos of Diego's rich friends, in order to get close to him. This wasn't merely opportunism. I felt deeply sorry for him, and was glad my companionship could ease at least some fraction of his grief. But it was a frenetic companionship. Diego could be quite manic.

The next afternoon and for many afternoons we sat drinking in his bar when his drinking companions went back to whatever work they did. His few friends were the social upper crust of Quito, the sons and daughters of the very richest ministers in government: businessmen, lawyers, and doctors. Most were about his age, thirty-five—a rather decadent crew, I thought, but at least they had jobs.

Diego lived outside the mainstream; he gave away far too much liquor to make his bar profitable, and I wondered where his money was coming from. For him the Wonder Bar North was a place for friends to meet and for Diego to brag about his next expedition to the Llanganatis. But only a few seemed to take Diego's "hobby" seriously. The rest merely humored him by pretending to listen to his treasure talk.

◆◆◆

One afternoon we went shopping for rain gear which I would need for the mountains. Diego made a list of essentials: rubber boots, wool hat, wool gloves, compass, rain poncho, and so forth.

I had difficulty finding size ten boots in Ecuador. The people were small, and I am six foot two. But I found a pair in a little kiosk in the old city along the market street, 24 de Mayo, where one could find absolutely anything.

Over and over Diego described for me his three trips into the Llanganatis, two of which had been with his former mentor, Andy. Whenever he spoke of Andy, the pain of losing his wife, Monica, resurfaced and he would quickly look for a drink, anything he could get his hands on. Alcohol was his medicine. But he always spoke of his father-in-law with reverence and nostalgia. Perhaps this made losing Monica that much harder. I met Monica once. She came into the bar late on a Saturday morning. Diego was suddenly very timid; you could tell he loved her very much. Monica was blonde and American-looking, which is a desirable trait in women in Ecuador. She worked for a TV news program in Guayaquil, and she took care of their two children. But she was hardened against Diego, and I hated to see him weak in her presence. He ran around trying desperately to please her; his breath reeked of booze. Even Monica seemed embarrassed by Diego. Love between them, I was sure, had died forever. But Diego was still hoping she'd come back.

◆◆◆

The first time he took me to his disco, which was a club for rich Quiteños, we sat in dark black light. The dance floor, sunken below us, was packed with what looked like gypsies—women with haunting eye shadow, black-haired Carmens in skintight jeans whose extreme sexuality weakened every cell in my flesh.

Knowing instantly what I was feeling, Diego leered up at me and shouted drunkenly, "You like these girls? You want one for the night?"

I longed to say yes, but this kind of woman made me nervous. I said, "No, thank you. Maybe later," and I pretended to want to hear about treasure, all the while hiding my fear of these Quitenian society women. They looked like whores, they were so made up.

Diego disappeared and I worried that one of these women now looking my way from the dance floor might beckon from below, entreating me to dance.

For the moment, I was more scared of those bouncing Latin bodies in perfect rhythm with the dance music than I was of the distant Llanganati Mountains.

Diego came back with drinks and shouted, "You mention to any Ecuadorian that you're going to the Llanganatis, and they tell you, 'Not me. I would not go there even if the treasure exists, señor.'"

I looked down at the women dancing.

"Spooky area. So many died there. Have you contacted Eugene Brunner yet? No? He's been in more times than anyone alive. Andy told me all about that fellow. What a character!"

Diego, who talked like a buccaneer, had never met Brunner, and I found this odd, too. But again the "crazy" German's name had surfaced, and I found that the name itself, spoken in this ghoulish light and pounding madness, seemed out of place.

"Where can I find him, Diego?" I screamed, and still my voice seemed like a whisper beneath the hypnotism of the music.

Diego's shoulders went up, his head cocked forward, eyebrows lifted.

"Some say he's *dead*, ha ha ha."

When I bought the next round at the bar, a tall Ecuadorian next to me threw his sports jacket over a chair and out tumbled the heaviest, largest revolver I have ever seen. It landed at my feet, so I picked it up and passed it back to him. He slipped it into some sort of holster and nodded a thank you, then went on talking with a friend. But I wondered what kind of place this "club" really was and became more cautious with my talk of treasure.

For the next few months Diego and I went often to his club, and I have never in the rest of my life drunk as much whiskey and brandy as I did during that time.

◆◆◆

Early one morning, having just dropped into bed without taking my clothes off, falling instantly into a lead-mine sleep, the earthquake hit. At three-fifteen A.M. my apartment began to shake with delirium tremens.

As I woke slowly from stupor, I had the distinct feeling that someone was in my room rifling through my closets. I struggled to stand but found it impossible to walk, not because of the alcohol I'd consumed, but from the anarchic tremble of the floor.

A deep rumbling rolled in the street outside, and when I scurried to the windows, and stared at the apartments across the street, there were lights flashing on and men and women scrambling for clothes and children. Dogs barking everywhere.

For four minutes I crouched under a doorway, not knowing if I should take to the streets or stay put. I heard car motors starting up in the dark, but where did the drivers plan to go if the earth opened up?

The worst part of the earthquake, one of Quito's longest in recent history, was the knowledge that somewhere (three hundred people on the Ecuador-Colombia border, the newspaper said later) someone was dying at the epicenter.

In those irrational heavings of floor and furniture, bucking in every direction at the same time, and as the walls threw pictures and glass onto the ground in violent rebellion, the world seemed malevolent, and I thought perhaps Atahualpa was warning me to stay away from his mountains.

But suddenly, the birds sang, and the earth froze. The stillness then was deeper than ever before, the walls of the house inert. And I pictured a whole city of people like me waiting in windows, beneath doorways, in stalled cars, waiting for the next terrestrial paroxysm. We all looked out at the Andes feebly with frightened eyes trying to steady the geology, praying it still. I held Pichincha's silhouette in my gaze as if to control any intention of aftermath. Fortunately there was no second shock.

Dogs kept barking, but the roar had ceased, and I felt my heart go still. Minutes passed; twenty minutes later I took off my clothes and tentatively, gratefully, slipped under the covers, waiting for a long time before I fell asleep again, not trusting anything anymore.

But something had happened to me during the earthquake: a realization of my own loneliness, a feeling of insignificance, and a longing to be truly in love with someone—anyone.

At one point in those long four minutes I thought how terrible it would be to die without ever having loved and committed to a woman. Since high school I'd had a few girlfriends, a number of lovers, but how comforting it would be to die loving only one woman, to be missed by her when I was gone, or to die together, loved even as the earth opened and took us down.

The idea of dying alone seemed so pointless.

I woke the next day feeling vulnerable and lonely, and Diego told scary stories about the 1949 earthquake that hit Píllaro, killing thousands. The Llanganati region, he said, was the worst for earthquakes in the whole country.

Diego told me three books were necessary reading for my journey. These were the only three ever written about the treasure and none of them is well known. Two were out of print, and it took quite an effort, a lot of excavating in old bookstores, to bring a copy of each book back to my apartment so I could study them.

The first, *Llanganati*, in Spanish, was written in 1937 by Luciano Andrade Marin, an Ecuadorian geographer and statesman. It was reprinted and updated in 1970 just before the author died. No English translation was made. Only a few copies of this quasi-scientific work remain.

Marin discussed his trip into the mountains in 1933 and the natural history he found in the area. He was extremely nationalistic about the treasure, claiming that too many foreigners, and not enough Ecuadorians (to whom the legend and the riches rightfully belonged) had searched for the gold.

The second book, *Fever, Famine and Gold*, was written in 1938 by a Scotsman, Captain Erskine Loch, a veteran of the Uganda Highlanders and an officer in the British Army who fought in India and Africa. Unlike Marin's book, only half of *Fever* was written about the treasure; the other half recorded his journey into Ecuador's Amazon region.

The third, *Buried Gold and Anacondas* by the Swedish travel
writer Rolf Blomberg, was printed first in 1954 and subsequently
translated into nine languages. It was also divided into two halves:
a search for Atahualpa's gold and a search for anacondas in the
jungles of Colombia.

All three books sat in front of me on my desk. Obscure works.
Some days I struggled like a monk through the arrogant convoluted sentences of Marin's seminal work, then I closed this and
opened one of the other two, both of which followed the quick-
paced, dynamic, adventure-travel format of books written in the
early part of this century. Other books in the same class were
Leonard Clark's *The Rivers Ran East* (in the Peruvian jungle the
author faces jaguars, piranhas, hostile Indians); Colonel Fawcett's
Lost Trails, Lost Cities (a journal compiled posthumously after
Fawcett disappeared in Brazil's Matto Grosso while searching for
Atlantis); and Commander Dyott's *Trail of the Unknown* (Dyott
begins his book surrounded by arrow-shooting Indians and attempting to make radio contact with the outside world).

All three of the Llanganati books were also works of pure
action by men who went to the mountains themselves, looking for
the treasure and facing great dangers.

With two partners Marin spent a month in the Llanganatis.
One died. Of the hardships they endured Marin wrote:

> For my part I must say my journey back to Píllaro represented
> a maximum of the exertions an already exhausted human being
> can put forward, summoning up his last remains of physical
> energy, to return to a life from a region which without doubt
> should be marked on the maps, as few others in the world, with
> the words FOREVER UNINHABITABLE. . . .

Loch, under the aegis of scientific financiers in New York
City, searched two years for the gold, wrote his book, then,
disappointed by not finding the treasure in what he termed a land

of "false lures and dashed hopes," lit a candle at each corner of his kitchen table, drank a bottle of whiskey, and shot himself with his army revolver.

Blomberg's book described his first three trips following Valverde's *Guide* into the Llanganatis where he and his partner, Luis Andrade (the old man who, Andy says, now feeds pigeons in the plaza and talks to himself) were foiled by inclement weather and misinterpretations of the *Guide*.

Later I would meet Blomberg in his Quito house. He was sixty-five and had made three additional expeditions since the publication of his book. His library was filled with practically every book ever written on treasure and he told me he'd like to go into the mountains again one of these days.

All three men, Marin, Loch, and Blomberg, followed the *Guide* with little difficulty past the Black Lake (Yanacocha), but were befuddled at the Margasitas Mountain, the Pyrite Mountain, which Valverde instructs to go around in a path resembling that hieroglyph . This was the section of the *Guide* which Andy claimed finally to have solved.

Sometimes at my desk in October and November I would close all three books, gaze out at Pichincha over the city, and dream of being in those mountains with Diego in December. Only a little while longer, I hoped, and I'd be there myself. Then I wouldn't have to read a book to feel the mystery and isolation of the place, the fog-cloaked land.

◆◆◆

But I wasn't dreaming of mountains and gold all the time, not twenty-four hours a day. Even as I began to visit with Diego every night—to drink and listen to his treasure talk until the early morning—I had my hands full for six enervating hours in the daytime.

As soon as I got back from my visit with Andy in Guayaquil,

needing a work visa to remain in the country, I looked for a job. An American friend told me that the Colegio Americano, a bilingual school for privileged Ecuadorians and foreigners, regularly hired teachers off the street. All one needed was a bachelor's degree from any American university.

The school wanted a teacher right away, and I began teaching English in their elementary school. I told the administration nothing about my treasure-hunting aspirations (in fact, I did everything to conceal this from them), for if they had known I was planning to leave for the Llanganatis just as soon as Diego was ready, sometime in the middle of the school year, they might not have hired me. Because my undergraduate degree was in classics and literature, the school had initially wanted me to take the English literature honors classes for grades ten, eleven, and twelve; but I chose a basic ESL, English as a Second Language, position in the elementary division, thinking—not particularly rationally—that these students, being younger, would be hurt less by my midyear disappearance.

But I discovered I loved teaching kids, even if it was exhausting work at that high altitude. I'd never taught children this young before, and the required concentration distanced me even further from graduate school and monkeys. Why had I been interested in anthropology in the first place? All those trips to the jungle, and those dreams of some future professorship at a college seemed remote, almost ludicrous now. Only the teaching was real.

How I used to look forward to the early mornings, when, no matter how haggard I was from lack of sleep, at seven I'd wake to brilliant sunshine, the incandescent eye of God in a huge ocean of sky, the city already bustling. After coffee I'd trot the few miles to school in a fresh clean spring air that made me feel more alive than I'd felt in years, happy I was busy with my new job, glad, when I thought about it, to get my mind off Diego's expedition, which seemed forever receding into the future like a specter.

From the city streets, too, I could see volcanoes half hidden in clouds like shy women in a distant sky, and I was very happy I'd come to live in this gem of a country, this Andean Shangri-la.

One night I told Diego how much I liked Ecuador and wanted to stay, and he smiled. We were eating dinner at the Hotel Colón, a large new hotel in the modern section of Quito where most tourists stay when they come to visit the Galápagos or travel up the Andes for a day or two.

"You must try our national soup," Diego grinned.

"And what's that?"

"*Caldo de pata.*" He kept smiling.

"Foot soup?"

"Pig's feet soup. Ha ha ha. You'll love it: very good for the stomach, ha. *Ecuador puro*, pure Ecuador. You must; I insist."

I said, "No, I'm going to pass on that one, but thanks, Diego." But Diego ordered me a soup. When it came I poked at the pig's foot sloshing around in broth. I slugged down the liquid, but refused to pick at the foot with my teeth. I passed it to Diego, who wasted no time gnawing off the bits of pig flesh around the toes.

"Now that's delicious," he said.

A group of pale-skinned tourists from Spain were sitting nearby around a large table, laughing boisterously. Diego sent the waiter out to buy a rose to be delivered "from an unknown admirer" to the ugliest matron among them, a fat Spaniard with grey hair; on her upper lip was the not-so-faint shadow of an Iberian mustache.

"A token from Ecuador, ha ha," Diego snorted. "I hate Spaniards."

I disliked Diego's mean streak and said, "But why, Diego?"

I had thought rich Ecuadorians identified more with their European ancestors than with their Indian counterparts, but I was wrong. Diego was the perfect example of an Ecuadorian caught in the middle, neither Spaniard, nor Indian, but some self-loathing combination of both.

"Spaniards are such weaklings," he hissed. "They're so arrogant. They are as pale as milk."

To take his mind off the tourists, I asked him to describe the daily routine of an expedition. He looked away from the Spaniards, and slipped easily, thank God, into the subject he loved most.

"There's a bush in there, remarkable. It's called *caspivela* and it burns even when it's wet. So we camp near these bushes for safety. We send some peons to get bunches of it, pile it under a little cover, and start to cook. We always bring little gas stoves for when it rains, and cook in our tents. But the gas, a couple of gallons, weighs much at that altitude and it's difficult to carry it in.

"Andy and I usually eat what the peons eat. Salt is one of the most important items. I don't know why. But the peons eat a ton of it. We drink the *pinol*, which is a raw cane-sugar powder and roasted barley-flour mixed together. Horrible taste, but it gives the energy you need.

"And rice, and tuna, and *máchica*, which is a corn flour. The peons eat shit-loads of it. Every meal. Outrageous! But they need the energy to carry that seventy pounds on their backs all day. The loads are packed in boxes, then strapped around their shoulders. We have special boxes for them. All supplies get divided evenly into each box so if one falls over a cliff there will be equal amounts of each supply in the other boxes. Pretty smart, eh?"

"Yes, very smart."

"I like to have a peon walk ahead of me in case there's a crevasse or ravine or precipice. They warn me before I get there.

"But the peons, shit, they steal! Man, do they steal! Have stolen for centuries. You have to take that into account when outfitting an expedition."

Diego, I noticed, was more paranoid about the Indian porters than Andy. And I wondered why. Perhaps it was because he was still a novice, with only three treks behind him. Merely an assistant professor in this department, a long way from tenure.

"Another thing you have to watch for is who you bring into the mountains in the first place. If someone freaks out, or panics in there, it's a long way back." I wondered if Diego was aiming this comment at me.

I asked, "Diego, have you had your appendix taken out?" I had had an appendectomy when I was twenty-one, and somewhere I'd read that before going into the wilderness it was a good idea for an explorer to take his appendix out.

Diego retorted, "What?" As if I were crazy.

"Your appendix, I don't know the word in Spanish."

"*Sí, apéndice.*" He smiled. "No. I have all my things inside me yet." He looked oddly at me as if he might now reconsider taking me along. "Why do you ask this, Peter?"

Embarrassed, but already committed, I explained. "Because if you get appendicitis in there, you'd really have a problem, wouldn't you? I've heard many explorers died because they hadn't had their appendixes taken care of."

The Spaniards were getting up to leave and Diego eyed them with hatred.

"*Sí,* yes, you die," Diego said. Then smugly, with his bandit's smirk: "Or you fix it yourself with your knife, ha ha ha." He slashed the air with an imaginary machete.

Thank God Diego changed the subject. "You, of course, know the story of the Scotsman, Captain Loch, do you not?"

"No." I lied. I'd read Loch's book at Andy's house, but I wanted to hear the story again. Diego's version, Diego's additions. Part of what fascinated me about the treasure story was the way in which it was embellished by each treasure hunter. Never the same story told twice in the same manner. Each person had his own signature—his own style, diction, choice of events to highlight.

"Well, he was a crazy man, obsessed with treasure. He hired many horses and porters and he set off. He had a lot of backing from the States. But the first fiasco was that the horses couldn't get in. They sank in the bogs. We call them 'quaking bogs' because they tremble when you step on the clumps of earth floating in pools of water and mud. Horses, mules, sometimes men can't get through these quaking bogs.

"Loch finally killed himself when he didn't find the gold. Drank a couple of bottles of booze and, poof poof, shot himself in the head. One doesn't read about this in the book, I can tell you that!"

Diego was laughing, using Loch's misfortune to bolster his own ego, drowning himself in another Fundador brandy.

Then he looked up at the ceiling and he seemed to change again. "No, really, this Captain Loch was a poor son of a bitch, a tragic man, *señor*, really and truly tragic." Diego's face softened as he told Loch's story.

The captain was a debonair and swashbuckling treasure hunter, the Errol Flynn of Ecuador. A veteran British Army officer, he was tall with a lean Scots face, a strong even nose, thin lips, a concisely trimmed military mustache, and a high forehead—the delicacy of which emphasized a calculating courage. He was arrogant, reclusive, and he drank heavily (what treasure hunter did not drink heavily?).

The purpose of his two-year expedition through the Amazon and through the Llanganatis was ostensibly to explore the unknown regions, collect ethnological and zoological specimens, and discover a viable land route which would join the Andes with the Amazon.

Talking with those who remembered Captain Loch, I discovered that the man's obsession with the treasure was the essential motivation behind all his expeditions. And his book seemed to be little more than an explorer's justification to his financial backers.

The gold was Loch's main (and, Diego contended, his only) reason for going into the Llanganatis.

The captain's first expedition left Píllaro in March 1936, the worst possible time of year for traveling in the region. At Píllaro, Loch had met an old man named José Ignacio Quinteros. All his life, "Old Q" (Quinteros's nickname) had searched for the treasure. And he begged Loch to let him accompany the expedition. He claimed to know where all the others had gone wrong and to have new clues which, certainly this time, would lead them to the treasure. He spoke mysteriously of a "mountain of gold."

A good treasure hunter considers every clue to be a possible breakthrough, and Loch took him along.

Rain, strong winds, and snow in the higher regions beset the expedition from the start. It rained thirty-nine days and nights with no letup. Porters complained and deserted. One night flooding was so bad, Loch was forced to sleep in a tree. Provisions and equipment were lost.

Old Q underwent a change—the same kind of mood swing, Diego said, as that of the porter who died on one of Andy's expeditions. Old Q grew listless and he lost his sense of direction. One day he collapsed.

"The Llanganatis are known to induce these altered states of consciousness. They cast a deep depression over those who enter them," said Diego. But it wasn't until much later back in Píllaro that Quinteros was able to shake loose of the odd mood which gripped him on the trek.

Loch continued in spite of the rain. He came to a lake on the bottom of which he saw shiny metal flakes glistening. One Indian porter madly flung himself into the water and came up with a handful of mica. It was the lowest point of the first expedition. Nothing had gone well.

Most of the porters, by this time, had deserted, so Loch had to return to Píllaro, then to Quito to request aid from President Páez. Promising to survey and map that part of unknown Ecuador,

Loch was able to get the assistance of the Ecuadorian Army
Engineers.

On June 12, 1936, with an officer from the Army, seventeen
engineers, a new "batch of Indians and half-breeds," and a train
of pack horses, Loch was "again on the familiar trail to the farm
of Moya, Guapa, and the Anteojos, pushing on into the land of
false lures and dashed hopes."

The idea of using horses to carry provisions and equipment
over the morass in high *páramo*, the "quaking bogs," was a
disaster. "The unfortunate beasts would wallow up to their mid-
dles, when panic could take possession of them; and, plunging
frantically, they would sink deeper and deeper into the mire.
Meanwhile the loads would have been scattered to the four winds.
Then the problem was to save not only them but also the
equipment."

Soon they came to the stream where Father Longo was said to
have disappeared on the aborted expedition sponsored by the King
of Spain in the late sixteenth century.

Advancing, the party moved behind Cerro Hermoso, east of
the sacred mountain, into an area between the White Llanganati
(the Cerro) and the Black, or "Yana," Llanganati. The weather
continued to be horrible and the porters deserted again for fear of
their lives. Only seven soldiers were fit to carry on. The main
body of the expedition was called off and returned to Píllaro,
but Loch himself and three men—one peon and two soldiers—
went doggedly onward toward the Río Napo, one of Ecuador's
main tributaries feeding the Amazon Basin. Loch hoped at this
point that, if the treasure could not be found, then at least
he might find gold in the fast-flowing upper streams of the
Amazon.

Their journey got worse than a nightmare. It was anything but
a feasible overland route that might join the Andes with the
Amazon. It took seventy days through treacherous uncharted
terrain to travel fewer than twenty miles:

Loch wrote:

The country ahead was the most dangerous we had yet en-
countered. Spur after spur of precipitous rock faces descending
almost perpendicularly into raging torrents below barricaded
our passage. These bald surfaces, to which we were forced to
cling, were covered by but a few inches of soil, out of which
from the constant rains a heavy foliage grew, though with
deceptively shallow roots. Everything we stood upon, everything we clutched, with the added weight of our loads, gave
way under us to fall hundreds of feet to the plunging river
below.

Loch himself fell down a precipice, breaking two ribs and
injuring a leg. One of the soldiers drowned while trying to cross a
swift-flowing river on a raft. The streams were swollen with the
season's heavy rains.

Once, it took thirty days for the small starving party to go
fifteen hundred yards. Hunger made them hear voices and dogs
barking. They were losing their minds.

Finally, Diego said, they reached an abandoned Indian plot,
scraped up a few roots, and a week later found a *hacienda* on the
upper Napo.

Diego called for another brandy, and the waiter looked at him
askance. He'd already had five.

"You know, Peter, his book, *Fever, Famine and Gold*, ends with
Loch returning to the area of the upper Napo where he discovers
a few gold nuggets—not nearly enough to cover the expense of
the last expedition. His records showed that of the eight months
in the mountains only nine days had been clear."

In his book Loch seemed to be trying to codify his life of
adventure, looking for the value in all of it:

There's no romance to this, nor to a battle—while one takes
part in it. Great physical effort and discomfort are one's sole

companions. Only with the passage of time, when one can relive scenes amid a life of ease, does the spirit of romance transform those memories into something glamorous and picturesque. . . .

Into stories to be told, he might have said. In fact, after his last disastrous expedition, there was little ease, and no glorious nostalgia. Though the story is still unclear, even to those I spoke with in Quito who'd known the captain, Loch apparently succumbed to the failure of his last expedition.

Some said he was dying of cancer or a tropical disease he'd contracted while fighting in Uganda, an insidious disease which was slowly constricting his esophagus. Some said he shot himself from absolute despair over the Llanganati ordeal.

Either way it was a sad story, one that horrified and thrilled me in that odd desire to frighten myself with morbid tales. As if to say, "Glad that wasn't me!"

When I first heard Diego's version of Loch, I wondered what the man had really accomplished. One minute it seemed a monumental feat (there was no record of anyone walking successfully from the Llanganatis to the Napo before Loch). The next minute, it seemed ludicrous, an absurdly self-destructive and blindly arrogant journey, conducted in the holy name of science but shoddily executed only for vanity and treasure.

◆◆◆

Diego and I walked through the cold night air the few blocks back to his bar.

Diego dug around behind the counter and pulled out a folder. Then he showed me the journal he'd kept on his last trip with Andy. It was only twenty pages long, written illegibly in pencil. I pretended to handle it with great care, as if it too were made of precious metal. But it was a mess, not unlike Diego's unruly life, the dirty dishes piled in the sink, his unmade bed, and month-old, dirty clothes littering his apartment.

He said he would like to collect and organize all the information about the gold because no book had been written about it since Blomberg's *Buried Gold and Anacondas* and even that, he thought, was nearly impossible to find anymore in the Quito bookstores.

But, I wondered, how could such an unorganized man, shattered by grief over the loss of his wife, write such a book? Diego said he planned to keep a detailed account of our journey, to incorporate the impending trek into the book. But when I left him in the morning, he was drunk and his old journal had slipped off the table and sprawled pathetically on the floor.

CHAPTER 5

◆◆◆◆◆

Already it was mid-November and the weather in the Llanganatis would be getting better.

For weeks now I had risen at five-thirty, stumbled around in the twilight for my running shoes and gone out to jog up the steep hill behind my apartment. Everywhere in Quito, the hills provided perfect endurance tests for someone trying to get into shape to face the mountains.

Out before the city had a chance to wake up, I got back at seven and the city was already a sunburst, noisy and booming in the bright activity of a new day.

Occasionally I passed timid Indians in the dawn, demurely wrapped in dark ponchos. With bright blue and red cloth around their shoulders they bound large heavy baskets to their backs. Their breath steamed in the cold morning air.

Running at that altitude was different from what I was used to, but I had to expand my lungs, to ready myself for the hardships of our expected twenty-one-day expedition through fourteen-thousand-foot jungle.

Though I felt in better shape than I had for years, sometimes the uselessness of all that preparation filled me with despair. So many strong, healthy army captains, colonels, explorers, commanders, mountain climbers had gone to where I wanted to go and many of those had died in spite of their physical self-reliance. What good was a strong body against flash floods, hypothermia, shifting earth, panic, and madness?

Andy had told me that many of his expeditions leaving Píllaro faced the villagers as they lined the streets, jeering: "You're going to die. All of you. You won't come back alive." They weren't talking about inclement weather only, but also about something else, a less tangible, more formidable enemy.

As I ran now past barking watchdogs, I knew it wasn't just strength I had to muster, but I was unable to say precisely what it was I'd need. Arriving home after an hour's run, gasping, sweating, lungs screaming for more oxygen, I would shower, then sit at my desk a few minutes before school began and, with an inexplicable terror swelling up inside me, just stare at my copy of Guzmán's fantastical map of 1803 and at the topographical maps I'd obtained from the Geographical Military Institute.

Fascination with fear is an odd yet addicting emotion. When I looked at my maps, it was like, as a child, running in the dark at breakneck speed, scaring myself but not so much I'd stop, only enough to keep running a little faster, seeking a greater thrill. Like running through the blackness of night, watching the dark ghastly trees and the ground as it loomed up to meet me. Like driving a car to its limit around a curve on a mountain road.

I stared just a little more intently at the maps. I was learning to read precipices, gorges, valleys, and peaks in those many convoluted lines of the topos. And I imagined the worst: What if I should get separated from Diego and the guides?

Often the names of Guzmán's map thrilled me with morbid anticipation: "Peñon de las Discordias," the Peak of Disagreements; "La Muerte de Romero," the Death of Romero; "Mina Cristal," Crystal Mine; "La Muerte de Padre Longo," the Death of Father Longo . . . —one explorer who got separated from the expedition party!

I wondered what sort of man Guzmán had been, who could

walk for months and months through jagged wet jungly terrain. His map was a child's nightmare. Volcanoes were drawn in wild pictures; some spewed ash. Mines were marked as squares, deaths as little crosses. It was a fantastical map, a cluttered nineteenth-century rendition of a New World Inferno.

Many of those names were in Quechua, too, the language of the Incas and the language that many Ecuadorian Indians still spoke. A very foreign, nearly African-sounding tongue: Ustu Rumi, for instance, which meant "stone face." Suni Cocha (long lake), Yurag Gurug (white worm), Ata Urca (great hill), and Guarro-Machai (falcon's refuge).

It was also frightening and thrilling that the Geographical Institute had not yet mapped certain parts of Ecuador, most of the Llanganatis included. The two relevant topographic maps (San José de Poaló and Sucre) showed the terrain as far east as 78' 15", so that only part of Valverde's "Way of the Inca" was visible in the bottom right corner of the Sucre projection. I could follow Valverde's route from Píllaro past the Anteojos and the Black Lake, the Golpe and the Pyrite Mountain (just below "Soguillas"), which were all clearly marked on the San José de Poaló quadrant.

Andy, Brunner, Dyott—no treasure hunter had had the benefit of these maps until 1968 when they were first published. How much time and wasted effort might have been spared?

One of the interesting things about those maps, I noted, was that the contour interval, the distance between two consecutive lines of altitude, was forty meters, 132 feet, and these lines were often so close to each other as to hardly distinguish one from another. Anyone with the minimum cartographic experience could immediately discern the hellish canyons and rugged land of the area.

My papers spread out before me, I turned and left for work anxiously.

Diego and I had set a tentative date for the start of the expedition: December 1. Only two weeks away.

◆◆◆

Diego Arias, I learned later, came from a treasure-hunting family. When his uncle Luis was sixteen, he went with Diego's grandfather to the eastern slopes of the mountains which border the lower Amazon jungle. One night the Indians deserted and Luis's father became ill. So Luis went on alone through torrential rivers and steep ravines. He found several gold nuggets, one as big as a walnut. When they returned to Quito, the grandfather died, but Luis (who later started a very successful flying company with Diego's father) continued his forays into Ecuador's back country for gold.

Diego inherited his grandfather's and uncle's zeal for treasure. But Diego's father, who was a more sober, domestic man, often worried about his son's sense of family and his emotional stability. Many of the senior members of the upper echelon of this small country worried about their children spending so much idle time drinking and partying.

I learned that on the day that Diego had planned to go into the Llanganatis in December a few years ago (he hadn't been back since), he had a premonition that something at home was wrong. From Píllaro he telephoned Quito. His brother told him their mother was in the hospital. So Diego instructed his guides to wait for his return, if all went well, within a day or two. Diego rushed to Quito, where his mother died soon after.

Later, he canceled the trip for that year and, though he assured me he wasn't superstitious, and that it had only been a strange coincidence, the death and the expedition coming at the same time made him shudder when he told me the story aloud. His face was ashen, his voice low. He tipped his head back and threw down a huge glass of brandy in one monstrous gulp.

Diego was like that. One minute he could be all enthusiastic in a gentle kind of way with a soft voice and a considerable empathy, but then suddenly he could change. A dark anger might strike out from deep inside.

Yet I never felt closer to Andy's son-in-law as I did the afternoon we hunted for Brunner together. Diego found a telephone directory. We looked through the names under B. One listing showed: Marta Brunner in Pifo, a small village near the city.

It was an unusual name for Ecuador. How many Brunners could there be in such a country? I couldn't help feeling this old man alone was the key to the treasure tale, a man who knew something greater than all the others.

"Go on, dial! You do the talking," I urged him. My Spanish was not perfect and I did not want to ruin our chances by confusing the language.

Diego dialed fearlessly, not without his usual affected, yet endearing laughter.

A woman's voice came on. Diego and I touched faces as we both put our ears on the receiver to hear Marta Brunner say in a haughty, almost frightened tone, "No," she was unrelated, and didn't know any Eugenio Brunner, no no. And she hung up quickly.

The terse exchange implied a kind of treasure hunter's paranoia. Diego and I immediately assumed we'd hit the mark.

That day we drove to Pifo but found only an old woman whose whole family had died years before. We were stumped. Both of us felt a little foolish standing before her doorway in the mountain sun, inquiring about treasure hunters.

Back in the bar Diego said, "Everyone is against you. They don't share your faith. They don't risk anything in their lives; they don't believe you. You, *you*, make all the risks. *You*, goddamn, you make the risks for *them*. There's so many stupid people."

Diego's cloud had descended, leaving him more vituperative than ever.

His violence, I think, welled up out of a concoction of self-doubt and a distorted sense of his own martyrdom. He'd lived a good deal of his life with failure. Perhaps he hadn't really ever expected to find the gold, not ever. The search itself obviously provided some sort of ego boost. But the search seemed empty for Diego, as if the failure of not finding the gold mimicked some deeper failure inside him. His was a doomed, frustrated quest, it seemed, and it was very painful when I finally began to see through Diego's facade—when I allowed myself to see clearly. In a way, his problems had become mine, so intertwined is the search for a story and the story itself. For weeks, I could not face up to my disillusionment.

As Diego set up a game of backgammon, he went on slowly: "There were other treasures before this one, *amigo*. I looked for an emerald mine on the coast of Esmeraldas. Then a sunken city in the western jungle. When I married Monica, Andy and I used to drink at his office in the middle of the day and just talk and talk for hours about Atahualpa's gold, speculating, studying the maps, sipping brandy."

Diego recalled the old camaraderie with Andy, now gone, and his voice went soft.

Monica, he said, wanted custody of his kids. She claimed he was a lousy father, always off looking for treasure.

Diego's face looked childish, his eyes wide and sad when he said, "But it was Andy who got me started."

Andy, I realized, by implanting in Diego such a treasure lust, had helped turn his daughter's husband away from his daughter. Maybe that's why Andy had looked so disappointed when he spoke of Diego.

Suddenly Diego grinned. He seemed superficially bright and cheery—the sudden typical mercurial flip-side metamorphosis of a young treasure hunter, I thought. I'd seen it in Andy a little. But now Diego was perversely jubilant, impetuous, and—I feared— even a little dangerous. There was venom in his veins.

"It is a terrible life! Yet what a beautiful way to live. Treasure hunters are so few among so many living dead. It's a unique life, let me tell you, *enchanted*." That word came off his tongue like a javelin.

We drank a toast to "enchantment."

"Do you drink alcohol in the Llanganatis?" I asked. "Isn't it dangerous to drink in there?"

Diego looked at me. "Shit yes, of course. I carry a bottle of Fundador brandy wherever I go and a knife in my belt. The peons carry my gear. And I drink, but in there you don't feel it, friend; it spurs you on. Ah, how it spurs you on, Peter."

"Here's to Fundador brandy, then," I said as I lifted my glass, feeling a bit like a traitor because I secretly worried about being drunk in those mountains. I didn't share Diego's heedlessness. Loch's tragedy was still very fresh in my mind—it would not happen to me, not if I could help it.

An acrid fire was in his eyes. I asked about the porters.

"Why, they're fucking impossible. You have to be stronger than they are, outdo them to gain their respect."

Diego filled his lungs with bravado. His eyes shone like black glass. And he began speaking clearly in his rage.

I used to cringe every time he spoke with such superiority about Indians. And I am not proud of myself for keeping quiet on the subject, but I was a guest in his country and I didn't feel it was my place to discuss his prejudices.

"And you can't let them become too friendly, either, Peter. When they start using the familiar *estás* you must look straight into their shifty eyes and say, *Como que estás, hombre?* It's *está usted,* damn it! Formal, I tell them, keep it formal. And when you drink with them, which is never a good idea, never!, the tendency is to become too friendly and then they get aggressive, unruly.

"At night, you sleep always with one eye open, your hand on your revolver. Remember that, Peter, if nothing else, remember to watch them as you watch hyenas. You can not trust the bastards."

A deeper shadow crossed Diego's face, highlighting the gleam from his eye.

"When we get to the area where the treasure is," he said, "I will send back my porters, and just keep one. Then after a few days the others will have orders to come back from Píllaro to take us out. I will have looked in an area I don't want them to know about, understand . . . ?"

The last time he went in, he took thirty-six peons, as he called them. Every time he used the word "peon" he practically hissed his hatred for the mountain Indians, as if they themselves had stood between him and the gold.

"We all got lost in the fog once. The weather hemmed us in for twenty days, no less. We were cooped up like moles in our tents until the damn stuff lifted. Eleven of my men went off. I tried to stop them with a shotgun. But those eleven got even more lost and they had to return to me in that ghastly mist. Ha, the fuckers, ha!"

We finished our game of backgammon. Diego, leering and drunk, had played recklessly, taking ridiculous risks, always leaving a man open for me to take out. He seemed to have a great proclivity for losing, yet all the while imagining himself daring and cool, wild and dashing. I think he saw himself a treasure hunter the likes of which the world had never witnessed. He reminded me of the hotheaded upstart in Westerns who is out to kill the veteran gunfighter, but inevitably gets killed himself.

Just before I left him that night he told me of his first trip with Andy. He spoke shyly, and I noticed he was using the present tense. As if he wanted it all to happen again.

"Yah, after each long day walking the Llanganatis, we pull out a bottle of Johnnie Walker or Fundador. Then Andy gets some water from the icy river and there we are sipping whiskey."

Diego's voice crescendoed into Raskolnikov laughter.

When I learned from the German owner of the Libri Mundi, Quito's only international bookstore, that the famous Brunner had been definitely sighted that week in the streets of Quito, I roamed the colonial quarter every single day with new resolve, manhunting for someone who, I just knew, would have to be a more sober treasure hunter than Diego Arias.

I did not tell Diego about my renewed search; I didn't want him to feel I was betraying him in any way. Treasure hunters are a skittish breed. They don't like you talking to other treasure hunters after they've told you their side of things. It was okay to hunt for Brunner together, but alone? I'm sure it would have bothered him.

A woman in a café told me she thought Brunner lived somewhere near Espejo and Montúfar, that he was a short man with silver-grey hair, a nose like a potato, and a suspicious mouth. I stood on that street corner for hours, unaware I was only ten feet from the clothing store owned by Brunner's landlady.

From two to four every afternoon after school let out, before Diego opened his bar, I strolled around the twisted passageways and cobblestone streets of colonial Quito. I didn't have nearly enough to go on, but I kept trying. Something had to turn up. Why was this man so difficult to locate? Why were all these treasure hunters so hard to pin down?

The old city was packed with men with silver-grey hair and large noses. And when you look for a suspicious mouth, all mouths look strangely sinister.

In one plaza five Indian women wore thick layers of gold and red beads around their chubby necks. Bright blue ponchos covered their laced blouses. The listless children strapped to their backs wore toy-miniature black fedora hats pulled way down over olive eyes, hiding their starched miserable faces.

Walking south, I peered timidly into dark doorways and saw there, in the sad recalcitrance of Indian faces in the shadows and the heavy smoke, where they were cooking pork in large metal pans, certain secrets these people seemed to harbor which I knew I would never uncover.

That odd sepulchral feeling came over me always in mountain

Quito. Mornings were bright as floodlights; nights were so bit-
terly morose and cold, you couldn't figure out the change that
came over the magic city at dusk. Quito was really two cities in
one, fraternal twins: day Quito and night Quito. But even in the
brightly dancing daylight, everywhere in that place I came up
against the dryness, the stagnation of a special mountain languor I
couldn't fathom.

In the plazas so many old men tarried the afternoon away
beneath the cobalt sky, a sky dotted with a disk-blaze of sun. Old
forgotten discarded men slowly ambled with hands clasped wisely
behind their crooked backs. Pigeons and old men walked in those
plazas by the hundreds. Some drunks stumbled in the brilliance,
and occasionally a priest, his head turned stubbornly to the
ground, moved intently through the paths in the flowered plazas
to his duties at one of the intricate gold-embellished churches.

If not today, then I would find that Swiss-German treasure
hunter some other day soon. I knew that much. It was a mad
mission, but my story seemed absolutely to depend on interview-
ing the expert. Did he know where the treasure was? Of course
he must. No one could search for forty-two years and find
nothing. So what had he found? I had to ask.

◆◆◆

Lying there in my Quito apartment late at night, I began to
suspect more and more that Andy's son-in-law would never bring
off this year's trip into the mountains. It was already November
26 and for four nights that week he'd partied until dawn. He had
done nothing concrete in preparation. No guides had yet been
contacted, no supplies organized into porters' boxes. We hadn't
even made a trip to Píllaro yet.

Then one night in thick fog we drove out to his mother's house
in a small village down the Pan American Highway. Diego made
sharp turns sluggishly. He'd borrowed a friend's car, and his slack
driving frightened me.

In the fog, suddenly, there was an accident. A small pickup had overturned and rolled. No one was hurt, but Diego hit his brakes. "Jesus," he swore as he parked our car in the middle of the road. Lucky it was so late, and there was little traffic.

Diego, in a lucid moment of glory, directed me and the three men who had jumped from the flatbed of the pickup to rock the truck and get it on its wheels. Diego was magnificent. Everyone else was stunned and would have done nothing. Diego's plan worked. Drunk as he was, he had risen to the crisis as I would not have expected him to.

"You have to act quickly," he said proudly as we raced away from the accident, "before the police arrive and the bribes start changing hands. They will throw anyone in jail if they feel like it, anyone at all, ha ha ha."

His family place was a huge estate, almost Gothic. His mother had been dead three years.

Diego's eyes sagged with brandy and pain. He wouldn't speak about his mother. In a kitchen cupboard he reached for a bottle of whiskey and giggled like a child. *"Como un tesorito, no?"* Like a little treasure, eh?

The house was empty and spooky. Sheets covered the furniture. The rooms smelled of ghosts. It was late, I had to sleep. So I lay down in a bedroom.

Then I heard the first shot. But I didn't want to move. Diego, I was sure, had committed suicide. He had seemed in pain for weeks, brooding and bragging to his friends about how this time he'd find the gold.

I forced myself up and ran to the kitchen and there in the open doorway he stood limply against the door frame. Behind him, in dawn's weak light, green pastures stretched out and cows stared back.

"I was trying to get Miguel! Miguel! *Miguel!*" Diego screamed. He fired another three shots into the air before the gun fell in his hand to his thigh. Miguel had been his mother's servant who had stayed on and tended the place for the sons who never remained here long because they preferred the action of Quito.

Miguel had worked for Diego's family twenty years and he knew the rampages of the rich. When he first heard us come in late, he had boarded his little cottage shut and now would probably not come out for anyone, for hours.

We slept a little and drove back to Quito, but Diego's gunfire had deflated some of the magic of this treasure story. I was tired of his constant ineffective talk.

Diego told me he absolutely had to go this year to the mountains; he had new "evidence," he called it. But when trust or loyalty—or was it conviction?—between partners is broken, it can not be mended so easily.

I'd collected boots and rubber pants and wool gloves, too, but as I expected, the treasure-hunting paraphernalia sat idly in my closet while the days slipped by like opportunities missed and I was more and more afraid the treasure story for me had come to an end. I was finding nothing in the plazas, no Brunner, no Luis Andrade (Blomberg's old guide, another needle in the Quito haystack). I'd begun to drink far too much, adopting the treasure hunter's propensity for swagger. I was burning out, fast.

I heard the slow deliberate clicking of the night frogs in my garden: *tluck tluuk, tluck tluuk* in the cool damp night air and I got to thinking I must be crazy. It was the lowest point of all my days in Quito. I almost decided to leave for the States.

But my landlady, Lilian Robinson, inoculated me with new information just in the nick of time, and once again I was eager to know more.

CHAPTER 6

••••

Lilian Robinson was one of those rare few who really understood the sadness of treasure hunters.

When I moved into the beautiful old house her father had built in 1914, before my week-long trip to Andy's house in Guayaquil, I knew nothing about Atahualpa's gold, nor could I have known that Lilian's mother had been an expert Llanganati woman herself.

I rented the front apartment in this mansion which in an another era must have agreed well with the importance of Enrique Robinson's position with the railroad company. He had come to Ecuador to construct the Quito–Guayaquil railroad, the first major link between the port and the sierra.

From my garden in the front of the house, the building seemed almost Victorian with its ornately festooned windows and tall white facade. Its garden, which hadn't been kept up in years, was nearly all brambles.

The mansion was isolated in a community of newer carelessly constructed apartment houses and reminded me of an old Victorian lady, properly dressed, standing with anachronistic dignity among a myriad of loud and impudent teenagers.

One evening when Lilian and I were invited to my next-door neighbor's apartment for a drink, she held a scotch in one hand and looked sadly around the darkly lacquered woodwork which lined the walls of what used to be the dining room. Her father had brought this wood all the way from the Oriente, she explained. Now the room was one of six apartments. The huge old structure had been just too much to maintain and Lilian had had to charge rent to meet payments.

The sun had just set behind Pichincha. Tiny emerald-green hummingbirds, some with long tails, some as small and bright as a silver dollar, fluttered in and out of the few orange flowers outside the door.

"This room," Lilian sighed, then tasted her drink. Her English, slightly British, was unflawed. "If you could only know the memories I have of this room." She seemed on the brink of tears.

In her fifties and portly, with an Irish sort of face, she was a demure, genteel lady. Her deep brown eyes had the depth of liquid glass, her face slightly flushed from the scotch. I don't think she'd ever been married, and she had no children. (I always had the impression, perhaps mistaken, that had she been thirty years younger, she might have made a play for me. Her eyes seemed girlish when she looked at me, and she blushed easily.)

"Tell me about your parents," I said.

"Father, of course, was British. A very civilized man. Mother was Ecuadorian, civilized, too, but very different. She was a treasure hunter, as I have told you. Most Ecuadorians are treasure hunters, you know. But Mother was maybe Ecuador's most flamboyant treasure hunter. She never gave up. Everyone knew her. She was on the track of hundreds of treasures. All at the same time. She would buy a house just to get at the treasure said to be buried beneath it. But she knew so little about handling money, Peter."

"Lilian," I said, "I really wish I had met her."

"Oh, yes."

Lilian glanced absently out the window at the slanted sun rays high up on the peak of Pichincha. She told me the story of her mother, slowly, carefully, yet not without a certain relish and pride.

Clara Pérez Robinson would take the money her husband gave her for the month and she would invest it in treasure hunts. She would disappear for weeks at a time. Lengthy telegrams, sent on railroad company telegraphs, would arrive at the Robinsons' Quito house informing the family they'd have to get their own dinner; she'd gone to Riobamba or Ibarra or Latacunga on urgent business and would be back in a week and not to worry. The telegrams never said anything about her true purpose. And little was said about Clara's trips, but the family all knew she was hunting for treasure.

When Clara was a child in Riobamba (Andy's birth city, too, south of Quito on the Pan American Highway), her father had infected her, talking endlessly at the dinner table about treasure. Lilian could remember one of Clara's father's stories. An Indian had taken him up Chimborazo searching for a cave where he had found human-sized statues of solid gold. Clara's father had gone with the man, but halfway up the mountain a great electrical storm broke and the Indian was sure God was angry. He decided then not to show Clara's father the cave and they descended. Her father went back later but found nothing.

Clara herself had financed many expeditions. Lilian said her mother would get excited and raise money for just about anyone who was young, strong, and willing to endure terrains as bad as the Llanganatis in order to find gold. Many years ago even Brunner himself, Lilian told me, had been financed by her mother "on numerous occasions."

"Ahh, Peter," Lilian sighed as she looked at me, "how my mother would have loved you."

As she spoke, Lilian took sips from her glass. Talk of her mother had revived neglected feelings both of pride and sorrow. Her eyes were moist to the brink of tears.

"I'd hoped, secretly I think, that if Mother had found Atahualpa's treasure—or any of them, for that matter—then she would have helped pay for the expenses of the house after Father died. I too went along with her schemes, we all did. I let her spend the money we needed for the house on treasures as she got older. I guess I thought a miracle might happen. Crazy, don't you think? To feed someone's obsession like that."

"Lilian," I said honestly, "I think it doesn't matter what you do in this world, as long as it hurts no one. Better to have a passion than none at all, don't you think?"

"Yes, perhaps. I sometimes wish I had my mother's passion.

"Mother hated it when I finally decided to divide the house into small rentals. But what could I do? She had absolutely no sense of money. I had to take responsibility . . ."

That word again! Andy had used "responsibility," a concept incompatible with treasure hunting, I thought.

"And even now it's nearly impossible to meet the bills. Taxes on old houses like this one are so so high. Oh, this was one great old place when Father built it in 1914. Then, it was on the northern outskirts of town. Can you believe it? In the country! Now you wouldn't guess, would you? The way the new city has consumed the area in the last twenty years. It's tragic, I tell you. I'll have to sell soon, I think. Very sad."

I agreed.

Lilian now had only two servants. Years ago her parents had had many. She spoke of all the great old families of Quito. It was a small, intimate town to her, and she knew them all: Diego's and Andy's families, the politicians, the bankers, the artists. The famous Indian painter, Guayasamín, for instance, "the Gauguin of Ecuador," had been a good friend of Lilian when she was young. She had many of his paintings upstairs.

Then, as she walked me to my apartment and stood in the garden, she asked me if I'd like to meet a Mr. Adderley, a man who had known Captain Loch personally. She was having him over for tea. I could come up to her apartment next Tuesday if I'd like.

"Ah, Peter," she said, "I'll see if I can get Brunner's telephone number for you." She must have seen my eyes widen.

When I told her I'd like to come for tea, I thought how good Lilian had been to me, how she must have liked me if only because she had, like her mother perhaps, a soft spot for adventurers.

Lilian knew Diego. She knew he drank. She knew what kind of treasure hunter he was. She had known the whole family, but she would not talk negatively about Diego himself.

"You must talk to Brunner," she said. "He's the only one left."

Before I moved here, I did not know Diego himself had lived for a while in this very apartment. This had been a treasure hunter's house, and maybe that's why I had such a hard time sleeping: ghosts. Never before in my life had I had the insomnia I had there. From time to time, too, I imagined I saw movement in the dead brambles outside my front door, and I got chills thinking about Lilian's mother, Clara.

Coincidences have a fascination all their own, and the coincidences I'd experienced since I came to Quito seemed symbolic of something important. Rolf Blomberg, for example, the Swedish travel writer who lived in Quito, had been married to Lilian's older sister, now deceased. In *Buried Gold and Anacondas,* Blomberg, after thinking he'd given up treasure hunting for good (he had only dabbled in it before), wrote about Clara Robinson, his mother-in-law:

But in 1947, when I returned to Ecuador after ten years' absence, the fever returned. And who was to blame for it? My Ecuadorian mother-in-law, of course! Her treasure-hunting fever is incurable, and she has a strange capacity for infecting others with the same fever.... My mother-in-law has an inexhaustible collection of treasure stories. Some are quite probable and supported by evidence, others are pure old wives' tales and legends, which her grandchildren love to hear but secretly laugh at. My mother-in-law herself believes in them firmly. The existence of all possible extraordinary and super- natural things such as enchanted mountains, wild men of the woods with feet turned backwards—so that they cannot be traced—hairy devils, people who can fly like birds, and so on, is in her world something quite natural and not particularly alarming....

In the last chapter of his book, after two unsuccessful treks into the Llanganatis, Blomberg tested a modern detector in what had now become my garden. Apparently, he and Clara buried silver bowls and then tried to locate them with the detecting device.

Some afternoons I found myself sitting on my front porch overlooking this garden with its tiny emerald hummingbirds and imagining the two kooky treasure hunters burying silver for the detector. That it was my garden now, almost thirty years after Clara Robinson and Rolf Blomberg had dug little holes and gauged the depth of buried fool's gold; that Diego had at one time lived in this very apartment—all this seemed providential. Through Clara, Blomberg, and Diego, during my first months working in Quito at the school, I felt secure in being a part of a special history. I was the novice, the trainee, the tyro in a great line of seekers of Atahualpa's gold.

Lilian (and her mother) added to this story a woman's compas- sion. She rounded out the idea of treasure and shaved off some of its jagged edges.

◆◆◆

At a reception one night that week at the U.S. Embassy, given for a friend of mine, Dave Hewitt, a twenty-eight-year-old

American painter from Palm Beach who was married to an Ecuadorian teacher at the American School, I was confronted by a strange woman.

Dave's watercolors of sierran villages were becoming well known in Quito. And the bold deep colors of his canvases filled the austere Embassy building with a kind of surreal joy. Dave was the only serious painter I knew in Quito, a man who drove his Land Rover daily into the Andes to small villages where he painted for eight to ten hours until the light finally died. His large canvases easily captured the open blue depth of Andean sky dominating the fine, parsimonious lines of small beige pueblos etched in a rocky-grey landscape. If I had had more money, I would have bought at least five.

But at the Embassy I didn't even get a chance to speak with Dave because an Argentine woman with haughty eyes, who smoked a cigarette from a long holder, demanded to hear what I was doing in this Indian-poor country.

"*Estoy aquí para buscar tesoro,*" I am here to look for treasure, I said.

"*Aaahh señor,*" she moaned in a masculine voice. "My boy, often I stop in Quito on my way to the New York. It is a quiet town here, I believe, this little city, nice for the sleeping."

She blew smoke in my face, and I tried in vain to catch the attention of Dave Hewitt's wife, to find refuge.

"But if *señor* wants to see civilized Latin country, he must come to the Argentina, my boy, where the people are blond and tall—like you." She batted her fake eyelashes. "But treasure? What is treasure? There are only *great treasures of art* in the world, in Paris, my boy: Cézanne, Rembrandt, Vermeer at Tate and Louvre. Give up wild ideas of gold in such dark country as Ecuador . . ." When she said Ecuador, her mouth looked like the mouth of a blowfish.

I grabbed my hat, apologized quickly to Dave for leaving so soon, gulped down my wine, then ducked out of that Embassy like a mad fugitive, passing two stolid Marines at attention by the front door. I walked happily into the secret streets of the Quito I loved. It had begun to rain and the air was cool and refreshing.

◆◆◆

The next Tuesday, upstairs, with one of Hewitt's bright paintings staring down at Lilian Robinson, Douglas von Rau-Adderley, and me, I heard more about the Scotsman, Erskine Loch. And I also got an interesting perspective on the British explorer, George Dyott.

As we drank tea and ate biscuits, I had no idea that Lilian's smile stemmed from a secret in her notebook, which she held in her hand.

Mr. Adderley had recently returned from England where he'd lived for the past ten years. Lilian had known him since childhood.

In his late fifties, Adderley had a fuzz of grey hair on his bald head. Light brown freckles were sprinkled on top. His face was serious. Two thick carpet eyebrows seemed pasted on the lower inside of a thick brow. His eyes were a delicate blue which contrasted sharply with his Germanic demeanor and the rigor of his sentences. Those eyes added a kindness to his strict military mien.

Unlike Lilian and her soft English, Adderley spoke the name Loch with a gutteral harshness: "Locchchchc."

When I asked him about the captain, he squinted at me and paused. He was a man obsessed with choosing his words.

He began, "I'm not a treasure hunter, you understand. I am a practical man. But Loch and my father were *socios*, partners. My father had a great deal of influence in this country and he helped Loch with his schemes. He helped the man get *permisos* here in the government and he was in charge, you might say, of Loch's affairs in Quito while the Scotsman was out looking for gold."

Adderley took out a cigarette with the precise motion of his

right hand, where he held it between the tips of the first two
fingers. Without lighting it, he stared at the far wall as if
searching for a word.

"But Loch," he went on, "was a drinker. Two or three bottles
a day, they say. He had cancer, you know. I can remember one of
the long lists my father had prepared for him, a list of provisions
for Loch's last and tragic journey to the Llanganatis. On that list
was marked one hundred cases of scotch. Twelve bottles in a
case!" Adderley's eyebrows jumped. "Loch was a haughty man. A
real loner, too. He drank instead of ate. The Scotsman lived on
scotch. Ninety percent of the horses he took on that last trip
carried scotch and that's why it was such a failure. From the very
beginning, a failure!"

Adderley stared accusingly at the smoke from his cigarette.

"I don't think I ever saw Loch sober. Some nights in Quito he
would come out of hiding and he would sing at the Majestic, a
club we had for men only. He was a good singer, too, but it was
always a surprise to hear him. Usually he was a quiet man.

"During the war, in 1941 I believe, I spent a night with Loch
at the British Embassy. In those years there weren't many of us in
Quito and we took turns guarding the Embassy. Loch brought
three bottles and by midnight he was out cold drunk and snoring
on one of the tables." A sad look came into Adderley's blue eyes.

"I suppose he was trying to get as far away as possible from
something; I do not know what. Yes, it was a great disappointment, Loch's last trip. After the desertion of his guides, the death
of some of his men, and the bad luck of finding no gold, Loch
just disappeared. Nobody thought much of it, though, because
he was usually by himself. He never used to tell anyone where
he'd gone.

"Six months later they found a man with a British passport on
a farm in Huigra. He'd committed suicide. Loch had had a friend,
a big financier from the States, I believe. The man had poured

thousands into Loch's schemes. But Loch never talked to him after that last trip. The disappointment killed him."

Adderley abruptly turned to speak to Lilian in Spanish. They talked briefly about the headlines: A staff member of the Ministry of Finance who had recently been fired had broken into the minister's office and fired a few shots. The minister caught a bullet in his arm, but another official got a bullet in his spine and would be paralyzed for life. Both Lilian and Adderley had known the minister a long time.

Ecuador had not changed since Loch's day, not really.

I asked if Adderley had known Dyott, too. He said yes, they all used to listen to the Valverde treasure story when they stayed with Dyott on his jungle farm. Dyott had been to the mountains a few times himself but had had "trouble with his shoes." Leather and rubber boots were both torn to shreds on the razor-sharp plants in the high altitude. He could never find the right boot for that terrain.

"You wouldn't get any sleep when you stopped for a night with Dyott. He was a real gentleman but he could talk for hours. He and Brunner made some deal, but he never told me the specifics. Dyott hinted often that he had some really good information about the treasure."

I asked him why he thought Dyott, this famous inventor, aviator, and explorer, had come to Ecuador of all places to live.

Adderley smiled. He said Dyott was a naturalist and Ecuador was a naturalist's paradise. But Dyott had come here also to get as far away from New York as he could.

"Why's that?" I asked.

"Because it was the farthest he could get from his wife." Adderley's misogynistic laugh, when it came, was like semiautomatic rifle fire. Lilian was embarrassed.

Andy had also known Adderley's father. It seemed to me all Quito had been a club in the early days. They had all met at a special café near the Plaza de la Independencia.

It was well past eight when I got up to go. Lilian walked me to the door to say good night; she kissed me on the cheek and said, "From Mother," as she slipped me a piece of paper, on which was written glory-be-to-God Brunner's six-digit telephone number.

I went downstairs, drummed up enough courage to dial, my fingers weak and fluttering like aspen leaves. No answer. I tried again before I went to sleep. Nothing. I'd try again in the morning. I'd try all day.

CHAPTER 7

◆◆◆◆◆

At Diego's bar, bits of afternoon sunlight scattered through the stained-glass windows like colored shavings over the wicker chairs. Mestizo waiters, *cholos,* carefully handed around bottles of cold beer and glasses of brandy as if they were vials of nitroglycerin.

At two-thirty Diego's friends filtered in as they did every day for lunch: for ceviche, an Ecuadorian seafood specialty of marinated shrimp, clams, oysters, or langoustines served in dainty dishes of tomato sauce and accompanied by another plate of popcorn or maize. Men and women in groups would come up to the bar and shout for ceviche and drinks, which were brought to them by the mestizos in dapper white shirts and black ties.

But today was different from most afternoons. It was a Sunday in December, the time of the famous Quito bullfights. El Cordobés, one of Spain's legendary matadors, had just fought in the Quito bullring, his first fight in South America since he came out of retirement. All agreed it had been a magnificent veteran's display fought in honor of the Fiesta de Quito, the week-long celebration of the city's establishment in 1534 by the conquistador Benalcázar. On his knees El Cordobés had reached over and gently touched the bull's horns again and again. The crowd had gone wild.

The bullfight was over, but the serious drinking continued, especially fierce now because the old master had fought brilliantly even at his age. Cars streamed honking from the bullring in the north of the city.

That morning I had called Brunner.

"*Se fue, señor, a Ibarra y no regresará dentro de tres semanas—lo siento mucho, señor,*" said Brunner's landlady. Which made me so angry I could have wrung her neck. As if she were the only one who stood between me and the great treasure hunter.

Brunner would be out of town for three more weeks. He'd gone to Ibarra, but his landlady didn't know how to get in touch with him there. "Please, *señora,* tell *Señor* Brunner that Mr. Lourie called." I spelled the name four times and gave my number, which I made her read back to me twice. "It is very urgent." And I hung up.

I decided to go to Diego's bar. Infuriated by Diego's delays, I'd tell him that if I didn't see some action soon I was going to switch treasure hunters—the way you switch insurance companies or family doctors.

Diego had promised that this week we would go to the tiny village of San José de Poaló, near Píllaro, to arrange guides. If he wanted to back out now, I'd use new leverage: Brunner and the rivalry between treasure hunters. I had Brunner up my sleeve, or so I pictured it.

Perhaps it seems improbable that I continued to put any faith at all in this man Diego, but it was really quite simple: I did not want to go into the Llanganatis alone. I didn't have enough money; my teaching salary was barely enough to cover rent and food. And I had spent a lot of time with Diego—mostly in bars, it's true—but time together forms bonds. I might have been able to organize some sort of weekend ramble in the mountains by myself, but I wanted to be in those mountains with a real treasure hunter, for safety, for companionship, and for the genuine experience. If I had gone alone with a guide, assuming it were possible, I would be as lost as all the rest of the poor souls who had wasted so much time in there.

Wonder Bar was busier than I'd ever seen it. I stepped right up to the counter and said, "Diego, I've talked with Brunner's landlady."

From behind the bar, Diego responded:

"So you finally got the old man's telephone number, Peter. Very very good for you. We will make a treasure hunter of you yet, *amigo* . . . Okay okay we go today, then, Peter. Have you met Francisco? No? Well, he too will be going with us into the mountains."

Diego pulled me aside and said, "Peter, we have to take him. He has his father's truck and we need a truck to transport all our gear, no?" Diego slapped me hard on the back.

"So we agree, *amigo*."

"Okay," I said. But I gave him the mean look of one who has come very close to being betrayed. He had never once mentioned taking another person with us.

Both Diego and Francisco had drunk a full *bota* of sherry at the bullfight. Each was talking about our impending trek, boasting to their friends about the size of Atahualpa's treasure, about how rich they would be in a month or so, and about the dangers we would face "inside."

Diego took out a bottle of cologne from a cabinet, opened it, and splashed in it like a bird in a birdbath on a hot summer's day. This was how Diego prepared for our journey.

He barked some orders at an Indian waiter and turned to me, his eyelids heavy over his pupils, and said,

"*Listo, caballero*. Ready as ever, Pedro! *Vámonos!*"

"Okay okay, very goooood very goooood," said Francisco, who didn't know much English but who had confidently thrust his thumb up in the air grinning like a maniac.

With a sharp military cock of his head, our leader Diego looked first at Francisco, then at me, and said, "Okay, *caballeros*, let's be off! Llanganatis or death!"

As we stepped out into blinding sunlight, I hardly believed we

were going, all of us together, a team. To Poaló. Like three
musketeers, we were off in a cloud of Quitenian dust.

Francisco drove the *camioneta*, a small Ford pickup truck, as fast
as it would go through the streets of Quito. He slowed minimally
for stop signs and stop lights. Suddenly Diego ordered, *"Para!
Stop, Paco!"* And the car skidded to a halt in front of a liquor
store. Diego ran in and bought a bottle of Fundador brandy.

The late afternoon sky was a perfect blue, deep as the Pacific.
The higher peaks, snowcapped, rose on either side of us as we
moved down the Pan-American Highway toward Latacunga, where
in the 1860's Richard Spruce had found the Valverde *Guide* in the
town archives.

Every time one of us took a long pull on the bottle, Diego
would let out a wicked cowboy cry. "Yiipppppppyyyyipppppppoo-
ooooo."

What the hell, I thought. We were adventurers. But even so, I
drank to calm my nerves, fearing a car wreck in a country I once
again realized I didn't understand.

As we raced along the badly paved highway, Francisco would
take both his hands off the wheel to point out the Benalcázar
family land stretching to our right, with the twin peaks of Illiniza
behind. Francisco was nineteen and petulant. He had been drunk
for the last three days of the fiesta. When twilight descended, his
face contorted with the excitement of going into the legendary
mountains. *"No puedo creerlo; no puedo creerlo.* I can't believe I'm
really going," he repeated. His long blond hair hung over his
eyes. He looked like a rich American prep school kid out on a
lark.

Raising the bottle, Diego said something I didn't understand,
though I remembered that Andy had said something similar. It
was one of those stray pieces in this treasure puzzle.

"You know, some say the treasure was taken from the mountains already. But it's totally untrue. I can verify that. But the story exists."

"What treasure? All of it?" I asked Diego what he was talking about, but he only wagged his head and said, "Bullshit. Don't bother."

The color of the distant foothills of the higher peaks was ashen, volcanic. Cotopaxi, at nearly twenty thousand feet, the world's highest active volcano, rose to our left. The highway followed the old Inca road that connected Atahualpa's Quito to Huáscar's Cuzco.

Within half an hour the light had darkened radically into twilight. We were all pretty tipsy by the time we passed through Latacunga. My partners had begun to tell each other jokes about who they knew in government and what scandals they could remember. Each was trying to outdo the other. Francisco displayed a family escutcheon on the gold ring on his small finger and we nearly ran off the road.

We passed through a sleepy village, the name of which I have forgotten. But it was the same as Francisco's middle name. His family, he said, had a factory there. So he saluted the town and that too was a joke.

I was ambivalent about our trip out of Quito. It felt great to be out of the city, but I was so unsure of Diego and Francisco. One minute I felt privileged to be a foreigner traveling with two Ecuadorians who had connections, but the next minute I was thinking we'd die in a car accident. The lawlessness of Ecuador wasn't so appealing when it suggested real death on some bad road, miles from hospitals with sterile instruments.

Yet I knew that Diego's connections were important in this country, and this gave me a temporary sense of power that I liked.

Ecuador could be a dangerous country if you didn't know the right people. A South African acquaintance (another teacher at my school) had been thrown into the Quito prison for suspected drug trafficking. Having been in the country only a few weeks, he

knew no one. With a three-thousand-dollar bribe to the judge he
was set free, but he had lived for three months with rats in jail.

Traveling with these well-connected, if dissolute, Ecuadorians
might have given me the same exuberant feeling I had had with
Andy on our trip to his ranch if it weren't for Francisco's deadly
driving and Diego's frightening and mounting inebriation.

The decadence of that idle Quito clique of Diego's (almost
every night they went to the same disco) seemed similar to the
problem the first Spanish settlers must have faced in an Indian
country. It had something to do with being torn between two
opposing worlds, feeling homeless and wild and wanting somehow
to soothe the pain of self-imposed privilege and power. In *Nostromo*,
Joseph Conrad wrote about the recklessness of colonials:

> Their talk was the talk of sordid buccaneers: it was reckless
> without hardihood, greedy without audacity, and cruel without
> courage; there was not an atom of foresight or of serious
> intention in the whole batch of them, and they did not seem
> aware these things are wanted for the work of the world.

That description fit Diego and Francisco perfectly: "not an
atom of foresight or of serious intention in the whole batch of
them." It was lawlessness to the point of anarchy and it made me
uncomfortable.

◆◆◆

Sometime later, Diego said suddenly, "The Llanganatis, God.
Beat the Indians with prudence." Diego was now talking to
himself. "We must all learn how to beat the Indian bastards with
prudence."

I looked over at Francisco.

"Diego . . ." Francisco said, "we know you in Quito, partying,
drinking, dancing, but, Diego, *no one* knows you in there, in those
mountains. . . ."

We made the turn-off to Píllaro.

"There are women back at the bullfight, such beautiful Quitenian women, Diego. . . . But in the Llanganatis there are no women, Diego. How will we last?" Francisco sighed, laughed, and sighed. Out of nowhere, he screamed: "Money means nothing to me. I am *myself*."

"What do you mean by that, Francisco?" I asked, curious what the gold meant to this arrogant rich kid.

"Mi familia tiene montones de dinero, pero yo no lo necesito, porque soy yo. Soy YO MISMO." He said he did not need his family's money, that he would be whatever he would be in spite of his family, that he had consumed every kind of drug and that drugs had defined his character. They were good for his heart, he said. *"Drogas son buenas para el corazón."*

Moonlight half illuminated his scowl as he spoke. Talk of his parents enraged him. Drugs, he said, had helped him become independent of his father, but the treasure was the ultimate drug and would free him, he was positive, because he would have the independence of great wealth.

I did not bother to point out the contradiction in what he had said. I was discovering that motive in the quest for treasure was not as simple as just wanting to be rich. Obsession with gold, perhaps like obsession with anything, was an organic thing. It began somewhere for a reason, but through some complicated personal process, it ended somewhere else. A treasure was a symbol for one person's solution to life's problems. For Andy, the gold seemed like a childhood memory of the sierra, the innocence of what he had lost and wished to regain. For Francisco, Atahualpa's treasure was a way of proving himself to his parents that he was beyond their money. And for Diego? I kept thinking that for Diego it was a way of filling up some personal loss with Monica. But what about me? I wondered. What was my own interest in this gold? What loss would I compensate for? What did I need to prove to myself or to the world? Why had I dropped my chance of a Ph.D. for this? I don't think I knew the real answer yet, but I was closer to knowing.

And what was the crazy German's idea of treasure—the man who had searched more than anyone alive? After forty-two years, what had his original idea of gold become? For wasn't it true that motives undergo metamorphoses? One might begin a pursuit for one reason, but then the pursuit itself takes on a life, and motivations change as one pursues.

I suddenly had a great desire to be back in Quito waiting for Brunner to come home. To talk to him about his motives.

◆◆◆

But finally we were in the vicinity of Poaló, and I was trying hard to shake the numbness of brandy.

The houses of the Indians were like phantom burial mounds or glacial drumlins. The moon cast bits of silver over the Indians' potato patches. I could just make out long shadows that must have been rows of plowed fields. And I could smell the heavy smoke coming from the Indian huts.

Diego had fallen silent and seemed to be looking for the right house. The moon had turned the narrow fields into corridors of platinum.

Clumsily we three great explorers from the big city barged into a poor Indian's hut. A woman with a child wearing a woolen hat lay in a simple bed in a far corner. It was smoky. The child was sick with fever. It moaned horribly.

Although startled by our intrusion, the woman tried to smile. She recognized Diego. Heraldo, her husband, had once guided him to the nearby mountains.

Thick smoke added a nefarious unreality to the scene. And the cold of the high plains swept unconditionally into the hut through minute cracks in the walls.

The Indian, tall for a man in these parts, rose to embrace Diego. He smiled guardedly when he looked at Francisco and me and then waved his arms for us to sit. He hit the air, batted the smoke around with his hand, as if to apologize for it, bullying the smoke into our brandy-weak eyes. There were no chairs.

The Indian put on his orange hat and came into the moonlight with us. The wife, beautiful, was smiling as we left. Was she happy because Diego promised money for the family? A three-week trip to the Llanganatis would pay the head guide, her husband, at least two hundred sucres (eight dollars) a day, promising an extra helping of food, a chicken, or a trip to Ambato, fifty miles away.

We stood in the moonglow, negotiating. Diego told Heraldo to arrange porters and supplies for an expedition soon. *"Pero no sé exactamente cuando,"* Diego said he could not be sure of the exact date. "But soon, *amigo,* later this month, so—will you be ready, Heraldo?"

Heraldo nodded his head. He could be ready anytime, he said. The men would go. They have need for work, he said softly.

But as we stood in the man's potato field I felt I should not have come here. Or, I wished I had come alone, without these rich Quiteños. I wanted to talk in private to Heraldo, to find out who he really was, to hear his true feelings about treasure and treasure hunters and about his wife and sick child and friends; and I didn't feel comfortable when Diego gave him orders. Diego did not ask Heraldo to help us. His questions were phrased in the imperative, and the imperative stemmed from the power of his money, Andy's money, and from a rich Ecuadorian's racism.

I could see Heraldo in the strange light, his Indian stone face in the moon, kind, serious, and patient. His hair was shortly cropped around the ears. He wore a thick store-bought jacket against the raw wind. He had that ageless knowing expression of Ecuador's rural Indians. He listened to Diego and seemed to be making mental notes of times and amounts of food to be carried by his men. But perhaps he was laughing at us or hating us for having enough money to be able to afford a trip to the Llanganatis.

After Diego had expatiated on our demands, Heraldo spoke one or two sentences, asked a few questions about the details, how many men exactly, how many weeks. His Spanish had that odd Quechua-accented bounce. Quechua, the language of the Incas, was spoken everywhere in these mountains. Heraldo's voice was mellifluous and distinct like river-worn pebbles.

Quiet, unassuming, and (it seemed to me then) deeply convinced we would be wasting our time (but not our money), intently he listened to Diego again as Diego made idle talk, pretending to be social. Then even Diego looked a little embarrassed, talking about the weather and the crops and ridiculous things like that. None of us belonged here, and I think we all knew it.

Suddenly Francisco dashed for the car, flung open the door, jammed the seat forward, and pulled out a shotgun. I stepped back.

"*Lo hemos hecho!* We did it! We did it!"—but his words were muffled by the moon. He shot into the air. The echo from the huge sky was loud. Again and again he shot into the blackness until Diego went right up to him, and, in what I thought was a very brave deed, yanked that gun away from the crazy kid like a hero.

Francisco calmed down immediately, a scolded schoolchild, and we drove back to Quito in silence, our hangovers setting into our bodies like the chill of mountain fog.

◆◆◆

A few days later, Diego disappeared from the streets of Quito, from the bars and from the disco.

I called Andy because I thought he might know what had happened. I could hardly believe that Diego would just leave town at the very moment our expedition seemed definite.

Andy had wired money to Heraldo and his porters for supplies and they had waited for us. Andy told me over the phone that

Diego was drinking heavily again. Certain problems with Monica had come up, and Heraldo and his men had waited for two whole days at a certain crossroads with all our food and gear. Andy was not happy. "This is my last time," he said over the phone.

The trip of course was canceled, but Diego had never contacted Heraldo because neither the Indian nor his men had telephones (so Diego told me weeks later when I bumped into him in a Quito street) and Diego was too damn lazy to go down there himself to tell them there would be no expedition this year.

I felt this was inexcusable. Heraldo had trusted us. He'd been paid for the supplies, but he and his men had left their fields, said goodbye to their families, and waited for us for days. But now they'd gone back to the fields, with precious time lost and no extra income from the *Quiteños ricos*. I felt guilty, as if I myself had cheated them.

I learned from a friend, too, that Diego had run into financial problems at the bar on the very next day after we got back to Quito. He was in serious debt, owed his landlord many months of rent. He'd been losing money since the Wonder Bar had opened.

Weeks later when I finally ran into Diego in the street and he said, "So, Pedro, we need to reorganize and get into the mountains before January is finished," he also told me that at the last minute Francisco couldn't get permission to go from his parents, who were then vacationing in Europe, which had meant that we did not have the use of his pickup and so we could not have gone to the mountains anyway. Diego was searching now for another car, he told me. His eyes were bloodshot and he looked terrible, gaunt and weak.

On that drive back to Quito from San José de Poaló, I had more or less decided that if anything went wrong this time, I would leave Diego alone. He was creating more anxiety in me than I could take. He was a playboy explorer, and not very good at either role.

So this episode was the final stroke, and I broke with him. A

clean break. I kept to myself and avoided his friends and disco-
theques. A few weeks later when I passed by the Wonder Bar I
noticed it had been boarded shut. There was a part of Diego I
would always feel sympathy for, I suppose. On one side he was a
pathetic little boy, but he had personality and he knew a lot of
stories. And I had truly enjoyed our talks and drinking times
together. But now after nearly three months, I wanted action, and
this required that I extricate myself, at least for a while, from
Diego's morass.

I still had another week until Brunner would be home. So I
called Andy.

I flew to Guyaquil on a weekend in mid-December. He seemed
about the same, a little quieter maybe. He told me he was going
to get married to his Peruvian girlfriend. His voice seemed timid.
I don't think he looked forward to marriage the way he said he
did—all his other ones had ended in divorce.

I told him I'd talked with Brunner's landlady.

"Very very good for you, I think, Peter," he said. "Brunner
goes any time of year. Maybe you'll get on an expedition in spite
of Diego." Andy was sincere about this. He really knew I had to
go into the mountains and he was sorry he was so busy this year,
or he might have taken me himself.

When I spoke of Diego, Andy did not look surprised. "Yes,
that is the last expedition," he said. "I have better ways to spend
my money." Diego had gone downhill. Sometimes, Andy said,
people just can't pick themselves up.

Sitting together that evening in Guyaquil listening to the
rustle of palms, I couldn't help thinking how much I'd wanted to
go into the Llanganatis with this man. He knew the porters, he
had sufficient money, he was more familiar with the terrain than
almost anyone. But most of all, Andy was a magnet, a perfect
companion, I thought, for a journey like the one I wanted to
make. I couldn't understand why he wouldn't be going this year
with me.

But that night he was sad. Tipsier and tipsier in the usual camaraderie of alcohol, Andy's inner feelings rose unhindered into the conversation. He wanted to show me a few combat holds out back in the grass by the pool. I remembered the last time he'd done this, but before I said no, he put his right arm around my neck and said, "Now, I won't hurt you, Peter. This won't hurt a bit." And he led me outside.

"All you've got to do is this," he said, and he clamped me into a half nelson, switched to some Korean headlock, then effortlessly tossed me onto the ground over his back like a sack of feed.

"Come on, Peter, I'm not going to hurt you! But you better get tough for the Llanganatis, mister!"

I started to back away, but he charged and grabbed me and we tumbled to the grass. Then he let go.

I could hear the wind rustling the fronds above us in the muggy night air but was too tired to look up. Andy's breathing changed tone and pitch, turning into a visceral moan. A jet flew overhead.

When its roar subsided I looked over at Andy, lying now on his back, and I saw he'd started to cry.

His gasps had turned to sobs. I felt my heart constrict.

He sat up despondently.

What had I done?

"I'm sorry," I said, not sure what to say.

His face contorted with pain.

Then, suddenly, he confessed, "Please please. Don't tell my daughters. Jesus! Don't tell them. I'm losing all my money at the tables. I've got nothing left. And nothing, nothing matters to me anymore. Nothing, you understand? Not even the fucking treasure!"

His wet face turned to me, his eyes powerful even in sorrow.

"If I didn't have my family now, I'd kill myself."

Next day Andy woke and, I was very glad, remembered nothing. But I knew what perhaps he had secretly known all along: Andy might never again find time to go into the Llanganatis. He would be married soon and it would be hard to leave his new bride.

When I had asked Andy months ago if he'd ever gone to Seville to research the original copy of Valverde's *Guide,* and he had told me he had not, for some reason I hadn't wondered why a man of Andy's wealth and obsession with treasure had not tried all the avenues. But now I thought that Brunner surely would not have left any such lead unexplored. Brunner was my last chance of finding the real thing.

Whether Andy's enemy, the treasure, had bewitched and defeated him, or whether it was something purely personal that had corroded his interest, I did not know for sure. I felt terribly sorry for him and for myself. Last night had felt like losing a father. I was growing away from Andy. He had given birth to my desire to know more about the gold, but that morning when I caught a plane back to my home in Quito, I understood that there had to be at least two kinds of treasure hunters in this world. The first group were the wealthy who looked for gold as a panacea, diversion, hobby, leverage, something to brag about. Diego and Andy fit that category. Perhaps they were the more common variety of treasure hunter.

They had initiated me, and for this I would always feel attached to them. But now I wanted to meet the other species, the one Brunner had to be. I did not want any more idle promises. No more pretension. No more drinking.

For so many, it seemed, the gold was nothing but an excuse. But for the one and only Brunner, that treasure had to be something entirely different—a life.

PART THREE
◆◆◆◆◆
BRUNNER

CHAPTER 8

◆◆◆◆◆

It was already January when the German returned my call. His blaring voice forced me to pull the receiver away from my ear. He had my name wrong.

"Mr. Lufa, I got your message. Good to *hear* you, yes yes yes. I can see you tomorrow if you'd like, no?"

"No, Mr. Brunner," I said, "I can't wait until tomorrow. It has to be today. I'm in a hurry."

"Okay. Then come by my studio at three. I am making an expedition to the Llanganatis very very soon, Mr. Lufa, no?" He gave me his exact address and hung up.

Those ancient streets of old Quito were steep and narrow. The afternoon sky was grey, and the wind strong from the north. A tattered Indian woman with bleeding feet rumaged through a garbage can and the air reeked of urine and rain.

I sat around three different cafés drinking coffee and watching the time.

At two-fifty-five exactly, I entered a small clothing store from the cobblestone sidewalk. A heavyset, kind-faced *señora* led me through a neat colonial courtyard with a fountain. Magenta bougainvilleas hung over iron balustrades above.

Brunner's inner sanctum was tucked away from the loud street like a crypt.

As I climbed his back stairs, even before I saw his face and the friendly sparkle in his eyes, I knew I'd hit home. This was as far as you could reach in a story like this one. This old man had searched deeper and longer for the gold than anyone alive. And here I was, at last. I hadn't given up. I'd stayed in Ecuador for this.

I was certain he knew where the gold was. All the doubts of months and months were clearing like cobwebs in wind.

The landlady left me at Brunner's door. I knocked but there was no answer. I opened it. The treasure hunter was hunched over his desk lit by a huge unshielded lightbulb. He did not hear me come in. Years ago he had lost most of his hearing in both ears while bivouacking on a mountain face in a winter gale.

Brunner's tiny room felt stuffy. There was little space to move around. There were no windows, and many books had been stacked carefully in corners.

On his desk Brunner's large rugged hands moved deftly through neatly arranged pencils, ink bottles, labels, and paintbrushes of every shape, size, and color. Before he came to Ecuador in 1937, Brunner had studied commercial drawing in Switzerland.

On the wall above the desk was a plastic print of classical Greek maenads dipping amphorae in a lake. On a shelf below, next to a wilting geranium were eleven miniature white elephants Brunner collected for good luck.

Resting on an easel beside his desk a large map of Ecuador showed blood-red dots pointing to locations of treasures; blue triangles off the coast indicated sunken galleons; yellow squares showed other interesting sites, still to be investigated: lost cities, burial mounds, emerald mines!

Brunner looked up.

His hair was steel grey and waved backwards in thick lines. His eyes were sprightly. Beneath his thick grey corduroy sport coat he wore a plaid wool shirt of faded green checks. He looked about sixty-five or so and barrel-chested, a short but solid man. His eyebrows were almost nonexistent, only three or four white strands apiece. His skimpy mustache was neither white nor black, but a ratty grey. A wart sat at the base of his right nostril.

Brunner stared at me with draftsman's eyes, his mind focused somewhere else. Then he smiled, lifting the volume he had meticulously been documenting as I walked in. He spoke English with a German accent, a Spanish inflection:

"All this will go to someone when I die," he said, "so my work will not be lost. I will carry on, even when I am dead."

I was probably wrong, but when he said this it crossed my mind that he was suggesting I might get those papers, someday, if I turned out to be a good partner or friend.

He rose and grabbed my hand, grinning.

When he spoke, his mouth formed words to one side of his face. He said, "Mr. Lufa, so good you have come. So good to see you."

"Peter Lourie," I corrected.

"Pete, ah, my friend Pete, come and sit down. The search is over, Pete." And he warmly patted me on the back with his thick adventurer's paw. And called to a woman in the nearby kitchen for coffee.

Perhaps I should have been wary of his almost obsequious friendliness, but after what I'd been through to find him, to me he was now the most trustworthy, the warmest, the best man I'd met since I'd come to Ecuador. I suppose I was a treasure hunter's perfect audience now, the way I gave him the benefit of the doubt. And when I shook his hand, he gripped it tightly and I pressed hard, too. I felt like the son who had been away from home for so many years traveling, and now I was back, reconciled; and more a son to Brunner than ever I could have been with Andy, whose son was (for better or worse) Diego.

Brunner's old German eyes were so warm, all my faith in why I'd stayed in Ecuador was renewed, and from that first meeting on, I was sure I had come to Ecuador in order to make the trek to Cerro Hermoso with no one but this man. He seemed earnest, devoted to the Llanganati treasure. These were sober, refreshing qualities—persuasive and endearing.

Right away I told him about not getting into the mountains with Diego or Andy. This drew me into his trust, for he too had been disappointed by Ecuador's wealthy. Many times, he said.

"Andy thinks you can just go in and take the treasure out, just like that, easy. Forget it, Pete. You cannot trust some people, no? He and I had an agreement years ago and now you tell me he sends his son-in-law there without coming first to Gino. So much has changed since 1966 with Dyott. So much. Well, I don't tell him my secrets anymore, do I now? No, I will not."

The first few days I sat with Brunner I had to begin all over again, as I had done with Diego. I worked hard to earn his trust in me. Yet it was not an easy task because underneath that friendly facade, I began to sense paranoia.

On the surface, however, he was like an old bulldog sitting at a desk, jovial, optimistic. At first he appeared infinitely ingenuous. Like a small child, Brunner assured me he had recently interested a Dane, the manager of a textile factory here in Quito, and we would be in the mountains by February 1. He would be glad to have me along, he said instantly. Right away he knew why I'd come to him.

"So, you need old Gino to get you to Cerro Hermoso," he said.

"Yes. I certainly do."

"I can see it in your eyes, Pete."

I said, "Does it show that much?", and he said it did.

The Dane, Mortenson, would fund a large expedition, perhaps eight gringos, forty Indian carriers, and an Ecuadorian Air Force helicopter, Brunner assured me. Any day now, with the advance from Mortenson, Brunner would hire Indians to open the trail to Cerro Hermoso and build camps along the way.

It seemed nothing less than a miracle that I'd found my Kurtz just when he was about to make a trip himself. But it wasn't only this that made me almost dance as I walked home that first evening from his house. No, it was also that I had found someone special, a charmer, a sober man who seemed proud of himself. Someone who I truly felt could be my friend; he was more open than Diego and Andy, more honest with his intentions, I think, and a philosopher, too. What a philosopher!

The first day I met him, he said, "To be born is not the beginning, Pete. To die is not the end. These are just doors. No one is afraid of being born or of dying. We are only afraid to lose our egos. But we do not know who we really are. We don't often look hard into the mirror at ourselves, do we? Some people think they are very important, big bosses, generals and politicians. But if these people could look into their mirrors, they would see only a shabby little creature. Maybe if they could see themselves as they really are, looking deeper into that mirror, maybe then they would spit into the reflection. And this, Pete, is exactly what Gino Brunner does not want. I want to be free of that self-hatred. In order to look into the eyes of others we must first look for a long time at our own eyes in the mirror and we must like what we see."

I told Brunner I too was trying to look into a mirror, and he said,

"You are? Ha! Pete—maybe it had to be that we met, after all!"

Again I loved Brunner. Not just because he could get me into the mountains, not only because I felt so safe with him as my expedition leader, not merely because he had accumulated four decades of expertise, but also because he seemed to have a larger vision, and I felt as if I'd stepped under a huge umbrella of wisdom where this treasure story would finally take on a proper perspective. I suppose I'd been searching for the perfect treasure hunter all along, and that January day I knew I'd struck gold.

When he rose from his desk, he was shorter than I'd imagined. He looked top-heavy as he reached for a leather-bound copy of *The Inca Treasure in the Llanganati Mountains and the Almost Unbelieveable History of the English,* which he'd written in Spanish.

"What's that, Mr. Brunner?"

"Call me Gino; my friends call me Gino." Shaking his manuscript gently, he said coyly, smiling: "Here is the whole story. With this, Pete, you would not need me, no?" He laughed and coughed simultaneously. Of course, he knew it wasn't true.

He held the sixty-seven-page manuscript as if it were marked top secret. That document contained Blake's maps and photographs of Cerro Hermoso and Lake Brunner. Few had ever seen those maps which had shed light on the treasure's location. Part of me, I admit, wanted to grab those maps and run, though God knows where I thought I might escape. And then what? What would I do with maps of an area I'd never been to?

Brunner paused to admire his own writing. He leafed through the pages delicately with those thick, undelicate hands. His eyes started to glaze, trance-like, and he suddenly began to read the Spanish aloud, in the elevated tone of a Homeric bard. Forty-two years of searching had produced this sixty-page booklet, all of which—if he'd let me—I could read in a few hours.

Brunner read on, pleased, I think, with the sound of his own voice filling the room with epic intonation.

Then it was time to go. I left him as I found him, leafing wistfully in the naked light from the strong bulb through histories of the Inca and through his own writings that he was so proud of.

As I said goodbye that first evening, I was afraid I'd never see him again, that I'd wake tomorrow and he'd be again lost. I didn't want to leave, but Brunner had started working busily even while I sat there. As if I had not even been there.

So I pulled myself away from him and said I'd be back tomorrow after school, if he didn't mind, which he said he didn't at all. "No, Pete, you come over here anytime you wish. I will tell you everything . . . almost everything." He laughed and I laughed with him.

He then said something that implied he hadn't enough money for bus fare, so I gave him a few dollars in sucres. I told him I had two hundred dollars which I'd saved for an expedition, and I could give him a hundred soon, if he needed to buy provisions. Brunner's eyes were full of the fire of kindness and thankfulness and he said, yes, he could use the money to buy our food and, yes, we also needed a new camping stove. "Thank you, thank you, Pete," he said earnestly.

Brunner appeared to work hard, spending all day and night on his projects, preparing pamphlets to present to those few who still listened to him, who would give their support and money for expeditions. In me he had found an ally.

I believed the old man knew where the gold was, all right, or was so very close ... He assured me, "The search is over, Pete. Now we must only learn how to get the treasure out."

"*We*, Lilian," I told her when I got home. "Brunner says *we* are going into the Llanganatis in February, bad weather or not! Makes no damn difference now! Thank you for everything." And I gave her a long solid kiss on her cheek and she flushed like a little girl.

◆◆◆

In Pollo Psychodelico, a small chicken restaurant near the American School, a teacher friend approached me a few days after I'd met Brunner and said, "Peter, I want you to talk to this man. He's interested in the same crazy things you are."

I hadn't realized how much I was getting a reputation as a treasure hunter, but some things I suppose you can't keep secret for long.

A balding, swarthy Israeli sat down. We shook hands and he said his name was Haack. He smiled incessantly.

Since he said very little at first—I wondered if he was having trouble with Spanish or English or both—I asked what kind of treasure he was interested in. His quick answer suggested none of the suspicion of a treasure hunter.

"Holes," he replied loudly in English.

"What?"

His English was fluent. "Holes, you know. I work with detectors. Your friend tells me you're into T's, too."

"T's?" I said. It was the only time I ever heard a treasure reduced to a letter. It made me think of J's or DT's or DJ's.

"No," I said, wishing the Israeli would disappear now. "I'm interested only in one treasure, the Llanganati gold." After I said it I wished I hadn't.

Haack's idiot smile never let go of his mouth. He took out a cigarette and held it in his hand for five minutes. Periodically he searched his jacket and trousers for matches.

I thought he might be on barbiturates, and I asked the waiter for my bill.

"I know the Llanganati T. Do you carry tools?"

"What do you mean 'tools'?"

"You know, metal detectors. I need someone with tools."

I got up to leave.

"I know Yuri Geller," Haack said, "We met in Belém. I had a diamond mine there. But I gave it up in Brazil to come here. There are so many T's in Ecuador. There are no T's in Israel that do not belong to the state. Ecuador is a powerful majestic place, man. I heard there's a man named Brunner . . ."

"I know Brunner," I blurted, and could have punched myself for doing so, but I had just met him and his name spoken anywhere by anyone evoked such an intense emotion.

Haack's smile evaporated. "You know Brunner? I hear he's the best treasure hunter in the country. Where can I find him? I've been looking for that man for months. Where is that man?"

Haack had followed me out the door and into the bright street. This fawning Israeli made me feel I was privy to inside information. Knowing Brunner had indeed put me on a new level in the pursuit of treasure.

But I refused to give Haack Brunner's address, to have the old man hounded by the likes of him. I wanted Brunner for myself.

So I embellished truth, distorted time. "I think he's on the coast now, looking for emeralds. He'll be back next month. Check the Libri Mundi in March."

"Oh, really!" Haack said, and I dashed off to my class. "I'll see you around," he said as I ran down the street, but I hoped we'd never meet again. He was searching for the greatest of all Ecuadorian T hunters—the very man I'd be talking with in person again when school let out in the afternoon.

The teaching itself, however, had become almost unbearable by January. I was not concentrating on my work.

My second-grade class, in which I'd managed to fend off anarchy through December, now by late January exploded out of my hands. The boys and girls knew my heart just wasn't there, and they did pretty much what they wanted to do in class.

One day suddenly the principal was at my door wondering why so much noise was coming from the classroom.

When I'd kept up with Diego, the school had been a life raft, a salvation of sobriety, a fixed purpose and discipline. I had worked hard at my job and had maintained some degree of order. But when I met Brunner, the job was superfluous, so certain was I the expedition would leave in a matter of weeks.

Brunner, on the other hand, was glad I was working (and had a work visa) because he wasn't yet sure the exact date our expedition would leave for Píllaro. "It is always good, Pete, to have a work visa in this country. For security," he said as he glanced furtively around the room.

But the quality of my teaching was worsening, and I knew I should resign if only for the students' sake. The school would have to find a replacement, too, which would take time. But I didn't tell Brunner I was thinking of quitting the school.

For hours I would just sit in what I called "my chair" beside the old treasure hunter's desk watching him work, listening to his stories. The woman who owned the clothing store downstairs had gotten to know me pretty well, although she and I never spoke much. I wondered if she had been a lover of Gino's, but I never did find out. I would come in off the street and she would smile and say either *"Está"* or *"No está,"* he's in, or he's not in. If Brunner was out somewhere I'd wait nearby in a small café until I'd see him limping up the steep incline of the street, and I'd hurry out to him and say something which often he couldn't hear, and I'd have to shout so loud, everyone on the street would look over at us. "Good to see you, Gino!" "Yes, you too," he always said.

Again up in his tiny office he told me the search was over.

"The search is finished, no?" He spoke softly in deep, deliberate, slightly nasal syllables. He claimed he'd found the gold but would only take it out if it could be used for the Indians of Ecuador, to redeem the blood it had cost in the four-hundred-year search.

Tacked onto his sentences was this curt Ecuadorian-Spanish "no?" It was uttered through the nose with an interrogative inflection yet with an exclamatory significance. The old man's speech was riddled with these little tags; they poked force into his ideas.

"It's a whole life's work, no?"

Brunner held two large volumes of maps, drawings, contracts, photographs—the evidence of his many expeditions into those mountains. Their density, literally thousands of photographs, lent credence to the man's endurance.

Brunner had been to the Llanganatis looking for the treasure for at least a month every year since 1938, until just a few years ago when the doctor advised him not to go again because of high blood pressure.

Brunner exclaimed he would go anyway. "How can I stop, now that I am certain where it is!

"I am not a rich man, Pete. Since I discovered where the

treasure is, they tried to kill me three times, no? You see, I have unraveled the biggest riddle in South America, but I have done it with shoestrings.

"Believe me, there are no more mysteries in the world like this one. For years I did it alone. But now they know I know, and they ask me to dinner. Finally I deserve a right to a steak and a cup of coffee." His words were bitter. His f's and s's shot a fine mist against the light. His face flushed anger, but then, unexpectedly, he smiled.

I tried a few times to get Brunner to talk about his European past, but he would speak little of his twenty-two years in Switzerland and Germany. It was a dark gap in the unfolding story.

I managed one day, however, after a month of afternoons with him, to glean a tiny bit. His mother was Swiss, his father German. He'd spent most of his early life in Switzerland. But on the thirtieth of June, 1934, "the Night of the Long Knives," he was in Berlin. The Nazis killed seven of his best friends and he escaped only because he jumped through a window. He had been part of an organization that smuggled people out of Germany into Switzerland. He spent six months in a concentration camp and he told me he'd known a lot of important people in the German resistance. "But that's another story," he said, and the subject returned to the treasure in South America as if I'd wandered into forbidden territory, asking questions I should not have asked.

"If I had had money, it would be out by now, no? But maybe then I wouldn't be here talking to you, would I? Until 1962, like all the other bastards, I went to the wrong mountain. I did not go to Cerro Hermoso. I followed Valverde's *Guide*. We all did and we were lost."

I asked, "And that's when you got Blake's maps, right?"

"You know about those?" Brunner looked worried.

"Only what Andy told me. Very little, Gino."

"Well, yes," Brunner relaxed, "I did receive new information from Commander Dyott about the British naval officer, Barth

Blake, who found the treasure in 1887. How much did Andy tell you?" Brunner looked worried again.

"Very little. He told me only that Blake died before he could take it out," I said. Not wishing to jeopardize my position, and wanting to know the whole story about Blake from Brunner himself, I said no more about what I knew or didn't know. I played dumb and just listened.

But for the moment, he switched abruptly to something else.

"I have a base camp at four thousand meters. It is beside my lake, Lake Brunner. That is the treasure lake, Pete, the one Valverde mentions in the first section of the *Guide,* no? I suppose Andy told you about my lake, too? Eh?"

I quickly said, "No. What lake?"

Brunner was pretty angry. The slightest bit of information concerning the lake itself was too precious, too close to the gold, to be discussed by others.

Relieved but wary, his anger submerging, Brunner now recited the *Guide* from memory, the way Andy had done, except Brunner knew it in English *and* Spanish and could rattle it off as quickly as a child says his ABC's. In fact, he knew it as well as I had learned the ancient Greek alphabet in my first-year classics course at college, in which my professor had demanded that each student be able to say the whole alphabet rapidly in reverse.

"Our work on this expedition will be to study how to get the gold out. We need to pull down a natural dam in such a way so it won't flood the people who live down below at Río Verde where the road between Baños and Puyo passes. There are a thousand people down there. And I don't want to be blamed for their deaths, no?

"Once the water is out, we put the mud to the side, then we start to take the gold. We wash the Inca artifacts, photograph them, number them, pack them, and on a clear day we take them out by helicopter."

"Helicopter?" I had to barge in. "But isn't the weather too horrible for helicopters?"

Brunner eyed me closely. "So," he said nodding his head wisely, "Andy told you about his accident, no? Well, he was very stupid for not bringing food and supplies with him. I myself would never go anywhere near the Llanganatis without supplies."

He kept nodding.

"Then there's another treasure in a cave. Yes. My dream is about a lake *and* a cave. I was only seven when I had that dream, no? I was deep in Europe and too young to know anything about Incas. How do you explain that, eh?"

"I had a treasure dream, too, Gino," I said to distract him from his suspicion that I was in any way in cahoots with Andy.

Brunner, I was surprised, listened carefully to my dream; he believed in dreams. So I told him last year I dreamed I came upon a stone slab in the earth in front of a cave, a prehistoric burial tomb, and on the stone was painted Leonardo's *Mona Lisa*. In my dream I was elated—I'd made the anthropological discovery of the century—but when I lifted the slab, from down in the grave, from a pile of very delicate bones, a mist rose suddenly, the essence of the spirit of dead cavemen, a subtle fog, a living shape that moved with evil intent as I shone my flashlight on it. But I was so terrified of that ghastly mist I dropped the stone slab and ran, and woke up in a sweat.

"Very interesting, Pete, yes. Now, let me tell you my dream," said Gino.

At the age of seven his nightmare was of a boy standing on a high cold mountain at the edge of a dark lake. On the far side of the lake, a cliff rose from which a waterfall cascaded. At the base on one side of the falls there was a cave's black entrance. A strange light emanated from deep inside. Descending stone steps to a subterranean cavern, the boy found animal and human figurines of gold and silver and huge amphorae filled with scintillating many-colored stones. Thousands of human skeletons and skulls were scattered about the floor. The boy fled in horror and woke screaming.

"So you see, Pete, these dreams of ours are similar, are they not?"

"Yes. Amazingly," I said. But I don't think I saw the similarity as he did.

Brunner had come to Ecuador and remembered his dream in 1938 when he read about the lake, the waterfall, the tunnel, and the treasure in Spruce's translation of the Valverde *Guide*, which was incorporated into Luciano Andrade Marín's 1937 edition of *Llanganati*. Since then, he had devoted his life to his dream. His other projects—the circles, squares, and triangles on the big map of Ecuador by his desk—these were merely tangential.

The veteran, when he spoke of gold, wove recklessly in and out of details like an exuberant child.

"In the morning everything in the Llanganatis is frozen. Some say those craggy mountains are cursed by the Incas. Many have died." Brunner frowned. "But they are stupid, careless people. They did not learn from the Indians who live at the western edge of that region."

"So how can people survive up there for months at a time?"

"You must learn how to make a hut out of *páramo* grass in a snowstorm, as the Indians do. You must learn to fix a place to sleep, under the thick rug of vegetation, which will keep you warm even when you are cold and sweating to death. And when you are lost, when you have lost your tents and sleeping gear in storms or down ravines, when your helicopter crashes, and when you have no supplies, you can be safe with Gene Brunner. The dead ones didn't know how to build fires with *caspivela*, candlewood they call it—did Andy tell you this?"

"No."

"It is a bush that burns even when it's wet, no? So some have died and they say the mountains are cursed. The dead ones are stupid and they give that region a bad name."

Other "experts" had disappeared mysteriously, and died or

gone mad. What did Brunner have, I wondered as I sat listening in my chair, that exempted him from death and madness after all those years? Was he immune to the curse that some say is on that treasure?

Almost everyone I'd talked to said the mountains were bewitched. Did Brunner think so?

"Gino." I was cautious with this question. "Are the Llanganatis cursed, as some say?"

"*No*. Absolutely not. But from the conditions up there, you might think so. To give you an idea of the weather, let me tell you about Colonel Brooks. He was a man who had come to Ecuador from New York to establish the Central Bank of Ecuador. They say he died in 1922. It's a lie! Brooks was in the Llanganatis in 1924. The first time, he was miserably lost and the Indian porters deserted him, no? But he got out with his Peruvian friend.

"The second time, he went to the Llanganatis with his wife, an Ecuadorian he met here. She is one of the very few women who've ever been inside those mountains.

"They made a camp in a beautiful green meadow. At the end of the Valverde *Guide*, just after the Margasitas Mountain. There was a small river, meandering through the lovely valley. But it began suddenly to rain high up in Las Torres Mountain and the camp was flooded. They crawled up the hillside, hanging there all night long, but his wife caught pneumonia and she died right there.

"In 1943 I found their campsite and two bone hair needles, just like those the Indians still use. And I also found the sole of a lady's slipper. It must have been hers.

"I had a guide with me then, Amado López. He was one of the men who had carried Isabella Brooks's body out. She is buried in the cemetery at Píllaro. You can check it, if you don't believe me."

"Why wouldn't I believe you, Gino?"

"Of course you do, Pete. But then Brooks went crazy, no? He didn't ever go back to the Llanganatis, but instead returned to the

United States, where he died shortly after in a madhouse. He never found the treasure, and he is just one of the many casualties of the weather and the mystery.

"But I'll say too that he did something good for Ecuador. He and his New York firm finally established one currency here where before there had been many. Each bank had printed its own—it was chaos. Brooks gave us something here before he died, no? So it was not all in vain, I believe."

Brunner looked wistfully at his desk, rose, then asked the two women in the kitchen that adjoined his office for two cups of coffee. One of the women was quite young and pretty and very very shy. (Was she the daughter of his landlady? I asked. "No," Gino told me, "she is my secretary.")

Gino sat down again and resumed in exactly the same barreling-on-through tone as before, as if the story about Brooks and whatever would come next were parts of one larger story. If you can imagine a series of extended anecdotes strung together like clauses in a monumental run-on sentence, you will know what it was to listen to Gene Brunner talk.

"So," I said, "we will be safe in those mountains. I'm glad, Gino."

"I never force anyone to do what I can not do myself, Pete. Sure, some got sick, but I always have the right medicine with me. And nobody, nobody ever died on any of my expeditions—but one did die on Andy's trip, that time. Did he tell you about that? Yes? Well, that kind of thing never happened to me.

"I made my first expedition in 1938. Naturally, it was a complete failure. I got pneumonia and the boxes of supplies fell down a rock face and into a river. But I kept going and going and going through the years. Why? Because of my dream. Until 1975, every year for a month, sometimes two or three, I went like some people go to church. And then, when I did not have the money to hire porters (in 1975, when I was sixty), I moved the boxes in by myself one at a time. Sixty pounds each! It took four days and I moved them in stages. Like this!"

Brunner stood up and bent over like a burdened Indian. He took small steps, his face wrinkling, as he struggled under the imaginary weight. He smiled as he stood up straight.

"And I think today, Pete, there is nobody on this planet who knows the Llanganatis as I know them. I have covered every inch of those mountains. Well, yes, there is one man perhaps. Luis Andrade is an old white-haired man like myself." Brunner frowned. "With snowy Chimborazo on his head like me, no? But Andrade has given up, gone crazy! He sits in the plaza all day with the pigeons and the retired generals and he tells them he's the only one who knows about the treasure, about those terrible mountains, he calls them. He is full of bitterness, Pete. He is *loco*. Why, just the other day he came running in here and wanted to go with me on my expedition. I told him no. He has no money, so what use is he?"

◆◆◆

As I left Brunner's inner sanctum on whatever night that was, down the rickety stairs, through the courtyard, and into the crowded street, I wondered what had passed between those two veterans of gold. I vowed to myself I'd begin soon a new search, this time for Andrade in the plaza. But I was in no rush, because I knew that Brunner was the final word on Atahualpa's treasure.

Still, I was curious about any other leads.

Andy called me one day in January to say that Diego was planning a trip in March. I thanked him for telling me, but I was all set with Brunner. Andy sounded distant, and—I might have read this wrong—disappointed. "When will you be in Guayaquil next?" he asked. I said, "Soon. I'll call." But I never did. Brunner had eclipsed my interest in Andy and Diego, as treasure hunters anyway. Andy rarely came to Quito, so I never saw him. We had drifted apart: My focus was purely on the sierra now. But I did miss Andy in a way. He had been the one who started all this for me. There was just no time to go to Guayaquil.

I did run into Diego on various occasions. He would simply say his plans were firming up. It was sad that I had had to drop him also as a companion, and for a few weeks I ended up going to see him in the mornings at his apartment. Often he was still in bed and terribly hung over. After a few visits I stopped seeing him again.

◆◆◆

From the international book store, Libri Mundi, I bought and was rereading a copy of *Nostromo,* Joseph Conrad's novel about a treasure in a mythical South American country. The hero, an Italian sailor named Nostromo, rescues, hides, and is corrupted by a shipload of silver. In the "most famous and desperate affair of his life," Nostromo takes the silver out to sea to avoid an attack by revolutionaries. When he returns to the town of Sulaco and discovers that everyone thinks the boat with the silver has sunk and that no one really cares about him and his brave deed, Nostromo, feeling betrayed, decides to keep the loot, knowing full well that it will be his undoing.

Nostromo was famous for his great honesty, but sneaking around in the dark to get his silver one night, he is shot by the father of the woman he loves.

Before I'd met Brunner I pictured him to be like Nostromo, living in this reclusive country, a man who had fallen from grace or who had been embittered by some dark festering secret and who had found a deadly salvation in the corrupting power of a treasure.

In Conrad's novel the silver feeds on Nostromo's integrity and drains the man of his nobility. Before he dies he acknowledges his decline:

There is something in a treasure that fastens upon a man's mind. He will pray and blaspheme and still persevere, and will

curse the day he ever heard of it, and will let his last hour
come upon him unawares, still believing that he missed it only
by a foot. He will see it every time he closes his eyes. He will
never forget it till he is dead and even then ... Ha! ha! ...
There is no getting away from a treasure that once fastens
upon your mind.

Before I met Brunner I was sure that when I finally found the
man, he would be the same kind of treasure slave venting such
self-damning pronouncements. He, too, I had thought, would be a
triumphantly cursed loser, plunging lustily toward his terrible
end.

But it turned out differently. What I hadn't considered was the
difference between having a treasure and searching for it. It is the
difference between excessive nourishment and craving food.
Nostromo had been overfed; he already had the loot and was
being strangled by his self-indulgence. But not yet having the
treasure filled Brunner with a horrible hunger, which, oddly,
ironically, had the invigorating power to sustain him and even
make him glorious.

In my first weeks with the old treasure hunter, I found that
Brunner was indeed obsessed, but unlike Nostromo the malig-
nancy of the obsession hadn't yet petrified the whole man. Or
perhaps more accurately, Brunner derived energy from the tumor
which at any moment had the power to kill him. Brunner had
constructed a daily routine, a strong sense of discipline around his
forty-two-year-old quest.

Conrad's novel, also, seemed to describe a place like Ecuador.
Of the country and the people in his book, he wrote: "great land
of plain and mountain people, suffering and mute, waiting for the
future in a pathetic immobility of patience." This too described
the poor, sad Ecuadorian peasant, the descendants of the Incan
people who witnessed the murder of their Sun King. These were
the peasants Brunner said he loved enough to find the treasure for

them, and for them alone. "To redeem their blood and their suffering," he had said.

The rainy season had begun. During those first weeks with Brunner the clouds moved onto the city like heavy mysteries. Quito closed down even earlier than usual, eight or nine o'clock. The frogs clicked loudly in my garden.

The old man had stopped talking one night, an unusual lull in the steam engine of his words. He stared at the ground for the longest time, oblivious to me. Then, finally, he looked up into my eyes and said very very carefully:

"We will not go unless we go with the Air Force this time. We need strong men. I'm too old now to do what I used to do, to climb cliffs with ropes and pitons, no? I have the scars to prove I've done all that." He pointed to a purple line as thick as a night crawler on the inside of his knuckles. "I got this when I slipped off a cliff and had to grab my machete to save my life. With the blade cutting into my hand I pulled myself up. It cut deeper. Only way to save myself."

Brunner said he was making all the preparations for our trek, and I believed him. Call me a fool, but I believed him mostly because I liked him. I did ask him for specifics, though.

"To get the treasure out now, we need helicopters and men. I have a very important meeting with a friend next week, a general in the Air Force. Then you and I will meet with some generals and with Mortenson, the Dane. I'm setting this up now. I have worked for the military so many years in the old days. They owe me. I made rescue missions in rugged mountain passes, taking bodies from airplane wrecks so the families could have a decent burial for their sons . . ."

"Did you recover bodies from the Quito-to-Cuenca airplane crashes?"

"Many of those, yes." Brunner paused, remembering, but was neither morbid nor heroic about his memories.

"After next week we will meet with the president himself. I think he is finally realizing the significance of finding this treasure. There's so much money involved here that they will have to revalue the sucre to somewhere near the dollar, I think."

Brunner again took a long pause, this time about five minutes. He stared at his desk. I began to squirm. Then in a soft distant voice, a new voice, like a muffled seashell, not at all his usual bulldog voice, he continued:

"I don't remember if I ever told you how much gold and silver this treasure contains, have I?" Brunner looked around the room. His secretary, as he called her, the shy woman with high cheekbones and no smile whatsoever, entered with more coffee, left us, and then he continued so softly I could hardly hear him.

"Oviedo wrote that Rumiñahui left Quito with twelve thousand armed guards and sixty thousand loads of gold. If each man, each of the sixty thousand carriers took only twenty-five pounds—an impossibly small amount for a strong mountain Indian who is accustomed to great burden!—how much is sixty thousand times twenty-five, Pete?"

"Ah . . . well . . ."

Brunner was poised on the edge of his seat.

"I'll tell you. It is nothing less than seven hundred and fifty tons exactly! Of gold! Fantastic, no!"

"But, Gino, will that be enough for the two of us?"

Brunner quickly saw I was joking and smiled.

"But most people think the treasure of Atahualpa was only what Rumiñahui took out of Quito and buried in the Llanganatis, no? Not true, my friend. Not true at all. There are other treasures of the Inca. Rumiñahui sent seven other hoards from all corners of Ecuador. Seven caravans were on the roads from here to Cajamarca when Pizarro stupidly killed the Inca King.

"You and I, Pete, we are only concerned with the one in the Llanganatis. The big one. You and I . . ." His voice now despotic, he might have been some fanatical priest delivering a peroration. "You and I now are going to extricate it. I've worked forty-two years for this moment. If we don't do it now, someone else will, you can be sure of that, Pete!"

I stared into Brunner's avid eyes and I believed everything the man said. I believed this expedition would be the last great plunge of his life's quest. I believed I would go with him to see the climax of four decades of searching.

I decided to give the school a month's notice. I would quit because we would be gone, and because I begrudged my six hours at school (time I wanted to spend with Brunner), and it was better for the Colegio Americano to start looking for another teacher now.

◆◆◆

But that was the week of the student riots. I didn't leave my house for forty-eight hours because I lived one block from the university's Faculty of Medicine where the rioting had been the fiercest.

Lilian said that at times like these it was best to stay indoors. Colegio Americano was closed for two weeks, delaying my giving notice, and the tear gas that covered my neighborhood seeped through the cracks in my door and stung my eyes. Many of the younger students roamed the city looking for mischief.

The reason for the disturbance was the government's hike in the price of milk and bus fares. The second day of the riots I heard the jeers of students taunting the police. The catcalls and whistling stopped suddenly and I heard running and hysterical laughter. A tank approached from the north. I could hear, but not see, the metal treads grating against the pavement, and suddenly a tear gas canister landed in my garden and exploded.

Hours later I went out into the still-acrid air and picked up the canister. Written on the side was "Federal Laboratories, Inc.,

Salzburg, Pennsylvania." The instructions in English said, "Federal Spedeheat Long Range Projectile Irritant—Warning: May start fires, for outdoor use only—for use by trained personnel only."

The police had not been issued bullets for their rifles, but on the first day of the riots a tenth-grade boy stood on a schoolyard wall above an officer, taunting him violently, "Come on, shoot me, go on, you pig! Shoot!" And with his pistol the policeman blasted him right through the heart.

Three days later, when I finally saw Brunner, he said, "This kind of thing, Pete, it happens here all the time." He seemed so uninterested in these riots that it made me once again realize how precarious was my presence in Ecuador, where my monthly salary of four hundred American dollars was greater than a peasant's annual income.

CHAPTER 9

◆◆◆◆◆

What really makes a man grope forty-two years in a godforsaken region of the world like the Llanganatis? Pizarro, too, not really knowing what he'd discover, worked his way down the west coast of South America in 1527 and again in 1532. Perhaps Brunner and Pizarro shared a resolve or fortitude I would never understand.

I called Rolf Blomberg, author of *Buried Gold and Anacondas*, because he knew both the Llanganatis and Brunner. Maybe he could explain things to me.

Over the phone came a slightly belligerent Swedish accent.

"You understand, Mr. Lourie, I have no more interest in the Llanganati. None. I was there already six times, but I've moved on to other things now. That book has been written." He repeated this more than once. I suspected he wanted to go with Brunner and me.

"Are you excited about the trip?" he asked with relish.

"Yes, very."

"Yes? Okay, come and visit me tomorrow. And do listen to Gino Brunner; he knows more than any man alive. He's the real pro."

The travel writer's Quito house was built on the cliff above the little village of Guápulo. I was met at the front door by a man in his sixties wearing thick-lensed glasses with heavy black frames. One eye seemed milky.

Spread out before us in his big picture window was a patch-work valley of green- and sand-colored checks, farms, and cattle ranches. Beyond the valley were mountains, the western Cordillera of the Andes through which Francisco Orellana had passed when he first went down the Amazon River to the Atlantic. The sky was a deep permanent blue. Hawks slit the air, circling way out above Guápulo and the valley. It was as if Blomberg's house were standing on the edge of a great cliff about to tumble into a fantastic painting by a mad dreamer.

Lilian's former brother-in-law spoke softly, slowly.

"Do you have any obligations? Are you a bachelor?"

"No, no obligations. Yes, a bachelor," I said. (What I didn't tell him was that my identical twin brother was getting married soon and one reason I was still a bachelor and why I liked to travel and not get tied down was that from early childhood, whatever my brother did, I did the opposite. Our twinship had drawn us apart; we needed to get away from each other in order to define ourselves. Jim had wanted to settle down and start a family, and I wanted to see foreign places. Jim had moved to Seattle for college and never came back to New York. We saw each other perhaps five days a year. When I received an invitation to his wedding, I wondered how I could afford to just drop everything down here in South America and fly all the way to Seattle for a fifteen-minute ceremony? I certainly didn't have the money. So Jim would be a married man. To me that was the end—I planned to live overseas for decades to come.)

"That's good. You're lucky, then. My wife likes me around but I like to be alone. Marriage creates these kinds of problems. She once told me, 'I wish I'd known before we got married that you were a treasure hunter.' Perhaps she's right, you know. We don't make good husbands. Brunner, too, was married."

So it must have been easier for Blomberg to be a treasure

hunter in the old days when he was married to Lilian's sister, before she died. With Clara around for a mother-in-law.

"So what are you writing now, Mr. Blomberg?"

"I'm working on a new book now, about the Galápagos Islands. But treasure was a part of my life for many years. Brunner and I have known each other a long time. By conventional standards he is a failure, a do-nothing who devotes his life to vanity, to schemes of gold, but you have seen the man. He's no slouch, you can see that. He works all day on his projects, and takes it all very seriously, his books, his treasure. He is an asocial kind of man, like me. In a way, he must be. It is a treasure hunter's life. But you know, he has gone deeper into this subject than any man and still he goes on. Why not write a book about *him?*"

"I might do that," I said, thinking how much more like these men I was than my twin brother could ever be. Just as Brunner and Blomberg were loners, I was a loner, too.

In Blomberg's library, treasure books lined the walls.

"We need the excitement of Brunner. I sometimes think I've given up all my fascination for treasures until, after two or three hours with him, I'm practically one hundred percent convinced again and I'm ready to hike off."

Silhouetted against that fantastical backdrop of distant plains, mountains, and crystal sky was the same man who on the phone had said he was absolutely through with the Llanganatis.

He said his book *Buried Gold and Anacondas* had sold better than any other he'd written. It had been translated into nine languages "because it is about a treasure, Mr. Lourie." He sighed deeply with pride.

"Yes, Brunner has had money problems recently, but he is a story in himself, don't you agree?"

"Of course I do."

"One could write a book about Brunner and call it *The Treasure Hunter*. He alone has the infectious magic."

"But, Mr. Blomberg, does Brunner ever lie?"

"Well, Mr. Lourie, I confess I can't believe all he says. For instance, the Sabela Indian story, the lost tribe of the Llanganatis. Brunner is convinced of their existence. Yet again . . . now that would be a project. What a discovery! If you could find that tribe. But lie? No. He molds the truth into Brunner's truth; that is all."

I asked Blomberg when he first came to Ecuador.

"In 1934. It was a country of colorful people in those days. Men like Brunner, Loch, and Enrique Robinson." Blomberg tried to smile.

"You know, you never find anything if you don't look for it."

What was this fascination with searching? I wondered as I stared into Blomberg's thick glasses. Simply to get rich? No. The mystery of it? To hope to find treasure seemed to justify all the delusions and hardships of looking for it.

As I listened to this man who had wrestled anacondas in Colombia and who had been into those mountains twice as many times as Diego, I began to see more clearly that the key to the idea of treasure lay in the *possibility* of finding it. What was important was not the solution to the puzzle, not the actual gold in the hand, but the suggestion of it, the aura a treasure radiates. A treasure hunter searches for an aura as much as he searches for artifacts. And to search for that aura requires a kind of faith.

Blomberg continued, his voice slightly defiant—filled with that faith of the search for the aura.

"Listen, I can always go if I want to. But Brunner has promised me the first photos. And I'm working on other things now. And there's no time for that business."

There it was again: the lie, the denial of the faith. The faith intact, but buried.

"Besides, my interest in the gold was never for the money. Never." I'd heard this before; they all said it. "I had an agreement with the government for half, but I knew they would never give a foreigner as much as that. Maybe none. No. And no Indian would ever see that money either, as Brunner would wish. I went because I wanted to write a book and because I hoped to do what no other person had done."

"And what," I asked, "ever happened to Luis Andrade, whom you describe in your book as a great guide?"

"He is the only man who's been in more than Brunner, but now he just sits on a park bench. He is nothing but the shade of his former self, a bitter man who thinks that Brunner is a liar and that I tricked him out of his share of the proceeds from my book. But he used to be incredible! That man could go up and down those mountains like you would not believe, Mr. Lourie. Now he's given up. Andrade only sneers and complains all day and he believes he will go again, but he is finished, I know. Brunner is never finished, but Andrade is. The doctors have told Brunner not to go again, but he is the kind of treasure hunter who will always go again. If there is money or not. Brunner will go on forever!"

For Blomberg, and for me, Brunner was a symbol of human perseverance and professionalism. Blomberg lived vicariously through the other man the way most people identify with sports heroes. But I was young. And I was going. And I did not have to live vicariously.

When I left Blomberg's house I came away feeling somehow closer to my goal. He had confirmed, if not my faith in the treasure itself, then at least my faith in Brunner.

Most days I'd find Brunner alone deftly pecking at his typewriter with his index fingers. Sometimes I just could not imagine him or anyone doing this so diligently for forty-two years.

Once he said to me, "When you go back to the States, Pete, tell your friends about Eugene Brunner, the poorest treasure hunter who ever lived." And he laughed. It was Brunner's own special brand of self-disparaging, self-accepting humor, as if those forty-two years had formed around his soul a carapace, a wonderful resilience to failure.

Some told me point-blank: Brunner is mad. And to be sure, the man was obsessed. He did nothing extraneous to his mission. Yet Pizarro had also been thought mad by the residents of Panama; the conquistador was so convinced an empire lay to the south.

And if Brunner was mad, he was crazy in a good way. He was kind, exuberant, involved, devoted, coherent, tenacious, generous, disciplined. He liked people, and I could see in the street when they greeted him in return that people greatly liked him. More than once I saw him give ten sucres (thirty cents, his last change) to a hungry Indian. Money had always been what Brunner lacked. He was so poor, one day I had to lend him money for coffee. I didn't have a lot of money either, but I had considerably more than he did. I liked to help him out, but often he would rather walk than spend a few cents for the bus, and sometimes he refused my generosity.

It was in late January that I gave him half my savings for our trip. He said he needed to start serious preparations, buy food, get us a stove. So I gave him the hundred dollars I'd promised. I didn't know then (and I'm glad I didn't) that Brunner was in debt in a big way with a few people. No. I was ignorant and happy to give the man money, not only because I thought this was the final countdown to expedition, but because when I handed him one of the twin hundred-dollar bills I kept in my money belt, I never saw a man so grateful. He beamed and thanked me and I thanked him for telling me so much of the treasure story and for sharing with me his life. It was a good trade, I said. And to this day I still think it was a good trade, even though I never saw that money again.

Brunner was not the greedy swashbuckling treasure hunter I had expected. And unlike Diego and Andy, he didn't drink. He was sober and sympathetic; he had control of his life. Yet there was no denying that a trace of something dangerously protean hid behind Brunner's words and actions.

"Some people, Pete," he told me, "have already said they will hang me by my balls until I tell them what Blake discovered, no?"

His words formed at one side of his mouth and were aimed at the floor. His voice was muffled and I had to ask him to speak up.

Those who would torture him, he said, were the ones who never looked you in the eyes. They shook hands limply and if they had thin lips, too, if you could not see their lips, then they could never be trusted. They would hang you by your balls to get the secrets, he said, "And even you, Pete, should be careful because the bastards are sure to know that you are learning a few of Brunner's secrets."

Brunner looked troubled. I put my hand over my mustache and asked him what would happen when we found the gold. How much would the government demand? How much for us?

He told me the new law stated that finders got twenty-five percent. That would be about two hundred tons to split between us. We laughed together like accomplices in a crime. Two hundred tons was not a figure I could touch; it was like infinity or the stars.

For some months now I had wondered what I would really do if we found that treasure. There were those who said the government would give us none, so I had devised a plan to hide a portion of my share, somewhere in the mountains, in a crevasse or behind or beneath a rock. I could go back for it later, I figured, when it was safe and no one would suspect.

Brunner banged his fist on the wall. I stood up.

Some demon had gotten hold of him; he had the capacity for violence.

"There *is* one ridiculous story, no?" His voice boomed.

"It was in the papers some years ago. A large treasure is reported to have left a port in Peru in 1807 bound for Europe.

But it could not be our treasure because Blake found it eighty years later. So forget it! Impossible!"

Brunner was addressing someone else. He wasn't even looking in my direction. This was the same vague reference the others had made about some treasure bound for Scotland. I didn't dare ask Brunner about it right then, but the next afternoon I went to the national library and asked the librarian, who was no help at all. Without a concrete reference I'd never find the articles Brunner, Andy, and Diego had vaguely alluded to.

A few days later I asked Brunner where the story had appeared and he pretended his hearing aid was not turned up. I knew better than to pursue it.

Peevishly, Brunner got up from his desk, put on his heavy coat, and said,

"Let's go out to my café."

◆◆◆

It was winter. That very morning the city had been drenched in bright sun-gold but now the temperature had fallen twenty degrees and storm clouds obscured the peak of Pichincha.

As we moved out into the street, the lead sky drizzled. Brunner, who never left the house without his valise of pamphlets and maps, buried his notes under his long coat. I followed him. He limped with dignity, his chest thrust out, head high, as we passed up the inclined cobblestone street through the crowd. Brunner looked the Indians full in the eyes and he greeted old toothless women selling fried pork and maize in smoky little shops.

The city was dark with storm and the descending dusk, and, I thought, there lingered the acrid smell in the air of the tear gas although the riots were long over. The government in the end had lowered the price of milk and bus fares, and the people again were quiet.

Yet Quito became a quick-paced city as the hour approached seven when the shops closed and offices disgorged great hordes of sprucely dressed clerks and secretaries. Ordinarily I came to the old city only to see Brunner.

The men who lingered in doorways when I'd come earlier still lingered there but seemed more alive now, drinking beer, gesticulating among friends. The air was cold. The women wore dark leather jackets and long skirts. It could have been a city in northern Germany. Reflections from cafés and stores angled off the cooling air, hard autumn angles. Plaintive flutes and ululant Andean love songs rose from radios in windows with old iron latticework. Brunner and I passed churches built in the late seventeenth century.

I could hear the German breathing loudly as we climbed the steep street. He did not complain, he never complained.

The light in his café was amber. Brunner greeted seven old men at a table by the door. Their faces warmed instantly to his smile, a reciprocity of upturned mouths and hearty handshakes, an exchange of old men's eyes and compassion.

We sat nearby in front of a mirror. Brunner's face was ruddy from the walk and he talked excitedly in the smoky room.

"Though I've never had money, Pete, not my own money, I have moved thousands of sucres, millions of sucres, for Llanganati research. A fortune in itself, no? But it's not the money I want from the treasure. But to find it would mean the confirmation of my life here. Do you see this, Pete?"

"Yes, I do." It was funny how every treasure hunter, even Brunner, talked about a treasure in terms of something other than simply the money.

"Forty-two years would have some applause, finally." Brunner's eyes glittered with that idea. We ordered two coffees. He stirred milk into his with the slow cautious turn of his spoon, which he then placed with a bear-paw hand neatly beside his cup. The old men all around us were talking, arguing, sipping coffee while outside a mass of working people moved like a human avalanche toward their suppers.

At the moment, I was trying but failing to imagine the overwhelming logistics of our journey: porters, helicopter, money, Army volunteers, medicine, equipment. Finally, reluctantly, surprisingly, I began to doubt Brunner, just a little.

"I like sitting here so I can see every movement in the place. CIA, you know." Brunner laughed as he gazed around the room in the mirror. "I guess, Pete, I can tell you because we are friends now ..." (this was good to hear) "... in the war I was a secret agent for the United States. The Nazis here tried to kill me two times, no?"

Another side of Brunner was about to unravel. From the war he wandered to the topic of the Second Coming. His world, I could see, was an elaborate tapestry of truth and untruth, real and prophetic. He was a devout Baha'i, he told me.

One minute he'd be talking about the faltering economy of Ecuador, then suddenly he'd slide into the subject of man's spaceship origins. He would say that scientists, for example, overlook many things; that humans came from another planet; that there existed advanced civilizations on earth forty thousand years ago; that all religions awaited the Second Coming; that Nostradamus claimed Armageddon would occur on the seventh day of the seventh month in 1999.

Brunner's paganism had come unleashed in the whiskey-colored light of the café. It poured out of him as if no one had ever listened.

I drank my coffee while his mind disgorged a ramshackle litany of religion, cliché, and fantasy. Brunner's talk made me apprehensive. I could see that Brunner had the universe all worked out. For him death was not scary because it was a part of larger systems. But death scared me a lot, and I wondered if it really would be so safe with this man in the mountains after all. There was no denying he had fanatic leanings.

I wanted very much to pull him back to the treasure, to the specifics of the trip. He refused.

The stubborn bulldog, over his third cup of coffee (which I had to buy), unraveled a life of rage and mystery, of bleak helplessness and wild optimism. Yet something down deep in his rambling voice, embedded in his very idea of treasure, hinted at more than fanaticism. As for Clara Robinson, "the existence of all possible extraordinary and supernatural things" was possible for Brunner, too. He appreciated magic. That's another thing I suddenly realized about him: Brunner believed in magic.

Magic, then, was the goal, the quality in this treasure story that counterbalanced the craziness, that justified whatever life a treasure hunter chose for himself, whether it be ascetic or sybaritic, Brunner's order or Diego's chaos. And this magic in a treasure story was what intrigued me most—more even than the gold Inca artifacts.

There was an acrobatic beauty in Brunner's ability to connect Von Daniken's theories, ancient Pakistani writings, Velikovsky dialectics, Easter Island mysteries, all together into the converging lines of a unified world view. In one breath, his myriad run-on-sentence stories blended. He kept talking, and I couldn't have stopped him if I had wanted to.

Now he said that Ecuador's people and the country itself were the true treasures. For one who had failed to bring out the gold, who lived in poverty, there appeared to be an endless resource of faith and wonder inside Brunner. And I felt this wonder grow inside me, too, just to be near him.

Brunner gazed magnificently at himself in the mirror. With a slight nod of the head, his eyelids drooped like a movie actor's: an oddly debonair bulldog.

"You're a real ham" is what I did not say but was thinking.

"My heart," he told me in jubilation, wrenching his eyes from the mirror for a moment, "my heart is one and a half the size of a normal person's heart, no?" He quickly pulled out a recent electrocardiogram, unfolded the tape over the table. The coffee cups were hidden by reams and reams of paper with a continuous,

erratic line running through it like a horizon of crooked mountains. I couldn't stop laughing.

"Like clockwork!" Brunner boasted. "The doctor told me,
Gino, you are a monster; you have a huge heart and you even
have one extra vertebra . . ."

"Stop, stop!" I called. If he had said another thing I would
have split from laughing so hard. But when I opened my eyes,
moist and clouded from laughter, I suddenly saw a terribly
sad-looking face staring at me. Brunner had metamorphosed in a
second, and now he'd turned serious and frightening, haunted
almost.

He said, "I'm not so young anymore." He was afraid that he'd
never again go to Cerro Hermoso in anything less than four days.
From now on he'd have to take it very very slowly. No racing up
there as he used to do when he was young. Perhaps it would
take him seven or eight days even. This is what had changed his
mood so suddenly to gloom.

His mind began to whirl again, and his ideas went wild.

"Jesus Christ was not as he was portrayed. He was a man
with muscles like this." Brunner rolled up his sleeve as if to
receive an injection and he flexed his biceps, still strong even
at his age. Some of the men at a nearby table watched him but did
not smile.

"I do not have to worry as long as I have this." With a nod for
verification, he motioned me to test the rock-hard flesh of the
arm he held up. He turned and smirked into the mirror, lightly
poking his nose with his elevated hand.

Then I knew why the clownish antics tonight. Apparently he
had talked earlier with Mortenson, our Danish financier, and was
telling me now what I wanted to hear so badly: The money would
be ours within a week, a thousand dollars. We would get the
Indians to open the trail to Cerro Hermoso, he said, and build the
camps soon. We had a big meeting with the Danes and the
generals all lined up for next week.

Brunner's voice was unpretentious, methodical, convinced and convincing.

We celebrated with a fourth coffee and he said:

"Pete, in two weeks you will be there. In those strange mountains where I made a life's research, where I will show you the old Inca mine shafts, and tell long tales around the fire."

"Gino," I said. "Fantastic." And he smiled proudly.

We finished our coffee and braced ourselves for the crowded street. Brunner collected his precious valise and tucked it tightly under his strong arm.

The lead sky had stopped drizzling. Before we walked into the dark damp air, Brunner, who had a wonderful sense of decorum, ceremoniously shook hands with each of the old men at the nearby table.

Then, with no more delays, the famous treasure hunter leading, we plunged blindly into the dark wet street.

CHAPTER 10

◆◆◆◆◆

When I got home from school two days later, I found a note from Lilian asking me to join her for dinner. She wanted to hear the latest news, about Brunner and the expedition.

Around six, as the sun set behind Pichincha and the darkening air was cooling rapidly, I climbed the stairs to Lilian's apartment and knocked. Lilian's maid, Piedad, opened the door. (An Indian woman who had been with Lilian for decades, Piedad sometimes cleaned my apartment and washed my clothes. We always smiled at each other, but her Spanish was difficult to understand. Even so, one day when I had been deathly sick, she had patiently communicated to me an old Quechua remedy for worms and amoebas. She told me to grind up twelve papaya seeds and swallow them in a milky solution, which was the most bitter but effective medicine I ever found for the amoebas I contracted regularly in Quito.)

She led me into Lilian's living room, and I waited until Lilian emerged from her bedroom looking as if she'd woken from a nap, sluggish, her face mottled.

At the dinner table I knew Lilian was apprehensive about my contact with Brunner and I asked her what was bothering her.

"Peter," she said in her soft voice as she put down her fork, "do you consider yourself a real treasure hunter?"

I hesitated, then said that I supposed I was, in a loose sense of the term, but that I was mostly interested in the story, in all the threads of the story and in the treasure hunters and why they searched.

"I'm not sure I believe that I myself will get the gold, or that I'll be a rich man soon. Is that what you mean?"

I too stopped eating. Lilian's question seemed to chip away at something that had been nagging me. In a way I had felt, these many months since I first heard about the treasure, like an impostor. (Could Lilian see this?) I didn't think I'd ever have the dedication of Brunner, or the swagger of Diego, or the gambling fixation of Andy.

Lilian nodded and was quiet for a while, but then said:

"You absolutely must make a trip to Píllaro. Near Poaló where you went with Diego. Píllaro's the town where all the expeditions set off—Rumiñahui's birthplace. I remember Píllaro, an interesting town you must see. From there you can sense the treasure, as if it were only a hundred feet from where you stand, but always invisible."

Later, over coffee, she said, "If for some reason Brunner does not go in this year, have you thought about going alone?"

"What do you mean if Brunner does not go?" The suggestion stung.

"No, Lilian." I shook my head. Once again I explained I didn't want to just stroll around in those mountains, or get lost, or die. I didn't have enough money or know-how, either. I wanted the real thing, the genuine expedition. Sure I was having great trouble organizing a journey, but this only revealed the true nature of treasure hunters.

Perhaps I sounded defensive; I'd been waiting such a long time to get to those mountains. Lilian's question really bothered me.

And there was a slight accusation in her tone of voice, I thought. Was she calling me a coward because I hadn't gone yet?

Lilian said, "You must go." I supposed she meant to Píllaro. And the dinner ended on the first bad note between us.

After a day thinking about what she had said, I decided she was right. I had to get out of Quito, to see the town where so many expeditions had begun, and also to see if there were any clues as to why Brunner no longer went to Píllaro. For years he'd approached the mountains from another side, from El Triunfo. Perhaps now he had enemies or competitors there. I had to find out what they thought about Brunner in Píllaro.

Brunner was sitting when I told him I was going to make a trip to Píllaro the next day.

He looked up from a volume of photos and then stood.

"What for?" he said. "I'm doing all the preparations from here in Quito, Pete."

In the glare of his desk light, his face was oddly blank.

Guardedly he asked, "So what do you plan to do there in Píllaro?"

I worried he might think I'd betrayed him, overstepped some enemy line.

"Just going to get to know the town a little. I'm only going for one night." I'd planned two but thought it better not to say so.

Suddenly Brunner's blue eyes nearly danced out of his face.

"I . . . I've been in this country a long time now, Gino, and I don't feel I know the people or the land itself. I've been too long in the cities. And I just want to have a look at Píllaro. I'm anxious for some action, I guess."

Brunner looked away. His secretary knocked and he grunted, *"Vayase!"* Go away! I really had no idea what he would do next. His face very red, he looked violent.

"I'll be back the day after," I said, hating my voice for its submission.

"So. It's like this, is it? No?" Brunner sat down and seemed to go on with his work. As if there were nothing more to discuss.

With his eyes on his papers he said, "In a week or so we will be very close to there. I do not see why you must go now. With me, next week, you will get to know the Indians better than perhaps you want to."

He looked up. "Okay, go! And good luck in your exploration. But be careful, gringo. You know very little what is out there."

I sat with him for a minute before I left. He had never used the word "gringo" before. We were both gringos. Coming from him it was a bitter, pejorative, wounding word. I tried to imagine what I might uncover or stir up in Píllaro that could possibly threaten the old treasure hunter.

As I walked to the door Brunner tried to assure me he was not bothered by my short trip, but I was wary of him now. Our relationship seemed more precarious the closer we got to our expedition.

◆◆◆

Yet it felt so good to be out of Quito, moving somewhere.

Ambato was a large town, a very up-and-coming brick and cement town. The connecting bus to Píllaro was here, a few hours south of the capital. Modern construction of four- and five-story apartment houses was everywhere. Hammering, sawing, and the loud grating of cement mixers filled the bright still air.

Atahualpa had defeated his half-brother's army near Ambato before he moved south to Cajamarca.

I boarded a decrepit red and white school bus. As I went up the bus steps, I entered an alien century. It was jam-packed with whispering Indians, Mongolian faces, copper skin, and defiantly protuberant cheekbones peering over torn leather seat backs. Brown button eyes gleamed at me from under pounded wool beige hats looking more like finely woven pith helmets. These were the Indians of Píllaro. They faced me like a jury.

Each Indian had a bundle or two of vegetables, fruit, grain, wrapped in a ragged dusty poncho. The bus smelled like a market, the early morning smell of maize and dust and goats.

There were no seats but a lady with a child in front awkwardly made room for me next to her. As I sat down I could hear many voices whispering.

I had been months in a foreign country, but now I was entering a country within a foreign country. Here were the eyes of innocents. Here were the many, the collective, not incredulous, not cynical, not ironic, but rather the suffering, infinite, earthbound eyes of a group of Indians who went to Ambato, to the big city, perhaps twice a year from Píllaro.

The whispering filled the bus like spiderwebs until we departed. Dust blew freely through open windows. Five or six of the young driver's family stood around him in front.

I was headed for Píllaro, the mecca of treasure hunting in the Andes. Many millions of sucres had been spent in Píllaro for booze and supplies. Failed expeditions by the hundreds had given up in those streets, penniless, their expedition leaders broken. Píllaro: where Benalcázar had looked for Rumiñahui after the Inca general hid the gold.

We moved sluggishly back up the Pan American Highway to the eastward turnoff. A Mercedes raced past us at five times our speed, sending dust and pebbles up at the many cracks in our windshield. The bus driver, perhaps sixteen or seventeen, smiled at me and tried but failed to pass a slow oil truck on a curved incline. I got the feeling he was doing it on my account. After all, how many gringos went to Píllaro by bus?

We turned onto the dirt road I remembered drunkenly negotiating in moonlight with Diego. That indented moonscape, the volcanic phantasm (I could see now) was actually a great *quebrada*, or gorge, down which the bus inched. In the sunlight the earth had the color of raw sienna, like the hide of a Serengeti elephant. The dramatic sweep downward reminded me of leaving Nairobi years ago, descending westward into the Great Rift Valley. Thin light scattered over the gorge here as it had in Africa over the plains and acacia trees. Here the distances were not as great, yet the feeling of vastness in time, of something mesmerizing and nostalgic that the landscape evoked, was the same. Eternity. But instead of acacia, stands of sprightly eucalyptus, straight poles with silver-green trimmed tops stuck out of the bare land. Cactus reached up out of the barren rocks.

I was taking notes. The little girl beside me, perhaps eight, with braided black hair, a smudged dirty face, modest earrings, and a dress that was torn everywhere, watched my pen form words on the page. Her head was bent low over my writing, her eyes maybe six inches from my scrawl, and I wondered what she was searching for. Perhaps a word, I thought, a letter she might recognize, a sign that gringos were not monsters. Or maybe she was searching for the opposite, for a meaningless Martian scribble, proof once and for all that our pale-faced intentions were in fact subversive, alien.

As the bus worked its way down and up, in and out of gorges, I pretended to write when I had nothing to say, only to keep her there. I switched to Greek letters, but she was unfazed. She was so fascinated and I was as intrigued by her fascination. It seemed like two worlds meeting for the first time, she and I. This was the closest I had ever come to the Incas. I was glad I had not let Brunner dissuade me from coming here.

At times the girl tired of my cryptic nonsense and looked up staring at me with wide expectant eyes, partly fearful, partly full of mute curiosity, her face so close to mine. I smiled at her; she didn't smile back. But I was in love.

Most of the wool-hatted Indians behind had fallen asleep. The child's mother told me the young men and women at the front of the bus were all family. The driver, she was proud, was her son.

She too had a burlap bag of vegetables and fruit. She began to ask me the English equivalent for various Spanish names. When she ran out of names she pondered heavily, scratched her coal-black medusa's hair and found another name with a smile. *"Cómo se dice Juan?"*

"John," I said.

"Cómo se dice María en inglés?" Mary. She must have gone through the names of everyone she knew. We played that game for an hour. I'd tell her the English, and she'd smile politely, with a small sense of triumph. Her smile was toothless, and a baby I hadn't noticed beneath her poncho sucked listlessly on her breast. I was sorry the English names weren't more exciting and exotic, more different from the Spanish; I would have liked to give her something new. I wanted to dazzle her as I thought she hoped to be dazzled.

About twenty minutes from San José de Poaló we turned right toward Píllaro.

More populated now, pedestrians, dogs, Indians like tenacious fixtures of the land, seemed frightened as we roared by them kicking up dust. The wind on the *páramo* was strong.

In a flurry of dogs and sunlit dust, the bus let me out onto the Píllaro square. When it reeled off I was deposited into a silence I'd heard in other parts of the sierra near Quito but which here was amplified by all the strange stories of treasure, and the Inca's ghost. It was an outback, outpost, frontier-town secrecy, the silence of a sierran village.

In Píllaro, I discovered quickly, no one cared. Almost every stranger who came by bus or Land Rover, any of the dozens of white men who came every month, arrived in this quaint, tucked-away town and were immediately suspected of being here only for gold. The townspeople, on the surface, had grown taciturn to the point of deaf muteness. They seemed to snicker silently at me from the moment I got out of the bus.

The handsome town square was lined with large well-groomed

bushes and pathways for strolling. The robin's-egg-blue church was the modern counterpart to the old colonial structure which had been destroyed in the 1949 earthquake. Along the edges of the plaza were pastel-shaded stores and saloons, aquamarines, deep blues, and blatant reds. Doors, windows, and trim were correspondingly gay colors. People lingered quietly on street corners and in bars.

Before the road was built eastward to San José de Poaló, it used to take eight days to go to Cerro Hermoso from Píllaro. Now, expeditions slept here in town and left the next day through San José for the three- or four-day walk to the Sacred Mountain.

One pension, which had five rooms, all vacant, from the outside looked just like someone's house. The owner was a large Indian woman with long braided hair, who told me that two men had left that very morning for the Llanganatis, probably to pan for gold.

"These rivers around here," the woman said with a wry kind of smile, "are full of gold. That is what they tell me, anyway."

My eyes lit up because she talked about treasure, which didn't feel so very far away from there (Lilian was right). I could feel my body lean toward the mountains, wanting to get to them right away.

They all stayed with her before they set out, she told me, the treasure hunters, the experts and the novices. On the word "novice" she squinted.

"It is a good business, *señor*," said the woman. She had seen them all, the experts and mostly the beginners. The rain, the fog and sleet were bad now, she said, and "You'd have to huddle close together so as not to lose yourselves in the fog," she said. She grinned, as if to say, Ah, so you too have come here for the gold.

Everyone in Píllaro smiled sooner or later. There seemed to be a long-evolved, poorly disguised joke about visitors like me. Everyone grinned. And when their faces didn't beam outright, their words laughed inside their mouths.

The town road was lined with mud walls, ancient, sagging, pitiful mud walls. Many of the houses were the old-style thatch and mud. Beyond, the snow-capped volcanoes Chimborazo and Tungurahua added a postcard setting. Each mountain seemed only an arm's reach through the chrome-blue sky. Beneath these glaring pinnacles were more of the burnt umber and black shades of smaller hills and distant plains and, on the lower slopes, mottled avocado fields. Nearer the village, the *páramo* was a sepia print and the silence absorbed everything like a great sponge.

I looked into the eyes of people who knew intuitively about the treasure. God, they'd lived with it so long. Eyes from a nearby field or a shaded doorway watched me. Wariness stalked Píllaro.

I asked a shriveled old man in a tienda where I could find Villacresis, who, Brunner had told me, had been outfitting expeditions for years. Perched like a parrot on his stool, the wizened old man looked deep into my eyes and smiled—that smile again. It made you think you'd just been admitted to an insane asylum. He told me to go up the street, Villacresis had a store up the street, I couldn't miss it.

I had to ask two more people for directions. Nothing in the sierra was as simple as it first appeared. "So, so, I know," the eyes in the street seemed to say, "I know, you are here for treasure." That made me think about Andy's expeditions leaving from this town for years. And the story about how the townsfolk would line the streets watching the sixty porters, Andy in the lead, headed off into the bewitched mountains, some of the bystanders jeering, "You will never get back alive. You are all going to die!"

Yet for hundreds of years the town had derived a considerable income from what some might call idiots. Perhaps that was why these smiles didn't laugh outright.

And what if these villagers, or some of them, knew exactly where the treasure was, but would never tell? Wasn't that quite possible? Walking those streets, seeing smug Indian smiles created that impression, anyway.

Finally I found the store, my eyes stinging from lack of light inside. When they adjusted, I saw boxes of nails, shelves of sandpaper, steel wool, bullets, all the clutter of a hardware store in an outpost.

The old man was reaching for a box of blank cartridges for three boys who bought five of them, then went out excitedly grabbing at the little metal pellets and hitting each other. When I asked Villacresis how he was, he replied, *"Luchando, luchando. Fighting, fighting, not great, but okay."* I told the white-haired man that I'd heard he outfitted expeditions to the mountains.

He was the one man in the whole town who did not smile. In fact, he looked vaguely offended. He was eighty or so. His head wobbled; his eyes seemed distracted by deeper thoughts. Here was another sucker, he must have been thinking, another idiot after gold.

He was quiet for a long time, and I thought of all the men who had come to him for supplies, who had ended up in this store, Andy, Brunner, Blomberg, Loch, Brooks, an endless list.

The old man wore thick baggy pants, a white shirt with the top button buttoned and a black fedora hat. His face was taut with age and his mustache was similar to Brunner's—black and grey hairs mixed into a sloppy bristle.

Hearing me he grumbled. He didn't want to talk about those mountains.

"Well, *hombre,*" he began, "I can't fit you out, no. Go up the road to San José de Poaló. There are at least ten men up in that place who can take you in." His eyes were fixed on the bright road outside. His head shook, and I thought he might be remembering something. I wondered if I should leave him now. And I worried that maybe he had heard from Heraldo or his men about Diego canceling our expedition, so I made sure not to mention Diego's name.

Then his sad eyes glanced quickly at me, and quickly away again and down onto the counter before him.

"You can ask in San José, *hombre*. I've got nothing to tell, *hombre*." He spoke with a sad, bitter voice. His eyes watered. Was it the dust in his eyes that swept in from the street?

I had come a long way. I persisted.

"Did you know Loch and Marin, too?"

"Yes, man, all of them, all of them, and many many others not so famous. I have been in myself a few times. But no more, no more. I am an old man, *hombre*." I kept prodding him and he continued to tell me that I should go to Poaló. He described a three-day jaunt to Cerro Hermoso in such a glib tone of voice it made the trip sound completely unnecessary, like a picnic—for tourists. Exactly what I'd told Lilian I did not want to do. A joke! Just hire a guide, he told me, and take a few supplies and go to the sacred mountain for a day, then come back.

"Nothing more to tell, *hombre*. *Nada*."

His head shook frantically. Then there was another very long and painful pause. He was waiting for me to leave, but I couldn't just yet.

I wasn't, on the other hand, willing to pester the old man with painful questions. So finally, disappointed, I thanked him and asked one more question about Brunner at which he looked up.

"Brunner has been treated badly. Many many people have stolen his equipment over the years, taken from a man who doesn't have money, too. It is a shame, a real shame." His eyes grew fierce.

I wondered about all the stories I would never hear from this store owner. He was like the source of a river, being so close to the mountains themselves, but he was locked up somehow. That was a shame, too: knowing that no matter how long I stayed in Ecuador I would never get *all* the stories about the treasure. Not from men like Villacresis who defied questioning. It was impossible.

I thanked him, walked into the street, into an eye-blast of sunlight.

Down from the store a street or two, I sat on the curb making notes. Blomberg's idea of writing a book with Brunner at the center seemed like a good idea. I had a lot of material now. So who needs that old man Villacresis, I thought.

That night I drank in a barren bar with red lightbulbs. The dark square outside filled with lingering pedestrians. Some had no qualms about peering in at me, the stranger, all alone in a flood of sad whorish light. Frogs, like the ones in Lilian's garden in Quito, clicked in the grass.

But there were other strangers here, too. There are strangers wherever there is gold. An American in a straw hat came in and sat down across the room. He seemed about fifty.

The owner-bartender pulled me aside to offer his information in a whisper. Rumors had it, this old gringo—Diablo, they called him in town, the devil—had found gold in the mountains. The bartender grinned; I knew he was pulling my leg, another Píllaro joke. Nevertheless I went over to the American and sat down.

"Mind if I sit?"

"It's a free country here, too." He didn't look at me. His accent was Midwestern.

I asked him what his work was but he didn't reply. I think he was very drunk; his head seemed flimsily attached to his neck. He had thick stevedore arms, and his skin was like rawhide. He looked like he'd faced gales at sea. He looked like Nostromo. Then, belligerently he told me he got up every day at four and drank a bottle of gin every night before bed.

Who might have warned me about this man? No one in Píllaro. The bartender had laughed and gone out. I should have felt a camaraderie with a fellow countryman, but he was like ice.

I asked how long he'd worked here in Ecuador and where he came from. I had a lot of questions—too many. I planned to lead up to the gold. Perhaps he had some new information.

But before I knew it, enraged, he turned to me and shouted, "Look, buddy, do you really want to know what I think? Well . . ."

He drew a large bowie knife from his belt sheath (which I hadn't noticed) and threw it against the wooden table where it firmly quivered. "You see that point?" He growled as he wrenched the blade out. "That's where you were born, friend, that little hole there. See it?"

"Yes, sir."

Lightning quick, he threw the knife at another spot to the left of the first. Violently he pulled it out again. "And that's where you die." Granular, his voice cursed: "We come into this fucking world alone, we cross to this other fucking point and we leave alone. So leave me alone, goddamn it." Diablo began waving the knife, and I left the bar in a hurry.

Diablo! It was a very serious kind of joke, another Píllaro sneer. Thank God he wasn't staying at my pension. I slept fitfully dreaming of mountains receding as I ran toward them; wondering if perhaps Lilian had wanted me to come here to dissuade me from going into the mountains at all.

The next day I returned to Quito and Brunner, hoping I had not offended the one treasure hunter I really liked.

On the bus from Ambato, an old, large flat-backed truck on the other side of the highway swung out of control on wet pavement and took a huge gash out of one side of our bus. It had been drizzling near Cotopaxi and the southbound truck had no treads on its old tires. Stunned, but for only a second, the bus driver jumped out and raced to the truck, which had turned upside down on the embankment, engine still running, wheels spinning. He grabbed the panicky truck driver and, holding him firmly, was screaming at him. I thought he would murder the man.

My half of the bus had a huge hole in it. The windows had shattered, covering our laps with glass like shavings of ice. Remarkably, I was not hurt. I had been sitting only inches from where the truck had hit. I had always suspected I might die in an Ecuadorian bus, but this time only a child had received a bloody nose. The rest of us were unhurt, but deeply shaken.

Atahualpa had spared me another time, that's what I was thinking as I hitched a ride with a schoolteacher from a nearby town. I thought about the curse on the Inca's treasure, about the earthquake, and now this. I wondered again why Brunner had been so upset about my going to Píllaro. Maybe he felt it was *his* town, or had been before he moved his operation to El Triunfo.

After four decades, the town of Píllaro was his in the way one lusts after an old girlfriend, having turned his back after he was satisfied, but always the lust there beneath the surface. Brunner was afraid that I'd steal the gold, use the old town like an old mistress to get his mysterious Blake maps, buy supplies from Villacresis, then run off to look for the treasure myself.

I had no intention of doing that. In making a trip to Píllaro I'd stepped out from underneath Brunner's protection—that umbrella of professional wisdom. I had to get back to Quito quickly now, to assure him I was only a minor figure in this story, no threat at all, and forever his partner. I'd give him my last hundred dollars, too, so he'd trust me again. I was sure he'd need it.

This man whom the curse could not touch.

CHAPTER 11

◆◆◆◆◆

Yet something had happened to the old man while I was away. A tragedy had hit Brunner in Quito.

I went to visit him the afternoon after I returned, the very day I quit my job at school, as an act of faith or desperation. But as I climbed the old stairs to his study I passed the *señora*, who looked very glum indeed. *"Está muy infermo,"* she mumbled, and she made the sign of the cross in the air.

I raced into Brunner's bedroom and found his hair all mussed up. The old verve had seeped out of his eyes. He was in great pain, his leg supported by three pillows. For once he was silent.

"Oh, no," I said. "Gino, what can I do?"

"Nothing, Pete, nothing." Brunner rolled around on the bed while I was helpless.

Again I was superstitious about the treasure. Something was indeed preventing me from entering those mountains.

Brunner was in no condition to talk, but in the clothing store below, his landlady told me the story of yesterday's accident. She was distraught and deeply worried. I could have sworn she was in love with Brunner.

Two students had been arguing in a crowded Quito bus. Brunner had gotten on and tried to prevent the boys from coming to blows. The quixotic old man then moved between the students and was, at the same time, trying to pay the conductor, who was standing beside the driver. The bus rounded a sharp corner and Brunner, reaching for the handrail to balance himself, scared the conductor, who, confused by all the arguing, in a defensive outthrust of an arm pushed Brunner right out and onto the street. The old man landed on his left leg, flipped over like a stick in a hurricane, his glasses flying, hearing aid disappearing, valise opening and precious papers scattering in the wind like confetti.

The bus stopped; passengers rushed out to help the old man, who had broken his leg. The tibia had come completely out of its socket.

Onlookers raced around collecting Brunner's strewn paraphernalia and returned them to him. A young boy brought the hearing aid "intact," Brunner told me later. Brunner refused to go to the hospital. He limped back onto the bus and the driver told him that he'd never seen anyone fall like that right out of a moving bus before. "If that didn't kill you," he told Brunner, "then nothing will." The driver drove on.

Brunner got home, called a chiropractor, who put the bone in place, then he lay in bed massaging his leg for hours.

I knew he didn't want me around. This was the only time Brunner did not want to see me, the pain was so bad. I went home, depressed.

◆◆◆

One of the bars I frequented was El Pub, across from the Intercontinental Hotel of Quito, adjacent to the British Embassy. El Pub attracted an equal number of hotel residents and permanent Quito exiles. The bartender, who was Bavarian, knew that I was depressed and kept my glass full of beer.

For the first time in nearly half a year, I felt heavy with homesickness. I'd been away longer than planned and I missed the ease of living in my own country where daily business, buying a paper, shopping, getting on a bus, everything is conducted in a language I don't have to struggle with. My Spanish was good but speaking it every day gradually wore me down, always such an effort from the moment I woke and had to speak it to Piedad or the local store owner, to buy a roll or some coffee.

The man next to me at the bar said, "I love Ecuador."

I didn't feel like talking to anyone, but it was clear he wanted someone to jabber at. Hugh MacDonald, from Chicago, spoke with those flat Midwestern vowels. He leaned forward, his elbows on the beer-soaked counter. His fierce, ebullient smile lifted me out of my gloom like a crane.

MacDonald had maniacal energy that ripped the late afternoon lethargy into shreds. Before long we were buying each other rounds and he was talking about treasure. I told him nothing about the recent delay or about Brunner. As it turned out, no one could tell MacDonald anything; he was not a listener.

He talked and drank rapidly. He was balding, and he had a middle-aged beer paunch. He bragged that he had been a Green Beret in Vietnam, that he'd seen a "ton of action in the jungle," that he had four kids and "a little wife," that he'd come down to Quito on vacation, but that he'd been here many times searching for information about the Incas.

"Inca history's my hobby," he said loudly.

"Ecuador's great. You can do anything you want down here. Anything at all. It's a mystical country." He couldn't really define it, but he was compelled to return here again and again. His son was coming down in a few days, he said, and they were going hiking in the Amazon.

"That's nice," I said.

Feeling so down about Brunner's accident, certain that it meant no trip this year to the Llanganatis, I let MacDonald carry the conversation.

"This country's got treasures, too." The word "treasure" sounded hollow, like a vain political maxim in the weakening afternoon sunlight coming through the windows.

"I work for a communications company. A few years ago they sent me here to do a story on these so-called treasure hunters in Ecuador who ran scams on the folks Stateside. Jeeeesssus. These guys were making out like bandits. But we stopped 'em, you betcha."

Drunk now, he ordered another beer, but the bartender was slow in bringing it. His voice had the ring of religion. He drew a pair of sunglasses out of his pocket, mirror shades. He put them on suavely.

"Yah, we stopped 'em. Thomas, Davidson ... Ever hear of them?"

"Nope."

"Well, lousy company—thieves, all of them."

"What kind of scam were they running?" I couldn't help asking. After all, it was treasure he was talking about.

"One of them would come to a city like Chicago. He'd bring photos, documents, Indian tapestries—for effect—and he'd set up in some hotel room. Wealthy businessmen who wanted a little adventure, who could spare a few thousand bucks, came and listened to stories about treasure. Not only the Llanganati treasure, but all the treasure stories in this country.

"The scam artist would end up getting fifteen or more suckers to pay their own way down to Quito with the idea that these 'treasure hunters' would guide them to the gold. Nothing was guaranteed. It was a risk for the rich man, but not too much of a risk. A group would come to Píllaro and then the organizers would disappear. Abandoned in Píllaro or Patate or a similar village, they would learn too late how they'd been gypped. Another kind of scam was to get these groups actually into the mountains and leave them there. I remember one story about how the Ecuadorian government had to airlift five American bankers out of the Llanganati Cordillera."

"I know a different kind of treasure hunter," I said.

"Who's that?"

"Eugene Brun—"

"Not Brunner, the king imposter himself?"

"What do you mean by 'imposter'! No, a different man. The treasure hunter I'm talking about is old."

"About sixty-five?"

MacDonald turned suddenly to a British expatriate on the other side of him and started talking about the devaluation of the British pound.

What surprised me the most was that I had never once considered Brunner might be a fraud, a charlatan, a thief. Of course, the nature of his work demanded that he infect others, get them to invest. But Brunner was not an imposter—no mountebank.

It could not be true. Even Diego, who had greatly disappointed me, was no scam artist. The treasure was Brunner's life's work. Convincing others helped convince himself of the worth of his difficult pursuit. After all, he was unraveling the greatest riddle in South America. Not a project he could do overnight. He was addicted, yes. But Brunner was not a maliciously deceitful man.

I turned to the ex–Green Beret to tell him he was wrong about Brunner, and if he wanted to make something about it, he could. But he was talking with the Brit. He looked clownish in the dim bar, with those mirror sunglasses, his bald head, his maniacal smile, his beer belly.

I paid and went home, distressed that I had no job and that Brunner's condition could not be worse.

Now I was really homesick for hamburgers and French fries, for Sunday drives with a six-pack of beer through the Maine countryside, for autumn or even winter in Vermont. The lawlessness of Ecuador, which had captured me initially, had turned by accident into some form of malicious fate keeping me out of the mountains. So I called Braniff Airlines and made a tentative reservation to New York City. I had very little money left. I certainly didn't think I'd make it to the mountains this year with a man who had a broken leg, and with the bad season coming on, the rivers in the Llanganatis swelling to impass. Perhaps next year.

No, never.

I went to Lilian's and told her I was leaving. Piedad opened the door. Lilian was eating lunch alone at her dining room table. Piedad brought me coffee. Lilian was sorry for me, she said. I knew she was thinking I should go alone to the Llanganatis, that I should not depend on anyone at all, that a true treasure hunter like her mother did not let someone else's broken leg deter him. But I gave no more excuses. I was tired, and I didn't discuss it. I just wouldn't get there this year, that's all. I needed to get away from Ecuador, I said. "Maybe I'll come back." I wanted order and action. Leaving was a kind of action, anyway. Staying would be quicksand.

I rode around Quito in a bus that night feeling sorry for myself. At eight o'clock the city was cold and intransigent. All the sadness of the sierra seemed trapped in the space of that empty bus, the mountain sadness I'd experienced so often late at night, a blue-black Andean sadness like a shroud.

The engine made a deep grinding-metal sound as the bus struggled up hills, a useless sound. The pavement was wet. It was drizzling again and gloomy.

I thought about Atahualpa, who had died four hundred and fifty years ago. The people of Ecuador still mourned their Inca's death. And I too was bogged down in their sadness. I had to leave.

But how would I tell Brunner I was leaving? I was afraid of him, his paranoia. I'd sensed it coiled tightly in him, camouflaged by that jovial optimism. I knew it wasn't going to be easy to break loose.

◆◆◆

A few days after the accident I mounted his steps, wondering if I would find him bandaged like an Egyptian mummy, or on the brink of death. But when I opened the door to his bedroom, his bed was empty. I found him sitting at his desk, hard at work.

A week later, the day our expedition party should have been closing in on Cerro Hermoso, Brunner was up and limping with a cane I'd bought for him. I could hardly believe how this man rebounded. He told me nothing would stop him this year from entering the Llanganatis. It was only a small delay, he said, nothing more. *"Nada más."*

A famous Quitenian fortune-teller had told him years ago that he would have a terrible series of accidents before his sixty-sixth birthday but that if he lived through them, he'd live to see ninety.

Brunner was munching sausage and a hard roll as he talked. He was eager as ever. He lifted his wrist to show me a bad cut from a fall he'd taken which, he mumbled with his mouth full, miraculously had not killed him. Last year, he and Rolf Blomberg, in fact, had been walking in the street when they fell into a manhole together. Both escaped with minor injuries.

Brunner would keep on tumbling, like an old rock. He was ready to fall again and again, and get up, too.

"Look, Pete," he yelled at me two days later, "no cane!" And then he limped across the room, repressing the pain, no doubt. Out of breath, he lumbered from one side of his little study to the other, back and forth, back and forth, his leg as bare and swollen from the kneecap to the ankle as the stump of a small tree. He assured me the swelling had gone down every night. Now he was bouncing on it like a child on a pogo stick, and smiling truculently. I cringed at the sight.

I leaned forward to catch him, should he fall. "Please, Gino, be careful. You're going to hurt yourself!"

"I'm going, don't you worry about that, Pete."

But weren't the Llanganatis a bit different than hobbling across a room in Quito? I asked.

Brunner's silence was his answer.

Then he said, "What you don't know, Pete, is that we have a

big meeting with the Ecuadorian Air Force generals and Mortenson this week, Wednesday at seven P.M. You must come. It will all be decided."

Like a child showing off to adults, he now threw his cane on the desk and ran on that leg to show that he could manage, "In the mountains, Pete!"

A flicker of hope started inside me. Maybe I was crazy, but this man was truly incredible. He could do anything. He was stronger than ten bulldogs. I thought, "I don't believe it. *This guy is going to make it!*"

◆◆◆

It was winter in Quito, the sky as steel and cold and grey as anything you might find in Newfoundland. Pichincha, above the city, had been continually obliterated by fog. It had rained every day for weeks.

Brunner received a phone call from a man named Clint Provost, a deep-sea diver from Georgia, who promised a thousand dollars for us to open up the camps and hire Indians.

Brunner was overjoyed. Now he had Mortenson ready to give us money, a meeting set up for Wednesday with the Air Force generals, and Clint, all in one serendipitous turnaround. Brunner had been into the Llanganatis with Clint three times before, and he was sure Clint was a man who made good on his promises.

◆◆◆

Brunner and I stood huddled in a small phone booth at the telephone office in downtown Quito. Returning Clint's call, we waited for a good connection and then, just as Diego and I had come together to find Brunner, Brunner and I now put our ears to the one receiver and we both were tense, elated, and nearly incredulous to hear one of Clint's partners talking all the way from Buford, Georgia.

"Hello, Eileen hello Eileen, yes yes yes," Brunner's voice

boomed over thousands of miles, nearly blasting me out of the booth.

"How are you? Yes, yes, we are ready to hire the porters and clear the trail to Cerro Hermoso, yes yes yes, Eileen. So good to *hear* you . . ."

I heard the woman's Southern accent. She was as excited as we were, saying the money was on the way and that she and five other partners would be coming down to stay at the Hotel Quito while we were in the mountains.

So it was true! Finally things were taking shape. "I'll buy you a coffee, Brunner," I said and we went to his café.

Blast the weather! Screw the leg, I thought. I canceled my plane reservation.

Lilian thought I was a little crazy when I told her my change in plans, but she was happy I was going through with the expedition, at last. She offered me a scotch, but I said I was in training. We laughed and I left her apartment feeling almost giddy, happy to be on good terms again.

"I knew you had to go," she said before she closed her door.

The meeting with the generals was postponed, but the expedition with Clint was on for tomorrow. Yet I had never been fully honest with Brunner, I suppose, nor with myself. And now that we were going, I owed him absolute honesty. I felt guilty because I had never told him precisely what interested me about Atahualpa's treasure—the people who surround a treasure. So, driven perhaps in part by my fear of dying in the mountains with an unclean conscience, I took a bus to the old city and, with every intention of sincerity, climbed the worn wooden stairway to his study—to confess. Just to say that for me anyway the treasure hunters were real and tangible and the gold was not. The gold was an aura. The thing that I had been able to love was the people infected by that aura.

He was extremely happy because of Clint and Mortenson and the generals. What luck, he said, to have all this happen after his accident. His leg was much better. Almost normal, he said.

"It's Providence, no?"

"Gino, I have something I must tell you," I began.

"Oh, what is that, Pete?" Brunner did not look up from his desk.

"Hope all is ready with your equipment for tomorrow, no?"

"Yes. But what I want to say is . . . it's . . . well, it's just that I haven't really come to Ecuador to get rich on treasure." This idea had become clearer to me than ever before. "Gino, I'm here to be with you, if that makes sense, to go on this expedition with Eugene Brunner . . . What I mean to say is that I don't believe that for me the gold is the key thing, as it is for you. What matters more to me is getting to see the mountains *with you.* Do you see what I mean? . . ." I could feel my words collapse. Why had I brought all of this up now, for God's sake? The day before the trip!

"I too have something to say," he began as he looked up with a good-natured smile that disintegrated as he spoke.

His mouth formed silent phrases at one side, his forehead wrinkled.

"I don't believe you," he stammered. "Don't tell me that, Pete! No! Anyone who goes to the Llanganatis is going because he has a hunch he might find the treasure." Brunner's eyes grew severe.

This room here had been dedicated to forty-two years of searching. How did I dare say what I'd said? For the second time since we'd met, I fell from grace.

"If you say you're not here for the treasure, I would not believe you! Because if you want to just go hiking, you can climb Pichincha right here above Quito and you can camp on the slopes and watch the city lights at night. But not in the horrible Llanganatis, no! Not a hike, Pete! Don't be one of them! Not one of those who make beautiful camouflage, no? *No!*"

His voice was lower than I'd ever heard it. His jaw jutted. I'd opened the door to his darkness. And I couldn't get it shut again.

"One guy I met once wanted to find a certain plant, no? And he hiked into the Llanganatis, five days through thunderstorms and snowstorms and hail, spending hundreds of dollars, thousands of sucres. Why? To find a plant, he said, which he could have grabbed out of his car window on the *páramo* of Carchi! A kind of geranium, that was all!

"So, I said to him, to this 'botanist,' I said, Why not go to Carchi? and he answered that, Well, maybe they weren't the same kinds of geraniums. And I said to him, Oh, yes, they are—"

"But, Gino—"

"No. Don't be one of them, Pete. That 'botanist' was after one thing only. The treasure. It's there. I know where it is! Spruce himself was after it, no? Spruce kept the original map of Guzmán. Why? Because he knew even in the nineteenth century that if he had not kept it, a guy like me would have gotten hold of the gold long before this. And it would have saved me years of research, with that map."

"But, Gino . . ."

"Remember, I was in the wrong area for twenty-five years. You weren't even born when I began, Pete. So I know why Spruce was there, Pete, and I know why you are here. You, Clint, and I, tomorrow we will go in and get it, finally, and you will see my camp, no? I will show you things you have never seen before!"

For an hour I tried, when he let me talk, to twist my words, to bend them backwards, to regain his trust in me, and I think I was able to earn my way back to a partial trust, an unsteady trust.

"You're right," I told him over and over. "Yes, I did come to find gold with you, too, Eugene Brunner. That's what I'm trying to tell you now, Gino. Listen to me, please . . ." I struggled to rebuild in an hour what a sentence had destroyed. But it was impossible to explain what I really meant.

After all, here was a man who had made this treasure the

fulcrum of his existence. Brunner was the gold, Blomberg had said. So how would he ever understand that I might be more fascinated with him, with the mountains, with the stories, than I was with a monetary Sweat of the Sun?

When I finally left him, he was smiling again, placated to a degree. Before I descended to the street—as if to remind me of my priorities—he quickly read out loud a description of the treasure: human figures of beaten gold, birds, animals, jewelry, vases, goblets, " 'so much I could not remove it alone, nor could thousands of men . . .' " This he said to tempt me. It was a quotation from Barth Blake, the mysterious naval captain who had found the treasure but died before he could take it out of the mountains.

◆◆◆

That night I couldn't sleep. We planned to leave at dawn. Brunner would meet me here at my apartment and we'd use a friend's pickup to carry our gear to El Triunfo. I hadn't met Clint yet, but the plan was for him to arrive that very day and then, to waste no time, we'd all rendezvous tomorrow at five-fifteen A.M. sharp at the Hotel Quito.

At eight P.M. that night, the street noises subsided. But a group of young boys had begun a soccer scrimmage in front of Lilian's house. They loved to use her driveway entrance for the goal.

It began to drizzle. I could hear the tapping of rain against the glass windows. The bright embers in the fireplace had dimmed. The boys kept playing soccer. Bam bam, went the ball against the iron. From my radio came the plaintive flutes and guitars and the sad, almost death-like throes of a Quechua love song.

I was in good shape. I'd been running every morning now for two months.

I thought about the man I would travel with. Twice he had spoken of his past. He had opened up only after months of friendship. Now ours seemed a precarious relationship at best.

"One never knows, Pete," he had said to me. "Believe me, I was born sixty-five years ago and I have seen the highest of the high and the lowest of the low. I have loaded wheelbarrows with human shit in prison, no? And I have done this with doctors, lawyers, and famous writers. People died in my arms in that concentration camp. I had people over my shoulders with their guts dangling out. And all this in peacetime. Not even a war on yet. When a man says he is big, I can tell you he is full of shit!

"I got out of the hospital after they shot me, I went back to Germany and on the eleventh of December, 1937, I came to Ecuador. The last time I had my mother and father in my arms, I kissed them in the railroad station in Zurich, then I crossed France to La Rochelle and took an English steamer to Ecuador. I have no family anymore. All dead now.

"It's a story, my life, of how you fight and you act, but sometimes I wonder why I did it. I could have been a Nazi, a general. But fortunately I was born in Switzerland and my mother was Swiss. And, besides, Pete, I didn't believe in the German superman, no? I could not understand the German carcass-obedience. 'My dear Captain, I beg your permission to die for the Fatherland.' No! Fuck them!

"But someday I will write a book about all this. Oh, I knew very famous people, Erica Mann, Hesse, and so many others . . .'

I asked Brunner if his family had been rich. To my surprise he answered:

"Yes, my father was, but he lost it all. And my grandfather broke the bank at Monte Carlo. Next day he arrived with a train of fifteen carriages drawn by horses. The first one arrived and he and his sweetheart got out. The second arrived with his hat, then his walking stick, etc. That was my grandfather. And my uncle was a major general against the Russians in World War One.

"But here in Ecuador, Pete, no one knows any of these things. Why should I tell the people here this shit? Here one does not need a past. One needs only a treasure!"

As I lay that night thinking of expatriates, of my own past in the States, of my friends whom I hadn't seen in a long time, of how I yearned for a friendly New York City bar, of the women I used to date and whose faces appeared before me now, of how distance had kept me from calling them just to see how they were doing—I wondered what it was like to bury your past in another country. I did not want to be exactly like Brunner. To crave a treasure and to thrive on solitude might be too much for me. He seemed so sad, too, and unconnected to his roots in Germany or Switzerland. Brunner was running from a dark Europe, from Hitler. Was I running, too? I supposed I was a little, but I wasn't exactly sure from what. Certainly from nothing so dark.

Brunner had said, "They told me a friend of ours was building a railway but when I got to this country, the government had already hired all the men they needed. So I lived by commission, painting murals and odd jobs like this."

Brunner had once shook a fist in the bright air of the plaza. We had gone together to look for Andrade. Like a sledgehammer his hand moved against the air and he said:

"Damn it! You can not keep millions of Indians like domestic animals. These people must be reincorporated into national life. It twists my heart to see Indians on Avenida Amazonas, begging, these men with muscles selling apples and newspapers and cassettes. The old Incas knew that you could not shit on the farmer, could not take away the pride of the man who feeds you! Because, Pete, each man is a link in the chain. If we must suffer, we must suffer all together.

"For this reason I will bring the treasure out of hiding and into the light—to give it back to the Indians of Ecuador, to restore their Inca self-esteem."

◆◆◆

The boys had stopped playing soccer in the street. My knapsack was propped against the door. For two hours I'd packed and repacked it, unable to decide whether two pairs of underwear was enough (what if they both got soaked in the mountains?), whether I needed three or four wool sweaters, or whether it didn't matter how much I brought because I'd be wet all day every day no matter what I had with me.

I turned off the radio and the garden frogs tapped the night air. I knew Clara would be outside somewhere, restless in the brambles, waiting to see me off. Lilian was upstairs sound asleep.

It stopped drizzling. And all I had to do now was wait a few more hours until the sun would begin to rise and Brunner would be here.

CHAPTER 12

◆◆◆◆◆

When Brunner had not phoned by eight A.M., I walked sluggishly to his apartment, stepping over the bodies of two Indians lying drunk in their own vomit on the cobblestones outside his landlady's clothing store.

As I walked through last night's Saturday litter of discarded corn cobs, broken bottles, and the dark patches of urine puddles on the rock, I wondered where the Incan "spirit of passive obedience and tranquility" had disappeared to.

I passed through Brunner's courtyard and all I could think about were those images of paralytic Indians in the street outside— the sierran Indian who had come such a long way down since that time when he had been fed and cared for by the Lord Inca, when he had worked for the harmony of the community, when he really believed that gold was Sweat of the Sun and silver was Tears of the Moon.

The treasure hunter was hunched over his desk, working on a pamphlet. Why hadn't he called? I demanded. Had the trip been for real?

Apologetically, he said he was very depressed today. Clint would not be going with us. Brunner saw my disappointment and looked away. "A change in plans," he said.

Apparently Clint had sent a telegram at the last minute, saying everything was canceled. Now Brunner worried that Clint might try to enter the Llanganatis without us, on the sly.

"If he comes by himself, behind my back, I will get the Army after him. I have my spies on the lookout right now, in Píllaro, no?"

I was too upset to speak.

"But don't despair, Pete, there is other news, too. I have talked to Mortenson again, the Danish owner of the textile factory here in Quito. Tonight at eight o'clock, Pete, you and I are meeting with Mortenson and a few generals in the Air Force. We will get to the famous mountains, soon, I promise. You will come tonight, yes?"

"Yes, of course, but, Gino," I said as calmly as I could, "I don't have a job at the school anymore. I quit a few days ago. I thought we would be gone by now."

"You did what! How could you do that!"

Brunner was furious. He'd found a focus for all his anger. "But you need a visa, Pete! They are not easy to get! I asked you to hold on to that job!"

I told Brunner I was running out of money. Maybe another job would come up, I lied.

"Let's hope so, for your sake, Pete."

I left Brunner, both of us in low low spirits. I had no desire to stay with him that morning.

I strolled past a small bookstore nearby. The owner, who knew I'd been looking for books on the Llanganatis, called to me and led me inside. He said proudly that he'd finally located a copy of Luciano Andrade Marin's updated 1970 version of *Llanganati*. Until now I had only seen the shorter, first edition of 1937.

But I hardly cared anymore and almost did not buy the book.

Lucky I did, though, because when I took it home I found the reference that Andy, Diego, and Brunner had vaguely alluded to, about a treasure that had been taken out through Peru. The articles were from a Quito newspaper, October and November of 1965.

Here was one of those lost fragments of the whole story. I decided I had to see it through, in spite of my disappointments. So I went to the National Library that afternoon.

Though it had rained heavily in the morning, the afternoon was unfalteringly blue. The bright stucco houses in the old quarter shimmered in a shock of light.

Indian women sat despondently on street corners selling vegetables and fruit. As I passed Brunner's café, one woman looked up demurely from her basket of avocados and apples. From her chubby face, with sad eyes, she whined, "Aaawwaaakaatiii" and "Maaaansaaaanaaaa," "Aaaavooooocaaadoos, Aaaaappleesss" in high piercing Quechua vowels.

One block from the Presidential Palace, the old brown building, the Biblioteca Nacional—The National Library—had two large pillars on each side of an iron gate.

A medley of stairs led through intricate corridors to the periodicals room. At rows of wooden desks sat young students. A man in a blue smock at the desk receded into the stacks to get me the October and November 1965 issues of *Últimas Noticias,* one of Quito's daily journals.

Sitting at the desk at five P.M., just as the library was shutting up, I found it.

ULTIMAS NOTICIAS, Thursday 28th October, 1965, No. 77, 167.
FABULOUS TREASURE, The Pástor family disputes a fabulous treasure which was left by a Spanish Magistrate [from Latacunga, Ecuador]. Peruvian descendants say they are nearly ready to collect the inheritance. Various Ecuadorians are shaking the dust off old papers and genealogical charts.

The Peruvian press publishes sensational information about three families residing in Lima who are the descendants of the

Puga Pástor family branch in Guayaquil. They are almost at the point of inheriting a fabulous treasure of twenty-eight thousand million sucres [about a billion dollars] which was deposited in the Royal Bank of Scotland in Edinburgh in 1803. Following the dates of ancestors, the family Puga Pástor is a direct descendant of the Magistrate Antonio Pástor y Marin de Segura, Marqués de Llosa.

The judicial proceedings have begun before the civil judicature of Lima—The Origin: The fortune is evaluated at 460,000,000 pounds sterling and originally was sent by the ship *El Pensamiento* which embarked from the port of Lambayeque under the command of Captains John Doigg and John Fanning. The cargo contained various crates of gold and silver bars, a great quantity of emeralds, other precious stones, gems, gold powder, gold Incan necklaces, masks, and vases. The deposit was made by Sir Francisco Mollison in accordance with the authorization given him. . . . Don Antonio Pástor y Marín de Segura was born in Cartagena, Spain, in 1772 and his parents were Don Bartolomé Pástor y Doña Rosa Maria de Segura. His godparents were King Charles the Third and the Queen. He came to America as Magistrate of Latacunga in 1794. Later he held other public offices in Chile and Lima. . . . The Magistrate died in 1804. His will requested that his great fortune be divided between his descendants in the fifth generation, several of whom reside in Ecuador and others in Peru. . . .

A similar article from November 8 continued to delineate the family dispute over inheritance. One page of the article was missing.

I looked up. So here it was: what everyone seemed anxious to ignore. I returned the bound issues to the man in the blue smock and walked like a sleepwalker to the front door.

Richard Spruce in the mid-nineteenth century had found evidence that the King of Spain had sent Valverde's *Guide* to the magistrate of Latacunga and that the expedition he formed had failed when Father Longo wandered off mysteriously. Here, in the article I'd just read, was the suggestion that the Magistrate of Latacunga had actually found the treasure and had shipped it secretly out through Lambayeque in northern Peru. Incredible! At first my mind refused to digest the material—the implications.

The treasure might not even be in the Llanganatis!

Whether it was or wasn't in a lake or a cave on Cerro Hermoso, as Brunner believed, didn't make any difference to me anymore. Nor was it important if this 1803 treasure was really the whole of the Llanganati gold or just part of it.

Pizarro had murdered Atahualpa. Benalcázar had tortured hundreds of Indians in search of the famous treasure of Quito. Men like Andy and Diego continued the conquistador injustice, and now it was more the symbolic meaning of what I had just read that struck me. The ugly irony that the gold could even now be locked in the Royal Bank of Scotland, a foreign bank, brought to mind all the senseless rape, plunder, and oppression of the conquering Spaniards against the Incas. Brought to mind, also, so many delays and disappointments of my wasted months in Quito.

Self-delusion propelled treasure hunters into fruitless journeys. I too had deluded myself. They all knew the Pástor story, but chose to ignore it. Andy with all his money had never been to Seville to check the original Valverde *Guide*. Diego had not really wanted to meet Brunner, the "aficionado." Everyone seemed to ignore hints of truth—and to fabricate his own fiction.

Outside, the afternoon sun slammed into my head. I squinted at a metallic-blue sky. After nearly six months of self-deception, suddenly I knew I had to go home, not to graduate school, but perhaps to teach in some rural high school—just go home, get out of here. I wanted a quieter life now. I was drinking heavily again. (One despondent night a few weeks before, I'd taken a taxi to a whorehouse on the edge of town where some friends used to go dancing, and just before we arrived the driver pulled out a gun and demanded money. I threatened to jump out: I opened the

door of the moving car and he put away the gun and let me out of
the taxi in a strange part of town saying, "Gringo *loco*.")

I was swamped. The treasure story and the mountains could
just keep receding from me forever. I'd never know the whole
tale, no matter how long I stayed in Quito. I knew also that I was
not a treasure hunter with Brunner's stamina, his endurance in
spite of the facts. I had no money, no job, no visa. I could wait no
longer.

The articles I'd read were vivid reminders of the vanity of a
four-hundred-year-old quest. And I was no Pizarro, and no
Brunner. Nor did I wish to go into debt for the rest of my life, or
end up a gambler. In all my months in Ecuador, I had not come
any closer to knowing the sierran people themselves. I'd fallen
fatuously for an Indian girl in a bus with whom I had said not one
word. If anything, the treasure had isolated me in a dream world.
And now I had to break away.

But how to tell Brunner I was leaving? Should I tell him
tonight at the meeting or wait until tomorrow? And what would
he do? Or say? Was Brunner really dangerous when he felt
betrayed?

I walked fearfully through the cool black courtyard with its
silent fountain and up the flight of stairs to the living room
adjoining Brunner's tiny studio. The excitement of finally meeting
the Air Force generals and Mr. Mortenson was undermined by
my decision to leave Ecuador and by my fear of Brunner's
reprisal. Even so, I kept wondering, What if the meeting proves
we will go to the Llanganatis this week? What then? Would I go?
No. I was finished now.

My mind was made up, but I felt like a traitor in the room
upstairs, deserted except for an almost palpable anticipation, a
restive silence. Against one wall stood an easel holding a fantasti-

cal painting by Brunner of the treasure cave, a Jules Verne representation of the cave that Blake found. On the tables between the ten or twelve empty chairs and sofas were neatly arranged platters of hors d'oeuvres, enough for fifty people. Had Brunner's landlady prepared all this for him? I wondered. Or was this opulence a vestige of a more wealthy past?

Full bowls of peanuts and popcorn were scattered around the room. A bottle of Johnnie Walker Black Label, two bottles of mineral water (Güitig of course), and a silver bucket of ice cubes sat on the bar table in a corner as if waiting for a proper bartender to go to work.

Freshly cut flowers protruded from Steuben-thick cut-glass vases, some rose-colored, some opaque: preparations for a major festivity, it seemed, for important people, who any moment now were ready to burst happiness upon that room. I decided I must tell the old treasure hunter my news tomorrow and not tonight. I could not tell him now. Not here.

Brunner bounded out of his studio smiling, wearing a coal-dark suit and silver-blue tie, his white hair immaculately combed back. His eyes sparkled, though he was a little disappointed to see it was only me and not the generals. As we greeted, his shoulders dropped, and he told me the generals and the Danes were due any moment and that I should help myself to the hors d'oeuvres. He was still limping slightly from his accident.

Brunner then left to wait for the others downstairs at the door, like an eager dog whose master is expected after an absence. I sat alone in the gala room scheming how to tell him tomorrow of my decision.

After ten minutes Brunner returned with two blond Nordic, thick-chested men. Alfredo Mortenson and Faun Laursen shook my hand and spoke in awkward Spanish. Because the generals could speak no English, the meeting would be held entirely in Spanish, but it was odd for two Danes, one American, and one Swiss-German, who all spoke perfect English, to be conversing in Spanish alone.

The Danes seemed jovial but cautious. They'd been drinking, and they too had brought a bottle of scotch.

Brunner said, "Please, everyone, be seated," and in his incantatory voice the old man began to recite Valverde's *Guide*, "... sleep then the first night ... the lake made by hand ..." and so on. From his serious and heroic tone, I realized that for Brunner the *Guide* was a poem and a catechism all in one.

"I've found that lake," he said, "and all we have to do now is take the treasure out." I was by now very tired of that sentence.

Mortenson's body swayed in slight inebriation as he listened to Brunner. His face was pudgy yet stern and ruddy, like a somber, beardless Santa Claus. Laursen, a wiry timid sailorly man, fiddled with a pencil and paper and stared at the floor with unusual disinterest—or disbelief.

Abruptly Brunner fell silent, waiting, it seemed, for a pledge of money from the Danes. Mortenson began telling some silly story about thieves who plundered a small village in the Andes. The townsfolk, he said, tried to hide the chapel bell by taking it out and dropping into the middle of a lake. They rowed out, dropped it, and when the thieves had gone, the villagers discovered in dismay that they had no means by which to retrieve their bell.

Brunner wasn't sure if the story was over, but Mortenson began to laugh recklessly as he pounded the old man's back. Then he tried to explain the droll humor of the joke, and Brunner smiled politely, but I knew Brunner was thinking only about investment money.

Brunner stood up and poured us all a whiskey and Güitig water. Mortenson, it was clear to me, didn't believe in Atahualpa's treasure. The Dane was flippant. Not for one second did Mortenson or Laursen believe the hoard was at the bottom of Brunner's lake.

"So, tell me, Mr. Mortenson, what interests do you have in this treasure story?" I asked.

My question seemed naked in the brightly lit room which cried out for more guests, more noise—action.

The Dane said, "I believe in Gino," and gave me a threatening glance.

Brunner brought over a platter of tiny bread triangles sprinkled with olive and sausage slices. The Danes nibbled and Brunner talked, as usual, filling the silence, repeating the same stories I'd heard so many times: Loch, Brooks, the Sabela Indians, Dyott, Andy and his helicopter crash. I could see that Mortenson and Laursen were embarrassed by Brunner's tales tonight.

I too had to struggle to appear enthusiastic. Brunner, I'm sure, could tell that the Danes had no intention of financing this year's expedition, and his voice grew shrill.

He gave us fragments of stories, and he rambled through the events of his forty-two-year-old quest, descriptions of the Llanganati terrain reeling off his tongue, along with a great list of the bastards who used him and betrayed him and tried to steal his secrets.

Hours passed, but the generals never came. At eleven P.M., the Danes became businessmen, assuring Brunner they wanted to finance an expedition but only if Brunner let me go and he stayed at home. ("You're too old, Gino," they said. "You're much more valuable to us in Quito. Let your American friend here go with your guides.") They wanted Brunner to sign a contract with some advertising agency.

Brunner's voice grew even more excited. It was humiliating for him and painful for me to be a part of this charade. The Danes' eyes moved from each other's to the floor, uncertain why the old man was being so stubborn.

I detested being a part of that paltry meeting with Mortenson and his sidekick, who for three hours humored the old bulldog with insipid jokes and false-hearted back-slapping. Why did Brunner put up with it?

"You're too old, Gino. Now you must sit home and tell your story to the world, and all of us will make a big stash, a treasure in itself, Gino. The gold isn't up there. Even if it is, you'll never get any of it after the government steals it all." Mortenson was, if nothing else, persistent. I looked at his duplicitous smile and I wondered how he could do this to the old man.

The fire in Brunner blazed. "No. I'm not giving up now, not when I'm this close. No. Not after all those years of going to the wrong mountain."

"But why go?" Mortenson was like a terrier with his prey in his teeth. "You take the gold out, and you kill the myth, too."

This was the truest thing the Dane said, and the truth of it made me get up to say it was time to leave. "I have to get to bed," I said.

Laursen jumped up to take a photograph of Brunner. The room flashed. A fake festivity. The photo session for a commercial. Brunner immortalized. Later that photo would be framed with a caption below reading, "Historic meeting with great treasure hunter of the Andes."

"Good night," I said to everyone, hoping to break up this absurd theater, but the no-longer-timid Laursen was busy with his camera, taking pictures of Mortenson, his arm flung around Brunner's shoulder, and the treasure hunter himself, so easily a vain man, was remarkably putting his anger aside and neatening his hair for a portrait. Perhaps Brunner thought it was his last chance at fame, these photos that would make him the Schliemann of South America.

"Oh," Brunner railed. "Do you think Heinrich Schliemann had any real facts? No. He had a dream like mine when I was seven in Germany. Mythology provides the facts, no? He found Troy."

So here were Schliemann and Brunner, misunderstood believers to the last, one famous and successful, and the other on the edge of fame.

"Goodbye," I said weakly, but went nowhere. I could not leave him with these piranha. The old man wildly gesticulating, arms and hands furiously slicing the stale party air, the meeting a failure, a farce, most of the snacks untouched, the Steuben glass a terrible joke.

Mortenson rose to make his speech: "We all here agree that Brunner's 'research' has great value and that it should not be thrown out as garbage . . ."

"Here here," piped in Laursen, waving his hands like a monkey. Laursen clapped me on the back, and I turned with a clenched fist to say in English, "Mr. Laursen, don't do that again."

What the Danes did not understand was that only through action would Brunner's faith be sustained. A story for Brunner had no value unless it contributed to the search for gold. What angered me was that the Danes had tried to destroy Brunner's magic.

"Yes!" Brunner cried. "There are times when the generals of the military do not show up because they are very busy men. They have great responsibility! I had this same problem before. But it means very little, for they will come perhaps tomorrow. And even without them, Pete and I are going to Lake Brunner this year, even if we must carry everything on our own shoulders. As poor men. We will go in spite of the generals."

I shuddered. If he only knew what I would tell him tomorrow, if he knew right then as he shouted this final pronouncement at the Danes, he might become so distraught that I could not bear to see him.

Brunner had not been defeated by his age or by time or by any curse on that gold. But on the night of the so-called meeting with the generals, he was indeed brought to near impotency by the incredulity of those impudent iconoclasts. Four decades of doubt had been buoyed up by the treasure hunter's ability to excite others about the treasure. But these idiot Danes were a kind of depressant to Brunner's life of action.

We all stood up and moved downstairs. I had done so little to help the old man. I too was impotent to defend him.

As we went outside, Brunner's face drooped; no longer the defiant face of Blomberg's statement: "He will go on looking until he dies."

The Danes got into their fancy new four-door Chevrolet pickup. Brunner and I stood on the cold stone street. Laursen leaned over to take one last photo. Mortenson warmly said goodbye through his window as if we had all agreed on something that night. As he said *"Hasta luego, amigos,"* he gunned the engine and roared off, his laughter lingering behind him like tear gas.

There was a fog rolling off the volcano, and the slopes of Pichincha were buried in cloud. Despair seeped into my skin like a slow-acting tranquilizer.

Brunner turned to his door. I said, "Good night, Gino. I'll be here in the morning, okay?" And my heart leapt when he said, "Yes, of course, Pete, we have so much to get done in the morning."

"Yes, sure, Gino," I said and walked off with a heavy heart, not bothering to look back as he rang his landlady's doorbell for someone to let him in. The bell sounded in the cool air like a call for help. It grated against the fog, but as I turned the corner the fog swallowed the sound.

When I got to my apartment, the frogs were especially loud in my garden, but it was the fog that kept me from sleeping. The fog seemed to come through the walls that night. A terrible dampness worked on my bones.

I lay down in my clothes and wondered if Brunner might go next year to the mountains, perhaps to die there. I hoped he wouldn't go now because it was the rainy season, the worst time of year, when the rivers are swollen, when even sturdy men like Captain Loch easily die in the Llanganati Cordillera.

The next morning I rose early, called Braniff, made a reservation for the following day, and then went up to Lilian's to say goodbye.

It was Piedad's day off, and Lilian did not answer my knocking for a long time. When she opened the door, she was still in her nightgown, and her eyes looked red. But she had me come in and wait while she dressed. Then she made coffee for us both.

When I told her I was leaving and that there was another teacher at the school who wanted to rent my apartment immediately, Lilian's whole face seemed to weaken; her eyes were troubled and her mouth turned down.

"You change your mind so often, so sudden," she said. But I had to go, I told her. She said she didn't understand; she wished I'd stay. I think she was terribly hurt, not only because I was giving up the treasure, but because she would miss me. She told me how much she liked to talk to me. I was sad, too, I said. But I couldn't stay. I told her I would come around tomorrow before I took a taxi to the airport. She said, "Well, truth is, I knew that someday you would go." She tried to smile.

Andean winter was in full force again. Dark platinum clouds hovered just over the tops of the taller buildings.

Decisively I walked to Brunner's. The hard light of his desk lamp seemed to tug at the old man's face. He looked older and more tired. He glanced up as I walked in.

"Pete. So you see how it is. But we're going anyway." He remained sitting. His smile was no longer convincing, his eyes limp. I'd never seen his desk so cluttered with papers, pens, and brushes. His hands rummaged through the refuse of his life's work and, for the first time since I'd come to him, I felt sorry for the old man. Perhaps he might get into the mountains next year—but not until he had practically begged his "financiers" for more money, so dependent was he on others. And the delays would be endless.

He shuffled some folders and, raising one to the light, said, "We will go."

The man would not give up. His eyes floated around the room as if he were trying to remember something, then they alighted on the map of Ecuador. He continued:

"I had a fortune once, you know, but I lost it all. I was forty-five thousand sucres in debt. It wasn't even two thousand dollars, no? But because of that they took my furniture, they took everything I owned. Because of the Llanganatis. I spent the money on those crazy mountains. And I came back one day to find everything was gone. And in that shuffle I had lost my photographs of Blake's maps. Yet I have compiled them again from memory."

Brunner grasped an old crumpled bank check and raised it to the light.

"Here is the check from that account, no? The dictators came to power and they took away a mine concession I had also. Nothing you can do, is there? I'm in the process now of getting it back."

It occurred to me that I had no right to feel pity or sorrow for this man before me. He had weathered so much. And he had another life's work of research ahead of him—mine concessions to regain, Inca emerald mines to locate and explore, money to raise, people to infect.

Cautiously Brunner put the check in a drawer. He only feigned a smile.

"But fortunes come and go." A long pause while his eyes gazed into the space between us.

"The only thing that you can not get back when you lose it is a man's trust, no?"

Oh, goddamn, I thought. Why had I put this off so long! How could I possibly tell him?

The treasure hunter stopped talking altogether as if listening to the invisible intentions of my heart, as if he could hear the whispering of betrayal inside me.

Brunner picked up a worn photo of a young man on top of a sharp rock peak in the Swiss Alps.

"Nineteen thirty-six," he said, "an old friend of mine." I held the photo but Brunner grabbed it out of my hands and threw it down. And cursed, "Shit! *Shit!* That man exists no longer."

Full of anguish and anger, Brunner spoke as if that young, able, muscular, happy, lost friend of his had in some way offended him, had betrayed or deserted him, too. Then suddenly I realized the man in the photo could have been Brunner himself when he was young and strong and when nothing could stop him from going anywhere he pleased.

More tranquil now, lifting one of the hulking great volumes of Llanganati memorabilia—photos, contracts, letters, maps, drawings—he wistfully leafed through the pages, pointing.

"Here is a picture of me in 1964 before I went in and here is one of me 127 days later. Here's Andy and me and Commander Dyott in 1965 at Dyott's farm in the jungle ... And look here, this is a picture of the 'Reclining Woman' of Barth Blake ... but you still do not know this story, Pete. I will tell it to you in the mountains when we are there ... and here is a picture of the so-called seven mouths of Cerro Hermoso, not volcanic openings as Guzmán thought but two old mine shafts which go straight down into the belly of the sacred mountain. In those days when these photos were taken, my carriers charged only fifty sucres a day, two dollars. Now they get a hundred, and cigarettes, too, and I buy for them rain gear and much much more. They are worth it, though. They are good people, my Indians, no?"

I'd seen all these photos so many times over the weeks. I was sick of them. And, I had to admit, of Brunner, too.

Yet I still admired Brunner's compassion for the Indians, whom he understood and to whom I had not come close, and I still believed that if this man had had more money he would go any time of the year into those mountains. They didn't intimidate this treasure hunter at all. But there would always be more problems, money, helicopters, friends, logistics, rain, hail, accidents.

Brunner's voice seemed like something from my distant past.

"And we'll probably have a helicopter from the Fuerza Aérea, no? I'm planning a definite date for a meeting with the president . . ."

I had to act fast. I could not take it any longer. I would appeal to the man's knowledge of financial difficulty.

So I lingered no more. I said I had to go home to the States. I was sorry, but I needed to make more money. I had none left. And I had to begin writing my book about Brunner, the greatest treasure hunter, and his quest.

I smiled and I waited.

Brunner went silent. He stared. Ten seconds, twenty. Then, thank God, he smiled back the most expansive, genuine smile I'd seen in Quito. His eyes twinkled. He got up. Thank God for the vanity of a treasure hunter.

He got up and he stood boldly on his two legs. He raised his chin and thrust out his chest like a statue. He still believed in his own magic. My desertion could not destroy him.

"You do that, Pete. You write a book and you tell them that Eugene Brunner has unraveled the greatest puzzle in the world. But tell them also that he is the poorest treasure hunter that ever lived. And someday, Pete, you will come back. I know it because they always do."

The old bulldog smile had resumed control of his face. He stood before me proud, vibrant, and sure of everything.

"Perhaps," I said.

And never before or after that moment of goodbye would I admire the man so. He seemed to know much more than he ever revealed. He had the unique wisdom of reaching for something elusive, reaching always with his best hand forward.

Perhaps the treasure had been taken out in 1803, perhaps part of it remained. But how would you know for sure if you did not make the search? Brunner appreciated the paradox of treasure hunting better than anyone else. What Brunner understood was that the quest was only an empty shell; one needed the unshakable belief in the attainability of the goal. One had to believe in the gold.

I simply did not believe enough in that treasure. So I had no place here, I thought.

I told Brunner I'd be in touch, but I didn't really think I'd ever see the old man again. We shook hands warmly, then I hugged him. I'd miss the old silver-haired treasure hunter. But I was thankful he was letting me go so easily.

Partly to outrun any second thoughts or paranoia, which could come over him in a tidal wave, I quickly turned and raced out of his studio, and down the stairs and past the fountain, into the squalor and the rain. But as I passed through the store below, my eyes caught the black, kind eyes of Brunner's landlady as she said, *"Hasta mañana, señor."* We waved goodbye.

And I truly thought I'd broken free.

PART FOUR

TEARS OF THE MOON

CHAPTER 13

◆◆◆◆◆

For two years I kept thinking about the treasure in that beautiful raw country that I'd left behind.

When I left Brunner in 1980 and arrived in New York excited about all the material I'd collected, I began to type out his stories. A month later it began to nag me that I hadn't gone into the mountains, not even for a day.

William Prescott, the blind historian, had written *The Conquest of Peru* without ever visiting South America. His descriptions of battles and scenery were full of the impassioned drama of a man who created from his imagination what he could not see. So why, I had asked myself more than once, couldn't I do the same with my story? Why did I have to see the mountains to write about them? Was my imagination so feeble?

After a year I realized I was stuck. I couldn't write about Atahualpa's gold at all without sounding a false note, or so it seemed to me. So I went on to teach and to other stories; traveled finally to another, less beautiful, far less haunting part of South America, but wherever I went I carried inside me the anxious feeling of incompleteness: I'd left the treasure story hanging.

Late in 1981 I traveled to Brazil to write about the devastation of the Amazon region on the Bolivian border. For three months I traveled with a Brazilian photographer and his wife, a well-known folk singer from São Paulo. They were on a Guggenheim grant to record the deforestation and the genocide of the Indians. It was difficult traveling. In the rain forest again, I grew lethargic. I dreamed often of the cool cobalt sky of the Andes, of Quito, City of Eternal Spring.

On my way back from Brazil to New York I arranged to meet my father in Cuzco, to make a trip with him to the Inca ruins of Machu Picchu in Peru. My father's recent blindness demanded that someone guide him when he traveled to such out-of-the-way places. Also this would be a chance for us to catch up with each other. I hadn't seen him in months.

From Rio de Janeiro I called and asked him to bring me a heavy coat, long underwear, wool socks, and a number of other necessities for a cold-climate journey. He made a list, then said, "I thought we were going to South America, not the North Pole!"

I told him the stuff was for a friend in Quito. I didn't want him or anyone to know I was planning a trip to the Llanganatis. This time I hoped not to jinx the journey I'd failed to make two years before.

So, after a few good days with my father at the Inca citadel of Machu Picchu (he had arrived with a huge suitcase filled with expedition supplies; in exchange, I was his eyes on those steep Peruvian slopes), and two years after my first trip to Ecuador, my airplane from Lima banked sharply for the difficult approach to the Quito runway, and I was looking out the window at the city I'd left behind. I said out loud, "Such is life in the tropics," thinking how sometimes you just have to do what you didn't think you had to do at all.

Pichincha was so clear its rocky summit was on fire, and the modern city below was encased in the same bright fossil air I remembered. Brunner had been right: I was back. But not for Atahualpa's gold. I was returning for something else.

I made a quick checklist on the plane, of what I had and what

I'd have to buy in Quito: two kinds of boots, two pair of socks, long underwear, hats, gloves, two pants, wool sweater, three heavy shirts, raincoat, aspirin, a bottle of cane liquor, notebook, and pen.

Those mountains had haunted, nagged, and laughed at me for never having tried them, so I was here to go alone, if I had to. Even in Brazil's territory of Rondônia, the Llanganatis had loomed up in my sleep, a behemoth to slay.

Andy had told me in the very beginning that if I wanted the real story, I would have to feel the frozen fog on my skin—to know the treasure from inside the Llanganatis. So Andy had been right and Lilian too had seen it all along.

As soon as I landed I called Lilian, who sounded happy to hear I was back.

"You're the first I'm calling. I'm at the airport," I said.

"I just knew it. When will you come see me?"

"How about right now?" I said, and I took a taxi to my old apartment in Enrique Robinson's mansion.

Not a bush in the garden, not one color on the permanent slopes of Pichincha, not even Piedad, who greeted me with her old, fine, toothless, ageless Indian face—nothing had changed. I spent an hour catching up with Lilian, but it might have been an hour taken from some afternoon visit two years before when I was living there. Quito was indeed a fossil.

"I'm going to Brunner's," I said. "I'm going into the mountains this time, I promise."

Lilian said, "I knew it," as she shook her head back and forth. Her eyes moistened with the inarticulate joy of a mother whose son has done something extremely kind and unexpected.

◆◆◆

I went directly to the old city, ducked into the clothing store (Brunner's landlady was out), and passed through the silent courtyard with the still-bright magenta bougainvilleas above. Anxiously I took my wallet out of my pocket and counted the money

I'd brought. Then I climbed the stairway to the treasure hunter's studio.

For a moment I was afraid of him, what he'd think. But then I saw that nothing here had changed, either. Brunner was leaning over a map, he was as poor as ever. Only one reason I came back, I said. "To make a short journey. Yes, I have money," I told him.

Brunner was happy to see me. Was it because he needed a friend or was it because of my money? With no self-righteousness, nor with any trace of condescension, but rather with only the extreme cool of a long-earned confidence about a certain subject, he nodded his head.

"Pete Pete Pete, you are back; they all come back. I have just spent two months at my lake on Cerro Hermoso. I have all sorts of new information. Now we're ready, Pete!" When he stood, I saw his leg had completely healed.

So the old bulldog had finally gone, after all, as he never doubted he would. It had taken two years, but he'd done it. And would again in another few years perhaps. But not right away, not with me.

"I want you to take me to Triunfo this week."

He said, "Sure I will take you to Triunfo."

He agreed to help with provisions and his own guides (who might keep an eye on me, no doubt). So I gave him money and we were friends again—as if no time had lapsed between us. The Quito air had preserved him perfectly.

At first I could not believe how helpful he was. Perhaps I was no threat to him anymore, or never had been.

Two days later (I was staying at a nearby hotel) Brunner came by for me and together we went shopping for all the provisions I'd need. Then we spent a day organizing, with Brunner showing me how to pack once I got to El Triunfo. Many of the things my father had brought from the States, Brunner told me to leave behind. "You must travel light," he admonished.

After equivocating, one afternoon I went to see Diego. I knocked for ten minutes on his apartment door until his neighbor told me he had gone away, hadn't been seen in a while. I was sorry to miss him really, because Diego, as much as he had disappointed me, had nevertheless been a large part of my good memory of reckless Quito days and nights. Many times since I'd severed our relationship, Diego's buccaneer words returned to me. Even in my sleep I saw his wild dark smile, that disembodied face afloat in my dreams.

I called Andy's house in Guayaquil but he too was not at home. Apparently, after he married he'd moved to his beach house in Salinas. I did not want to bother him, so I didn't call him there. Perhaps his marriage wasn't going so well.

One week after landing in Quito, at five A.M., Brunner was waiting in the street. I picked him up in a friend's Land Rover. He was dressed in mountain clothes, wool sweater, thick hiking boots, Alpine knickers. Two huge knives were strapped to his belt. He threw a large duffle into the back of the jeep and jumped into the passenger seat and slammed the door.

"I have everything you will possibly need, no? Don't you worry, Pete. With Gino, you are safe." He was going to lend me everything I needed, from stoves, to tents, to emergency flares and matches. When we reached El Triunfo, an eight-hour drive, he'd arrange my guides for me, too, he said, "The very best mountain men for a Llanganati trek."

I was right about one thing: It was better not to think about what the hell I was doing—just do it.

Brunner's assurances did not help much. In the eight-hour drive on terrible Ecuadorian roads, I had to fight down that old fear. Brunner talked and talked and I listened as best I could. He spoke of old times, of stories I'd heard before and of new stories, too, of Blake and Dyott (finally the whole story) and the death of Old Q and the lost tribe of the Sabelas. But it wasn't until I got into the Llanganatis, there in the stillness of those freezing nights, when I lay almost paralyzed from climbing all day in cold rain, that I recalled most of what the man said in the Land Rover as we raced down the Pan American, the sun coming up over the spikes of the Andes.

◆◆◆

El Triunfo got its name when the peasants, who had been squatters, rebelled against a rich landowner and won their farms. The village was the last, the smallest, the most out-of-the-way pueblo at the very end of the road from Pelileo and Patate. There were perhaps sixty inhabitants here. One telephone, donkeys braying, chickens pecking at mud. Edge of the world. A subsistence Andean agricultural village with no running water, some wood-cutting business, a few cows, one generator. A poor village in the cloud forest on the very brink of unknown territory.

Tungurahua, a nineteen-thousand-foot volcanic extrusion, was visible three miles away on the horizon, snow at its peak. Often you heard it rumble—it shook the whole village.

"Well, this is it," said Brunner, who, it terrified me to think, would be leaving with the Land Rover in a few hours, after everything was settled.

We stopped in the mud in front of a two-story wood shack which was the town's only general store. Immediately people gathered around the strangers and shook our hands. Some eyed us but kept their distance. Some smiled at Brunner. He'd been here many times. A lot of the men in town had once carried goods to Brunner's camp on Cerro Hermoso.

Brunner was jovial. Imperiously he yelled at some children to go fetch Segundo and the other men, his guides, to bring them from their fields, get them right away, very important! A little girl ran off to fetch Segundo, who was up in the hills tending his corn.

The floors in the tienda were packed dirt. We were at nine thousand feet and because it rained here almost every day, the corn stalks in the field opposite the store were deep green, healthy and tall. Avocados, peas, and potatoes grew on the steeply sloping hills behind the corn. And there were dogs, whole gangs of skinny undernourished mangy canines sniffing around the store and the streets for scraps. This was the kind of town where you had to worry about rabies.

Men in fedoras and ragged old dark ponchos, carrying machetes, came into the store to gawk at us. One barefooted man without an arm had huge holes in his pants. Another had no teeth. In the corner a few young men leaned on each other's shoulders like lovers.

Brunner talked to one González about taking me up to Cerro Hermoso. González nodded. Segundo didn't arrive, and Brunner and I waited an hour.

"Don't worry, Pete. I have arranged it all with my man González here. He is quiet, but a good man, too. Segundo and González will go with you. You will be perfectly safe, no?"

Brunner had to hurry back to Quito. "I have a very important meeting with an Army general tonight. You're in good hands here now, Pete. I will see you in a week or two, no?" Brunner drank a large steaming cup of coffee that the *señora* of the tienda made for him and in the smoky darkness of the store he smiled at her and at me and asked her to take care of me and then as if he had never come at all he was gone. As if I'd dreamed the man.

The noise of the Land Rover winding down the twisted road from that village was the loneliest dream-like sound I'd ever heard.

The town grew silent. I was the only white man within miles and there would be no more English for at least a week. The store owner's daughter, a beautiful Indian girl of seventeen, was embroidering green and scarlet flowers on a white cloth on the spartan wood bench in front of the store. She had polio and couldn't walk. Her mother offered me coffee, which I drank in the damp cold air, making nervous conversation with the girl.

Segundo still had not come out of the fields, so I worried about meeting Brunner's head guide. Would he take me?

González had stood nearby as Brunner drove away. He was a strange-looking man of forty; the features of his face were twisted. When his eyes fell upon mine, they seemed to prod and poke at me. I can't explain it. Perhaps his eyes were too far apart or too intent. He frowned with such spite, I believed he wanted to harm me in some way.

When the sound of the Land Rover faded completely and the wind rustled the corn stalks, I asked him if he believed in the treasure.

"No," he said as he leaned on one leg, his face twisted.

"But Brunner comes here to find it, yes?"

"Yes." He started to smile, I think.

"And his money is good?"

His smile expanded into a snarl. "Yes, of course." Then, like an anchor that comes free in a stormy harbor, González walked off and abandoned me.

I called to him, "Will you be back with Segundo tonight to pack our equipment for an early departure in the morning?"

"Make ready, gringo," he said sternly from twenty yards, not even bothering to look back.

Most treasure expeditions still set out from Píllaro and San José de Poaló, just north of here. Brunner was the only man who began from El Triunfo. He'd opened the trail in 1970, which took forty men from the village fifteen days to blaze. The doctors had told Brunner that he could no longer sustain a three-day trip at *páramo* altitude, fourteen thousand feet; the old route would be too harsh on his ailing physique. Rather than giving up altogether, Brunner had studied the maps and noticed that if he approached the Sacred Mountain from El Triunfo he would climb steadily uphill and spend only one day, or two at most, in reaching his destination. The trip to Lake Brunner on this route would be easier on his blood pressure.

So in 1970 he came to El Triunfo armed with topographic maps and aerial photos and hired forty men to cut the trail I would take in the morning.

◆◆◆

At seven P.M. Segundo came in briefly and shook my hand. I'd taken the spare room above the store, the only extra room in town. Segundo agreed to go and said he'd be back soon to pack up all the gear that I'd begun to lay out across the wood floor.

Less pure Indian, Brunner's leader was more a mestizo, short, a strong face, his hair flecked with grey and his mustache thin, almost menacing. We did not speak to each other much and I worried I'd forgotten too much Spanish to communicate effectively. Coming from half a year speaking Portuguese in Brazil, I found it difficult to switch back to the less exotic and simpler sounding Quechua-inflected Spanish. For at least a week I'd be with men who understood not a word of Portuguese or English.

I sat on the bench in front of the store. An Indian woman passed by, holding the hand of a completely blond, fair-skinned little boy who looked more like a gringo than an Indian. I wondered if it could be Brunner's child.

A man with a gold tooth sat down on the bench. Eagerly he said,

"*Norteamericano?*"

"*Sí.*"

The man was panting like a puppy. "*Se va por Los Llanganatis?*" Headed to the mountains?

"*Sí.*"

"Well, *norteamericano*, I have been inside five times." He held up five stumpy fingers. "Did you know a man died two years ago, a German named Hanz? One of Brunner's men." His breath reeked of alcohol.

"No. I did not know this." Brunner had told me that no one had ever died on his expeditions.

"*Sí. Se murió, señor.* He died in there. Wandered off. Because he found gold nuggets and was filling his pockets with gold when he drowned in a freezing river."

The man left me hanging. "*Se murió*" were the words in which he planted more seeds of fear. "*Buenas noches.*" He smiled and stumbled down the muddy street, the dogs following him into the wet darkness.

The wind picked up and howled through the corn and rattled the boards of the general store. I sat upstairs and listened to men and women come and go and I thought about taking the truck out of town the next morning.

Until this very moment I had had real excuses, but now there was not one excuse left.

Did I think the treasure was still up there? Well, I did and I didn't. But the gold seemed somehow secondary, I was so anxious to get going.

I steered my mind to the practical. I sorted the equipment on the floor of my room. We would bring cans of tuna fish, rice, *máchica* (the local powdered wheat), *pinol* (the Andean dark sugar mixed with barley flower and cinnamon), grease for frying, coffee, tea, sugar, salt, and candies for quick energy. Since everything in the Llanganatis would get wet, Brunner had carefully wrapped each meal in a separate plastic bag.

Now I put all my gear, sweaters, extra leather boots, extra shirt and pants, in plastic bags, too. I wore high black rubber boots which were light and durable.

Brunner told me he kept extra supplies hidden up at the treasure lake, enough food for thirty men for four months, though this was hard to believe. Over the years he had Segundo and others carry them up. I hoped it was not one of Brunner's fictions.

Climbing up and down to my room in the little store, already my legs felt heavy and weak. I hadn't slept well since landing in Quito, a few hours a night, maybe more; it was hard to tell. I tossed all night. And as I waited for Segundo to return to help me pack, I wondered how I'd make it up to Cerro Hermoso. In the upper Amazon of Brazil I had lost at least fifteen pounds and a lot of my old strength. I had done no formal exercise for three months, and I think I had amoebas from drinking the Amazon waters.

The isolation of El Triunfo was like a cloak around that mountain community. The sharp smell of mules and cows was in the air. Women in colorful robes walked by in the street like phantoms. Their rubber boots squeaked. Now there was music downstairs. The general store had its own little generator and a few men sat drinking and playing cards below me; I could see pieces of arms and hats and bottles on tables through the wide cracks in the floorboards. When night came to El Triunfo, the villagers always gathered around the store.

A clique of eight teenagers drank rotgut cane alcohol on the bench outside and I could hear them joking, laughing. Two bottles of Cristal were passed between them. The sad music grew louder against the cold night. The guitar strings impressed the mountain air as delicately as frost.

More and more people in ponchos gathered outside. As if by spontaneous combustion, ten pairs of men and women, all young, began to dance silently in the mud of the street, a line dance to the sad music. I stood on my little balcony and watched as the couples, oblivious to all but the flutes and the guitars, weaved back and forth.

I had forgotten it was Saturday night.

A drunk screamed at them, but they danced heedless of him

and of the gathering onlookers. The one politician of El Triunfo, "El Teniente Político" as he was called by everyone, came swooping into my room wearing a thick, long, red woman's overcoat which made him extremely proud. His face was flushed and lined, an alcoholic's face. Very seriously he made small talk with me, his words slurred.

"When you rrreturn from Los Llanganatis, *señor*, you must come to see me and file a rrreport." He said I had to state the purpose of my journey. All foreigners who entered the mountains had to do the same.

"Strangers mmmust be mmmonitored, *señor*. You can understand us, can you not, *señor*? It is the lllaw."

Yes, I said, I understood very well.

At nine P.M. Segundo came to weigh all my gear and said it would require three guides: himself, González, and Washington, a young quiet boy, hardly twenty. "Washington?" I said. "How did he get that name?" Segundo said that he was an honest boy and that he was more like a gringo than anyone in his family, he was so tall. "So they named him after the capital of your great country." Segundo smiled broadly.

Silently, he then divided the gear into three sacks. González, who had slipped into the room like a thief and who hung back by the door as if he were ready to bolt any second, looked at me with distrust, I thought, intimidating me with his diffidence. He was downright unfriendly compared to Segundo, who was now telling me how El Triunfo first got its name.

Segundo was a curious and intelligent man. He asked me right away why I wanted to go to Cerro Hermoso alone. First, I told him I had not come for treasure, as Brunner did. At this, Segundo did not smile, but he kept looking at me with wide brown eyes.

Then I told him I'd tried to write a book but that I couldn't finish it because I was writing about an area I'd never seen. I'd tried to get into these mountains, I said, but something had prevented my journey. Brunner had broken his leg; I'd run out of money. But now here I was.

Segundo's face was the handsome middle-aged face of a wise man. He was still staring, not saying a word, as if he knew there were parts I had left out.

I fumbled in Spanish.

Segundo did not comment. Perhaps he saw that I was nervous trying to explain. He listened as he packed the rest of the gear.

"*Hasta mañana, señor,*" he said. He would be back at five A.M. He and the others were gone, and I felt empty.

Village children came quietly into my room, a swarm of little boys and girls, all brothers and sisters, barefooted, dirty-faced, wide black and brown eyes of wonder, some horror on their faces, too. When I smiled at them, only two smiled in return.

One little girl absentmindedly chewed on an apple as she stared, her face smudged with dirt and charcoal. Outside, it was a damp night, no stars, and only the sad music below where the fathers of the children drank and played cards.

After the children disappeared, I lay awake in the darkness until three-thirty, when finally the owner of the store told the drunken men to go home. He turned off the generator, the music stopped, and a rooster began to crow.

Segundo had told how Hanz really died. Segundo himself had been there when Hanz broke his legs in the Río Topo, on the other side of the Cerro. It was Hanz's first trek. Brunner had not been along on that trip but had arranged for Segundo to take Hanz in. Hanz wandered off, fell into the river, developed gangrene, and when he finally got back to Quito they sent him to a Miami hospital where both his legs were amputated. He died a week later. Segundo said he liked the man. He was sorry he had died.

Packing up at five-thirty in the morning, Segundo looked up at me with big curious eyes. He said, "Rarely do gringos come all alone to Triunfo to go to the Llanganatis. You must have a good plan." I nodded. Perhaps he had understood something from yesterday.

CHAPTER 14

◆◆◆◆◆

The morning of our journey we gathered in the weak light outside the general store. Segundo said with a straight face, "González is not coming with us." Juan would take his place.

But I wanted to know, Why not González? Was it because of me?

Segundo said that he was sick. And I gathered by inference that he was one of the men drinking in the store last night and was hung over.

In the grey cool morning gloom I was relieved. I had enough worries about the difficult trek without fearing one of my guides, too.

Juan was much the better man, I knew right away. He was a short (perhaps four-foot-six-inch) Indian with half of his upper row of teeth missing and a ready smile. Juan's Spanish was so rudimentary I easily understood him when he spoke. Segundo too was easy to understand because he talked deliberately and slowly. But young Washington was incomprehensible. Maybe it was his adolescent apathy that made his words run together like liquid. It seemed incredible that anyone could understand him at all. He didn't speak; he mumbled.

Washington was scared of me. Maybe he just didn't trust me. He was thirty years younger than the others. Segundo and Juan were well over fifty but looked so vibrant they might have passed for thirty-five. Their attitude toward young Washington was paternal.

Brunner had planned our trip to last anywhere between a few days and three weeks. Juan and Washington each would get two hundred sucres a day (six dollars) for carrying approximately sixty pounds of gear. Segundo, who would get four hundred sucres, had been in more times than anyone in town: fifteen trips, and all for Brunner. Juan had gone to the mountains, he thought, only nine or ten times altogether; he couldn't remember now. These two men were old hands and good friends. They joked a lot and laughed easily between themselves. This would only be Washington's fourth trip. Seriously quiet, more uncertain perhaps, he set himself apart from the other two from the very beginning.

◆◆◆

When we walked up the street, no one said, "You will die. Don't go to the Llanganatis." The only creatures that cared about our journey, it seemed, were the dogs. They barked from the fields and from the few huts scattered up and down the street. Segundo and Juan set the pace and we were already a mile up the path before I had time to think. As we passed near a few more village huts, a woman was cooking something over a very smoky fire. Little boys collected firewood. Business was as usual.

We skirted pastures, then dove into virgin forest, elevation about ten thousand feet. But as we were leaving town, Segundo's sister, who was going to check her cows, followed us for a long time. She was stocky, buxom, her legs sturdy, her face oddly round, cherubic, a Welsh face but darker. It seemed I had never really looked into Indian women's faces in all that time I'd lived in the Andes a few years before. Segundo's sister was beautiful. Her smile was radiant, and she reminded me a little of the girl I'd seen two years ago on the bus from Ambato to Píllaro.

Before she headed off on another trail, she grinned and said, "Hope you come back with your life, gringo." She meant it, too. I detected no sarcasm in her voice.

I replied with the truth. "I hope I come back with a new life, *señora."* Because that was why I was doing this, wasn't it? To complete my investigation of the treasure story, for which I'd given up anthropology—to complete myself, what I had begun and not quite finished. To put the disappointments of Andy, Diego, and Brunner, and of myself—to place these failures of the past—behind me and move onward.

Although she separated from our expedition party, her flirtatious smile lingered with me.

◆◆◆

It was twenty-five kilometers to Cerro Hermoso from El Triunfo, a rugged climb of seven thousand feet through jungle and *páramo*. Brunner's first camp was at 10,000 feet, the second at 14,000, and the last, on Lake Brunner, was at 14,500. Segundo thought we could make it in one day to the second camp, doing two days in one, if I was able and willing.

"You look big and strong, *Don* Pedro," he said.

I said, *"Cierto,"* but I wasn't so sure. Segundo wanted to get out of the jungle quickly and up to the *páramo,* "Where one can think clearly," he said.

For someone so out of shape as I was then, I knew it was risky to take on too much in one day, but unlike two years before, now I didn't care so much for caution. I'd climb until I couldn't climb, and it was better to get as much over with as soon as possible.

So we began walking briskly, nearly a trot. I followed directly behind Segundo, the others behind me, up the valley along a Colorado-pure, very loud, swiftly flowing river called Río Verde Chiquito.

For an hour or so the air warmed as the morning passed. The trail grew muddy, knee-deep in places, and then we plunged into the dark purple light of the cloud forest. The vegetation grew thick above us.

Hour passed hour as we strode up and down the sides of the valley wall, now along the river, now five hundred feet above it, now back down into the river and across it and back again. But always upward. I began with a nice easy stride, breathing slowly, not pushing myself, but pacing every step. I let my legs do the thinking, perhaps wishful thinking.

It seemed remarkable that this high jungle on the west slope of the Llanganati Cordillera, unlike the lower rain forest I'd just come from in Brazil, was almost a benign presence. Here there were no malarial mosquitoes, no deadly snakes, none of the normal dangers we associate with the word "jungle." The real danger, though I didn't think about it, was simply the damp cold.

As we walked, Segundo said in his customary soft voice, "*Don Pedro, one can sleep anywhere here on the jungle floor and not worry about death.*"

The absence of jungle stereotypes added a ghostly feeling to the start of my trek—as if I'd been so prepared to feel terror I had to invent it where it didn't exist.

The trail narrowed and grew nasty with prickers and mud and lianas. It didn't seem like a trail at all.

Segundo and the others were amazing. They carried no guns, only machetes, which they used like third arms.

I followed Segundo like a shadow. He and the others leaned into the climb as it grew steeper, hands folded in front, machetes tucked under their arms, the ungainly loads of their backpacks towering way above their heads. The pace quickened—we had so many miles to cover. When the pain began in my legs, I pretended to ignore it. For a while it could be ignored. And then I'd never felt such agony in my life.

Above the forest the sky seemed low, pressing down on us, pregnant with rain. February was a bad month to make a trip to the mountains but I prayed for good weather. Juan told me at a resting place that I was lucky to get guides this time of year. A few treasure hunters, who had come to El Triunfo one February, said they'd pay anything to get guides for the Llanganatis. But he and Segundo refused; all the villagers refused. After December no one liked to go in, except Brunner and sometimes Segundo. "We value our lives. After February," Juan said, "you can be sure of someone dying. The weather is that bad, *señor*."

Segundo stopped to point at a huge boulder and a shelter beneath it. There were caves all through the area, he said, and here was an old Inca stopover. "Human bones lie hidden beneath that rock, *Don* Pedro, ancient Inca bones. But no archaeologist comes here from Quito to make research."

◆◆◆

A trek into the Llanganatis could not exist for me without one of Brunner's famous stories. I remembered them clearly, the old ones and the new ones, as I walked. They came to life for me out there in a way they had never lived in Quito.

The word "bones" reminded me of yesterday's drive from Quito. Brunner had talked the whole way. One tale he told was about the death of Old Q.

As we raced down the Pan American, Brunner had said: "I will tell you the story of Quinteros now, Old Q, the man Captain Loch brought with him on his 1936 expedition. Old Q had a horrible death, Pete."

Brunner said Old Q was a screwball, but somehow, on one of his many trips he had found a green stone, a very peculiar discovery. Quinteros went to a friend of Brunner's, a *Señor* Monge, and asked what kind of stone it was. Monge, who was the owner of the hacienda La Moya, which Valverde mentions, told Q he hadn't ever seen anything like it, and he should take it to Quito to have it analyzed. Well, instead of going himself, Old Q, who hated the city, sent his brother on the mission. And his brother met a jeweler in Ambato, a Colombian, and sold him the precious stone.

"Months later, the jeweler went to Píllaro to the store of *Señor* Villacresis. And, well, Old Q discovered that he had been cheated by his own brother, that the stone had not been lost, as his brother had told him.

"The jeweler said he'd come to give Old Q fifty thousand sucres to make an expedition to get more stones like the first. But Old Q went crazy. He didn't accept the money. He asked Villacresis for provisions, wheelbarrows, and food for two months. He said he wanted to dig up a landslide where he'd found the green stone. Everyone said he seemed *loco*. And Villacresis gave Old Q nothing.

"So," Brunner continued in his usual epic mode, "the last known words of José Ingacio Quinteros were, 'Well, there is no one anymore in the world you can trust.' And he took a little raw sugar, you know this *panela,* and some *máchica,* barley flour, and a few other items. And he went alone to the Llanganatis with a mute and deaf idiot Indian. One of these aberrations you find in the sierra.

"Together they went down to the valley of San José de Poaló, where Old Q slipped on a rock and broke one of his legs. This was before the road went through there. So they made a thatched roof, and put a little firewood beside him. And they put Old Q's things near him while the idiot Indian went off to Píllaro to get help."

"Too bad you were not there to show him everything about the *páramo,*" I said, and Brunner smiled just as he had smiled for Laursen's photograph session two years before, the old vanity intact.

"But instead of two and a half days, it took the idiot nine days to get out. And fifteen days to organize a search party. When they finally got into the Llanganatis again, the idiot had forgotten where he had left Old Q. They looked all over but couldn't find him."

Then Brunner read the whole story in the Quito newspaper, that Old Q was lost and probably dead. And in 1943 another treasure hunter, a man named D'Orsay, found the skeleton of Old Q sitting against a tree. The thatch roof was in shambles. He still had his water poncho on but the pants had almost rotted away.

And he still had his rubber hat on, too. He was just sitting there with his shotgun in his arms, underneath the tree, a bandolier across his chest.

Brunner had unzipped his famous valise in the car as we raced down the highway near Salcedo and pulled out a horribly detailed drawing of old Q propped under that tree in the Llanganatis, shotgun across his arms, his skull glowering from beneath an old rubber hat.

Whenever Segundo disappeared from sight a few yards in the brush, I hurried so I wouldn't lose him. I certainly didn't want to end up like Old Q.

These mountainmen who farmed on steep inclines had no difficulty in the mud. They literally skated on the dark slick stuff while I was so overcautious I'd slip and slide, exerting twice the necessary energy just to keep from falling down and looking like a fool in front of them.

The steep mud track ran along the edge of a precipice, the river far below like a pencil line. Deep greens in the forest turned light olive. The vegetation at eleven thousand feet was fiercely tenacious, violently adaptable to the capricious weather—just as Loch had described it.

The sun slit its way out of the clouds for a moment and smashed the river below, turning the grey liquid to chartreuse, a pure-freezing emerald water crashing over granite boulders. At a rest stop, Segundo joked about a journalist from Quito who had come out to El Triunfo and misreported a statement the Teniente Político had made. Then Segundo lifted his great bulky pack onto his back, and said, "But we are wasting our breath joking here when we haven't even begun to climb yet."

After four hours I fell behind, but whenever I got too far back, Segundo would wait for me. When I caught up to him, he'd ask how I felt. I liked Segundo for his concern.

Being over six feet tall, I had to bend down low to squeeze through the thick jungle, through little tunnels in the vegetation. And Brunner called this a trail! Leaves with poisonous prickles like tiny razor blades cut my hands until I bled.

My body hurt, but I felt good heading to the Cerro.

Then doubts set in. Why am I doing this? Why go? Why?

For some crazy reason I thought of Vietnam. I'd never gone to Vietnam. My lottery number for the draft was too high. It was pure bingo chance that my twin brother and I were so lucky. And now, years later, like some of us left behind who, if we had actually been drafted at the time, might well have cut off toes or escaped to Canada, like some of us who had built up histories of allergies and psychiatric excuses, I felt a kind of guilt—as if I'd missed something crucial, a lesson of some sort.

To me those men who came back and were not treated like heroes because they'd fought an ignominious losing war, to me they had always been better and bigger than heroes. They'd faced absurdity, and survived. The pitiful tragedy of it was that when they returned some went mad, were forgotten, ignored, hated by others who had fought in a cleaner John Wayne war two decades earlier, hated by those who could not bear to see dear old U.S.A. wallow in shame.

All through adolescence I'd wondered if I could handle army life, the routine, the authority, the physical demands, life under pressure fighting a crazy war in a jungle thousands of miles from home. I had decided I could not handle war, but at the same time I wished I could. To face true madness and come out whole, this seemed like the real test of manhood. Vietnam could have been a testing ground. And I still felt untested.

So, walking into those crazy mountains unprepared would be my testing ground, I thought. There was something absurd about forcing myself into the Llanganatis even after I'd decided I was not the kind of person who would ever find the gold. Risking my life going where I'd thought I would never have to go. All I knew for sure was that I wanted to get to the lake, get in and get out—perform a cold kind of commando foray. No attachment to speak of, not months and months of wandering these hills for clues. Just a one-night stand in the mountains, a weak man's proof to himself that he could do it, so that he would never have to do it again, so no one and not even himself could call him a coward.

I realized I was confronting the heart of Ecuador's lawlessness for the first time. Until now I had never really confronted it myself. Always hiding behind Andy's expensive pickup, or Diego's boozy nights, or Brunner's expertise, hiding behind other people's disappointing me, never able to just make this trip on my own. Now I was alone in the lawless country, and it felt wonderful and terrifying, for it was my own inner lawlessness that I was confronting.

My legs were robots; my mind ran in circles. Then, thank God, Segundo interrupted my thinking. He said he didn't kill animals like so many others from El Triunfo who had completely hunted out this cloud forest over the years. All the tapir had been shot. Only a few birds were left. Thanks, he said, to the lack of concern of his government, the poorly enforced existing laws remained slack.

"Such is Ecuador, such is poor Ecuador," he sighed. A steadfast, honest, hardworking man, Segundo was well respected back in El Triunfo for his candor. When I asked him if he would consider being the politician for the pueblo, he said, "No, I am too egotistical. My family comes first. There are too many stupidities I would have to contend with. It is not for me."

◆◆◆

We moved under the double cover of jungle and cloud. I was glad I did not know the terrain ahead of us. For now, the trees were typical of lowland jungles, with high canopies. The jungle here was benign, the temperature cool but not yet cold. I was wearing a rain poncho over a heavy wool sweater I'd bought in Quito for ten dollars. I had long underwear on and wished I didn't because I began to sweat. I was tired and sweaty even though I was carrying only a small knapsack.

Washington never made any jokes himself. But Segundo and Juan made me laugh often with the idle kind of jokes men make when they are busy doing serious work, when there is an element of worry that it is better to ignore.

I felt remarkably close to Juan and Segundo. These were the first Indians I'd really talked to in Ecuador. The mud and the climb united us. Those men were like the plants all around us, too. They clung to the mountain walls with the same professional loyalty I imagined they also felt for me, and I had the feeling they would help me no matter what trouble I was in. They embraced the hills, and leaned deeper and deeper into them like Sisyphus with his stone.

We passed a nook in a huge rock where, Segundo told me, Brunner had had to sleep one night when he was not able to get down from camp before night set in. "He is not what he used to be, *Don* Pedro. No, he is not."

But Segundo spoke of the old man with great respect and affection. His voice had that adult-to-a-little-child gentleness when he talked of Brunner, and I greatly admired his tolerance for the old treasure hunter. It assured me once again I was in good hands and also that I had not completely misjudged Brunner over the years.

At one point Segundo said, "*Señor* Brunner has been kind to you, too, I think." And I caught Segundo's eyes with a twinkle in them.

"Yes," I agreed, "*muy amable.*"

"*Soy pobre.* I am a poor man. I suffer a lot," said Segundo, who was a great commentator on his own life. Much of his talk was about the imbecility of the local and state governments. His kids were all entering school age, but El Triunfo had only a small primary school and no secondary school. The government had promised more funds but never delivered. "*Como whiskey en la mesa*" was Segundo's expression for describing the idle rich, idle promises, idle government. Like whiskey on the table. The wealthy of Quito, he knew, drank whiskey, "The rich have whiskey always on the table. They talk and talk and talk and promise but only drink the rich man's scotch and talk some more." Segundo might also have been alluding to certain treasure hunters, I thought.

"I cannot even speak Spanish correctly," Segundo told me. "I never learned my own language." Segundo was serious as he said it. This sad truth hurt him deeply.

It was true. Segundo and the others used present forms to express the past and they said things like *"más mejor,"* the equivalent in English to "more better." Their tenses were often incorrect and they almost never used the subjunctive. Segundo apologized for his poor education. He was convinced Ecuador could only improve as a country when it better educated its people, and I agreed.

I noticed Segundo's belt buckle was something he'd fashioned himself out of five bullet cartridges.

At one point when we had climbed back down to the river and sat, popping candies into our mouths for quick energy, I asked if he and the others in El Triunfo believed in the gold of the Inca.

"No, not really," was his reply. "We have no real evidence for it. We have not read any books, nor have we seen the *Guide* Brunner speaks of," he said, shrugging his shoulders.

I felt strangely guilty, for in my pocket I was carrying a copy of Valverde's *Guide*. But I also knew I would not show it to him.

"Perhaps if we read the books which all you gringos read, then maybe we might know enough to believe, *jefe*." He was staring at me. His raised eyebrows said something different: they told me he had no real interest in the gold, and later he verified this.

Segundo made me laugh, and he laughed after I did. Segundo knew I liked his sense of humor. And there was something in Segundo's attitude toward treasure that seemed healthy. I wondered why, for instance, he didn't have any crazy stories to tell as Andy and Diego did, and why the tales that surround a treasure hadn't been passed down to him, and why he didn't believe in this treasure, especially since it was a part of his own heritage. He seemed somehow free of the lust for treasure, and yet he was here and he might be coming very close to the gold and to the legends every time he brought people like me into these mountains. Maybe the old idea of the Incas was manifesting itself even today, the idea that gold and silver were not "valuable" in the way that Andy or Pizarro thought of them. After all, the Incas had not been completely wiped out by the Spaniards, only conquered.

Segundo was a descendant of the Incas. Perhaps it was this fact that explained why he wasn't even interested in solving any puzzle or mystery of the treasure. He merely accepted or did not accept it. I never had the feeling the gold mattered to him one way or the other. Segundo was free of it all.

Men had come to the Llanganatis armed with guns and all the modern equipment of war, treasure-seeking macho men infected by Brunner and books, lusting for gold. But these guides with me now, Segundo, Juan, and even young Washington, were the quiet heroes of the Llanganatis. Heraldo also, in the north, was a silent hero. They were brave and they carried the loads of treasure hunters and they themselves didn't even believe in the gold. For six dollars a day they would leave their fields and their sons and daughters and wives and the safety of their homes, to risk their lives with sixty or seventy pounds strapped to their backs. And the whole time, they called me *"jefe,"* chief!

While I drank from the river I noticed none of the others were drinking. They hadn't even begun to sweat, and already I was drenched.

Segundo saw me gulping and advised wisely against too much cold mountain water. If I drank too much, my body would fall out of tune with itself, and I'd grow sluggish. So I had to pull myself away from that beautifully icy river.

We reached Brunner's first camp, where we would not stop for the night. Near the loud river, the camp seemed diminutive and abandoned, a few poles, the remains of campfires, a torn tarpaulin, bits of plastic for a roof.

We moved by the roar of the river, too loud to hear each other's footsteps. I told Segundo, "Tomorrow my legs will not work. I am sure of that."

Segundo replied, "Hanz, before he died, after he broke his legs in the river, told me, 'Segundo, my legs want to make a matrimony with Cerro Hermoso; they don't want to leave this mountain.' And it would have been true if we had not gotten a helicopter to go in there and bring him out."

◆◆◆

Then: cold gloom of rain, a cloudburst of it when the sky seemed to be falling on us.

Segundo stopped in the trail in the rain. He ripped his pack off his back in one motion and, with the others now, searched the jungle floor for little green seeds everywhere which he squashed in his fingers to suck a white milky fluid.

"*Droga,* a drug," he said, while the rainwater flowed off his face, "for going up there!"

Segundo pointed straight up, to a jungle-carpeted wall. Three thousand feet, a three-hour climb if you were in good shape. It might take me five.

I tried the seeds. They were tasteless. Segundo was smiling to himself ever so slightly.

I shoved five candies into my mouth from desperation.

Lianas drooped from the sky and moss seemed to grow in the air, on the rocks, and on the sides of the trees. This was high, high jungle between eleven and fourteen thousand feet. This was the jungle Andy had told me about years ago when I first heard his story; the "beard of the world" he called it.

I couldn't get my breath. My lungs would not open to receive that extra crucial inch of oxygen I needed. Brunner had often explained to me how the Andean Indian was a wonder of physical adaptation. His heart was twenty percent larger than a lowlander's. His lungs too were bigger than mine, and he had two quarts more blood in his body "to process the little oxygen of high altitudes. His stamina is Olympian," Brunner had said. Of the Píllaro Indians Luciano Andrade Marin had written:

> After this experience, I think that the roughness of Andean Ecuador has the potential to be conquered, colonized and civilized with the help of the Indian. Since Pizarro and Orellana, to modern times, the heroism of adventurers would have amounted to little without the anonymous aid of the Indians. . . . On our expedition . . . those who endured to the last, noble and loyal, were the pure Indians.

Washington, as we were getting ready for the big surge, suddenly felt sick. He dropped to his knees and buried his head in his hands.

I had that sudden panicky feeling I get when I first detect disaster. But Segundo went to him and spoke softly to him and I felt my body relax when I saw that things were under control. But we had to wait half an hour while Washington rolled on the ground holding his stomach, then his head again. He said he wanted to turn back. Apparently he had been drinking heavily last night.

I suddenly felt that our trip was doomed, and that we should turn back immediately. Even if we could convince Washington to continue, this display of agony in so quiet a young man made me shake with fear that Atahualpa did not want me to go forward. I really thought this was a sign.

But another part of me, the part that had waited for this moment for years, was terrified that the expedition might be called off. So I went up to Washington, spoke kindly to him, entreated him, and gave him two aspirin. Finally, he got better and stood up, not happy by any means, but at least not rolling in pain anymore. He agreed to go onward.

We each drank a glass of *pinol*, mixed with river water, and I filled my canteen because up on the *páramo*, Segundo said, there would be no potable water.

Segundo looked troubled. I could see he was trying to form ideas in his mind. What he said came out thoughtfully.

"You know, some men do not understand at all, *Don* Pedro. They do not know what these mountains can offer us. Like the governor of Ambato who came to me one day and asked me to lead a trip to the treasure lake. 'How long will it take?' he wanted to know. And I told him three weeks for a good journey. 'But how many kilometers is it?' he asked again. And I told him twenty-five. 'But that is impossible, Segundo,' he complained. 'Twenty-five kilometers in three weeks! What, we will inch our way there? Do I look so weak it will take me that long?' No, I tried to explain to this man, Cerro Hermoso is very shy and to know her well one must wander over her sides, her back and front, to see the magic of the place, the waterfalls, the lagoons, the tunnels, the vistas, to see all of Ecuador's skyline from there and to feel the mountain itself. It takes time because it is so rarely clear up there. But when the fog lifts it is like precious stone, diamonds in the eyes. That's what I tried to tell the governor.

"Well, he said I was crazy and I was trying to cheat him. He said I was only saying three weeks because I wanted more money. So he never came here, *jefe*. He is a stupid man. I think he wants only the Inca gold and he will not spend time to see the beauty of the region. But, *señor*, what else is there in this life of ours, eh?"

"*Sí, pues.*" I smiled and agreed, because here again was Segundo, the descendant of the Incas.

◆◆◆

Any false feelings I'd had a few hours before that I was an agile, surefooted youth who could make it up any mountain that a fifty-year-old could climb, faded when we started up for the *páramo,* up a seventy-degree incline with roots sticking out of mud like fractured glass. Sharp plants dug into my hands. The tentacles of squid-like bushes peeped out of mud to grab my feet. There seemed no order in that anarchy of stunted life. Within minutes I clutched anything I could get my hands on, roots, leaves, mud, miniature trees—those dwarf trees, covered in beards looking so deceptively soft. You could touch one of those cobwebs and draw blood as easily as on a coral reef.

Hours later I was still grabbing prickle bushes, taking my hand away suddenly swollen, inflamed, and limp. Mosquitoes came out in squadrons. At one point while trailing the others, who had scurried up the wall like goats, I sat in a nest of tiny ticks the size of pin heads. I spent a half hour picking and brushing them off me before the night would fall. Segundo said they could bury their heads deep in my skin and itch like a thousand flea bites.

Here now was all the homeless, vagabond, black-sheep vegetation of the grey and brown world, the grey floral rejects from below—arrow plants with spikes that ripped into my rubber rain gear and gashed my boots. Tiny dark brown trees like tarantulas. Branches and bushes that poked deliberately at the eyes. Every imaginable plant cried out, "Go back, you don't belong." But I kept pushing. Because in some masochistic way I enjoyed the pain. I was headed for the lake and for the mountain. My legs, arms, and hands were telling me I was close.

On that incline, in that jungle of mud, I found it remarkable that Segundo could stop, look at a root blocking the trail and say, shaking his head, "No no, *feo feo,* ugly ugly," and then he would spend ten or twenty minutes of hard labor slashing at it. When he finished, like the craftsman who cares profoundly for details, having only just begun to perspire, he would sigh and say, "Now that is much better." A look of contentment shone in his eyes as he regarded the cleared path, the stumps he'd created and the bright fresh woodchips sprinkled on the mud all around us. It was a job well done.

When my legs cramped one time and I was paralyzed for at least fifteen minutes, I struggled to explain. I couldn't remember the word for *muscles* in Spanish. Not recalling enough of the language to communicate the details of an emergency was a distinct problem I was glad I didn't dwell on. I couldn't remember the word for *cramp* and I never had learned the word for *charley horse,* if there was one. So the Indians from El Triunfo stared in disbelief at me lying prone in the muck, trying to stretch out my legs, moaning.

Segundo asked if I needed to make camp right there in that very spot for the night. He looked worried as I lay in the mud. He said he had a tarpaulin for emergencies.

"No no no," I said. "Thank you but I want to get to the *páramo.* I'll take longer rests. We have to go on," I said. But I must have been a pitiful sight, lying there for fifteen minutes, pulling, pumping, rubbing my dead legs back to semilife.

"Mind and heart want to go on," I told Segundo when the others went ahead, "but legs rebel."

It seemed the climb would never end. It was as if the world had turned over and all the weight was on my back.

"Take your time," Segundo assured me. "We will wait for you. *No se preocupa.* Do not worry, *Don* Pedro."

It was no good slapping mosquitoes because I needed both my hands to hang on. Once or twice I did let go, and I dropped the twenty or thirty feet it took me so long to conquer, and I had to start again. When Segundo saw the mosquitoes on my face he said, "They think you are a cow, with that blue hat you are wearing. One mosquito says to all the others, 'Hey you guys, over here: a GRINGO with gringo blood.' And all the others come over for the feast, a rich *norteamericano* delicacy." Juan laughed and even Washington laughed at this.

Perhaps it *was* ridiculous, me here on the edge of the world, my legs defunct. And not even for gold! But for what? In order to prove something to myself, I would risk all this?

Resting again a little while later, Segundo, who was smoking a cigarette, said, "This will be good for your book, *jefe,* suffering like this." He wasn't even breathing hard, which angered me a little.

Panting, I blurted, "You know, Segundo, I didn't really have to come up here. But all those months expecting to come and then never seeing the Cerro itself—it seemed like a lie. I was afraid I was weak. So I had to come back, *entiende usted?* I am not after the gold, Segundo. But here I am nevertheless."

"Then you must dedicate your book to *las chicas,* the girls, eh?" Segundo the thinker said, "The good girls, the ones who will marry you not for your money but because they believe you had to come here, the ones who will believe you came and that you came back a different man."

◆◆◆

At 13,500 feet I crawled, clawed, grappled, clutched, clenched, grasped out with any part of my body that dared reach a little farther—arm, leg, elbow, finger, toe stretching for holds in the mud. I was a crab on the bottom of the ocean which had lost all feeling in its claws. At all costs I had to move from where I was.

A fantasy scene surrounded us as we approached the *páramo,* something out of the Swiss Family Robinson. The sun broke cloud, illuminating the deep valley below. I could see that we were on a ridge with open air and jungle slopes all around.

Then, thank God—the *páramo.* You sensed it coming up ahead because the trees changed from tarantulas to knots of bark. They grew taller, drier, scrawnier. We sat on the edge now between the sandpapery toothpick trees of the *páramo* and the *páramo* grass spreading out for miles in more or less flatness. God, to climb out of that bearded forest and onto the flat top of the world, of bog and high grass where I could see for a great distance without the cluttered vegetative claustrophobia of below. It was bliss.

A tremor from the earth exploded in the valley like somebody dynamiting a mountain.

"*Temblor*," Segundo said in a deep voice. It was a good word for it, I thought.

In the air above the valley, protean clouds formed, moving fast, mutating, then unforming to disappear like silk in the wind. My legs had shut down and I had to wait an hour before I could get up to stumble behind the others.

Segundo said, "This is where all the winds of the world meet."

CHAPTER 15

◆◆◆◆◆

But the *páramo*, at fourteen thousand feet, had its own devious traps in store. A sharp pain now ran from my feet up the back of my legs into my spine as I stumbled behind the others. On the trail for ten hours, we had climbed seven thousand feet.

The trees were twisted and charred from a recent fire, Segundo thought. We had difficulty lifting our feet because our boots got stuck in the slime of the bogs, the famous quaking bogs that Loch's mules had had such difficulty negotiating. Sometimes our boots slipped off, and before we knew it our stocking feet had plunged into the black ooze, which was very cold.

The trees were lifeless; they stood in the cold damp air like spooks, like shadows of real trees. Thank God it was only an hour to camp.

Brunner had built three thatch huts nestled against the base of a small hill. Incredible to come upon these signs of humanity in all that broad bleakness.

One hut was for sleeping. Plastic sheets lined the roof. I changed my clothes as it began to pour again. The hut was remarkably dry inside. Juan made a fire in the kitchen hut; the thick smoke billowed into our eyes.

We drew our water from the bog and boiled it to have tea.

Near camp there were no running streams, only putrid sulfur-smelling, stagnant water.

At first I could do nothing but lie down. In an agony of thirst, altitude sickness, leg cramps, and general wretchedness, whenever I tried to move I wanted to vomit. The others had gathered around the fire, chatting, joking, and laughing, happy we were already up on the *páramo* with only six or seven hours' trek tomorrow. I wanted to ask them to stop laughing. Their laughter nauseated me.

Segundo said, "Hope you're better," and he brought me a big cup of tea. After a rice and tuna dinner, we all crawled into our beds on the straw floor of the hut. The freezing darkness had fallen fast. I was feeling a little better after the tea and after a glass of Alka-Seltzer, which was much better than aspirin for altitude sickness because it worked fast to take away the feeling of vomit, but I had to keep taking it or the nausea returned with the dry heaves.

Segundo loved to talk. In the candle-lit darkness he said, "I don't want the gold, no. Gold is for war. Yes, I need money but I want money by sweat of work. Money is for my children to go to school with books and pencils. These mountains are full of minerals, which means a lot of money, too, but the metal detectors can't find them because the dials on the machines go crazy."

Segundo was tired. With half-closed eyelids he rambled on.

"There was a Norwegian who came here with sixty carriers from Píllaro and started looking in the bushes for the treasure. After a few days when he couldn't find anything, he said, 'No, no gold here,' and he left. Pretty stupid, if you ask me. What do you think, *Don* Pedro?"

"*Muy estúpido,*" I said.

When we had first come into camp in the dwindling afternoon Segundo had found a small dead bird on the floor of the sleeping hut. It was the size of a little hummingbird, and Segundo, who had picked it up in his thick rough hands, said, "Poor thing, died of the cold, you can see the way it's all bunched up."

Now the temperature plummeted. Before we put the candle out we talked some more, our breath steaming in the coldness, our voices somehow distant, like the faint voices of other people in another room. Segundo said, "In Triunfo there is a golden Inca doll, *jefe,* sleeping on its side."

I asked where it was and if anyone knew about it from the city. "Oh no no (he put his finger to his mouth), just me and a few others," Segundo whispered. "We will tell no one. We do not need that gold. Gold is for war and the doll is very beautiful, *señor.*"

"Can I see it when we return to the village, Segundo, please?" I asked, but Segundo only shook his head. And I thought that the Inca belief in gold as a religious quality, not of any fiscal value, was here once again manifesting itself. And I did not pester him about wanting to see that golden doll, perhaps of great anthropological significance. I realized how much I'd changed over the past few years: My former interest in monkeys and archaeology had dwindled so much.

The *páramo* outside was soaked in cold silence. Yet up here as I started to feel a little better, getting accustomed to the fourteen thousand feet, I felt a strange freedom coming from the land outside, though it was completely dark and fog had set in to block out even the embers of the dwindling fire. Yet there was a distinct breathlessness up so high, as if a burden had lifted, as if I'd just met the woman I knew I would marry one day. I thought I heard an occasional chirp of a bird, a lost lonely sound. My muscles stiffened, then grew limp.

I couldn't keep my eyes open but I heard Segundo say, "Everyone who hears I come to the Llanganatis thinks I am a rich man. But out here, nature and mountains and the *páramo* are the only treasures."

"Tomorrow we will find gold, Segundo," I said as a joke.

"Friendship is gold," I think I heard him say. Segundo was still talking. "Pizarro and the conquistadors," he was hardly audible, "were killers, rapists, illegitimate, uneducated bastards. And this is Ecuador's heritage. It goes on still with these local corrupt politicos. And the treasure of Lord Atahualpa is a symbol. The devil has two burning emeralds in his eyes, *Señor*. But the Inca has these mountains . . ."

"Segundo," I said softly in the frozen blackness, "what about the spell that comes over men up here. I feel strange. Is it the altitude really that affects me so?"

"Personally, I do not believe in the curse on these mountains, *jefe*. I think it is what one brings to the region. But who can really say for sure."

When a few hours ago Segundo had first seen me unroll my bulky green sleeping bag, he had said, "I have one of those bags, too, but I did not bring it because I will sleep together with the others tonight. To sleep alone is very sad." And as I crawled into my cocoon of American goose down, the three men from El Triunfo had joked and laughed like brothers lined up under one wool blanket between them, huddling close to one another against the icy air.

I was deeply impressed by the bond between these mountain men. Earlier as we had talked over dinner, even Washington, who I discovered was Segundo's nephew, leaned his head on the older man's knees just as naturally as a man and woman touch each other after years of marriage. Those rugged men sometimes touched each other like babies.

That night it dropped well below freezing. Before I slept I took a shot of cane liquor I'd secretly stored in my pack for emergencies, hoping the liquor would melt the pain in my body. Tomorrow the treasure lake at last, I thought, congratulating myself for getting out of the jungle.

Brunner had told me the rest of the Blake/Dyott story in the Land Rover. That ride down from Quito seemed so far away, but the story came back to me now.

I slept poorly. Brunner's story ran through my mind like frames from a movie. All night in fragments, then in one continuous sweep, as if I were living through the whole saga myself, but in a dream. So this was the tale I'd gleaned over the years of how Brunner finally zeroed in on the treasure.

"You see, Pete," Brunner had said in the Land Rover racing south on the Pan Am, as he intertwined his thick stubby fingers and turned them slowly like gears working, "I know where the gold is because of Commander George Miller Dyott. He was a famous British explorer who came to live with us in Ecuador. You know some things about him already, I think. He had a little farm outside Santo Domingo de los Colorados in the western jungle, no? In 1965 he told me a strange tale and he showed me the maps of Barth Blake, the sea captain. And suddenly, Pete, for the first time in thirty years of research, finally, by God! the cogs in all the gears fell neatly into place."

As with Marin, Loch, Blomberg, Andy, and all the rest, Brunner had gone to the wrong area for years. He couldn't get past the Pyrite Mountain into Valverde's "Way of the Inca."

"But, you see, two officers in the British Royal Navy discovered the treasure in 1887 and Dyott, who was a great sleuth, received all that information, all the maps, and none of us knew anything about them at the time."

Dyott was a perfect man for solving this mystery, too. The North American Newspaper Alliance had hired Dyott in 1928 to search for Colonel Fawcett, who got lost in the Matto Grosso of

Brazil while looking for the lost city of Atlantis. That famous search was in all the world's newspapers. And it took Dyott quite some time, but he found out in the end that Fawcett and his son had been killed by a hostile tribe. The Commander wrote a book about it! *Man Hunting in the Jungle*.

"Dyott was another of those men who know how to enthrall you with stories," Brunner, the quintessential storyteller, told me. "I used to listen for hours without ever getting a word in, not wanting to interrupt the stories he could tell about his marvelous life. He was a short amiable fellow, of the old school. I miss him a great deal, Dyott, I do. What a man!"

To tell how Dyott first got involved with Atahualpa's treasure, Brunner said he must begin in the year 1887. A cousin of the botanist Richard Spruce who was studying to be an officer in the British Royal Navy told his two superior officers about his uncle's adventures in Ecuador and about the lost treasure of Atahualpa in the Llanganati Mountains.

The two officers, who were immediately taken with the story, decided to make an expedition to Ecuador to investigate. In January 1887 Captain Barth Blake and Lieutenant George Edwin Chapman embarked for Panama, then sailed to Guayaquil on Ecuador's coast. From there they traveled up the sierra to Ambato, where they spent some weeks outfitting their expedition.

In 1886, before Blake had left, he had written to a friend in New England:

My dear friend,
Very soon I shall be in South America. I must perform some secret mission in the Republic of Ecuador. I am not allowed to tell you more at this time, but it is a critical operation. I shall write you often, and if I have some information, I will send it to you. You must guard it for me with your life. . . .

From Ambato the two friends made their way to Píllaro where they hired carriers and mules to take supplies to the Spectacle Lakes ("Anteojos" in Valverde's *Guide*). They inquired as to the terrain or routes, which indicates they had special information (Brunner believed) supplied by Spruce or his family.

The second week in March they began their journey passing directly over the Pongo de Guapa without going to the mountain with the same name, as Valverde indicated to do in the *Guide*.

At the Spectacle Lakes they sent the mules back to Píllaro and left Yanacocha, the Black Lake, on their left as they descended the Golpe, then passed on the right side of the Río Desaguadero to Parca Yacu (Two Rivers). Then the two crossed to the left bank to the Cascadas de las Tundas, entered the thick cloud forest, and there (writes Captain Blake on his first map) discovered the "location of probably the world's biggest gold mine."

From this spot—the mine—which until then was known only in local legends, Blake knew that the "Way of the Inca" proceeded to the third Cerro Llanganati. To find the mines, he reasoned, was to discover the ancient road used to transport the gold to the melting "Guayras," or ovens, on the Cerro where the ancients had used the trade winds to regulate the temperatures of the fires.

Blake and Chapman returned then to Parca Yacu (which was the joining of the Río Desaguadero and Río Rivera de Llanganati on the Guzmán map), then on to a place called Soguillas where for many years Brunner said he had camped without knowing he was only a hundred paces from the "Way of the Inca," which was much broader than Brunner had previously imagined.

Blake marked the Inca path on his first map. From here, the two must have seen the *socabón,* or tunnel, that Valverde mentions. Continuing on, they climbed up the east face of the third mountain, the sacred Cerro Hermoso, or "Volcan del Topo" on Guzmán's map.

Through the first and second peaks they passed to Cerro Hermoso's west face where Blake marked on his map (between the main peak and the adjacent pyramid rock structure): "Gold in hidden cave here."

He and Chapman entered the cave and discovered Atahualpa's hoard on the fourth of April, 1887. They had sent their porters back to Píllaro before entering the cave, of course, and when they went inside, they found emeralds and figures of gold and silver. Blake later wrote his friend in New England:

> It is impossible for me to describe to you the wealth that now lies in that hidden cave marked on my map, but I could not remove it alone, nor could thousands of men. I have to go back to sea for a while, and I beg of you to take good care of my maps and papers. . . .

and later, in 1889:

> Maybe you don't believe me when I tell you. There are thousands of gold and silver pieces of Inca and pre-Inca handicraft, the most beautiful goldsmith works you can imagine: life-sized human figures beaten out of gold and silver; birds; animals; corn stalks of silver with golden ears of corn; gold and silver flowers; pots full of the most incredible jewelry; golden vases filled with emeralds in gilded goblets and a thousand other artifacts. . . .

Grabbing eighteen pieces of gold and a handful of emeralds, the two men packed up only four days' supplies to lighten their loads for the way out. They didn't leave the same way they had come in, but moved west instead, using a compass. They went along the rocky knife edges to facilitate walking rather than struggle through the valleys thick with dense cloud forest. After the region of the three María Lakes, snow, rain, and hail obscured their journey and they got lost in the labyrinthine area now known as Auca Cocha, Savage Lake.

For days they wandered through deep *quebradas,* ravines, and gorges. They were nearly starving. The weather continued to be bad as it is usually that time of year. Somewhere along the way, Chapman, who (Blake later wrote to his friend) was suffering from a tropical disease, sickened and died. Blake buried him in "a tomb of rocks," marked also on the map.

Blake continued on alone until from a high ridge he finally saw Lake Pisayambo in San José de Poaló and evidence of habitation below. Back in Píllaro he recuperated and then returned to Guayaquil and England. A letter from the British consulate in Guayaquil states, "By the merest chance he [Blake] found Atahualpa's hoard in a cave next to an extinct lake."

Brunner was suspicious of Chapman's death. He told me:

"In 1966 I met the ancient grandmother of the owner of the Hotel Villa Hilda in Ambato. She claimed to be 128 years old. She had good eyesight, however, and a sharp memory even then. Manuel, the owner, her grandson, brought me to meet her because she had known the two British mariners, no?

"And the *señora* told me many things about the 'Señores Misters' as she called them. She knew a lot about them because they had come to her parents' house. She said one had died in the Llanganatis, that he'd fallen over a precipice because a rope which was tied to him had broken, and that the other, the captain, had shown her eighteen pieces of gold and some green stones. Her family was sure that the gringo had bought the articles from someone in Píllaro, where many of the villagers often made a living by selling fake relics to tourists.

"So there are two versions of Chapman's death, Pete. What really happened up there? Tropical disease, as Blake wrote to his friend? Or rope breaking? Or murder? You tell me."

"I really cannot tell, Gino," I said. "You tell me."

After selling the gold pieces in London, in 1892 Blake again

embarked from Liverpool to return to take the treasure out. His
first destination was New York. But when the ship entered New
York harbor, Blake was not on board. The captain of the clipper
informed the port authority that his passenger, the retired naval
officer, had fallen overboard while drunk in a violent storm, and
although they had tried, they couldn't save the man. So they had
given him a burial at sea.

Commander Dyott believed that Blake had indeed been drunk
and had blabbed the story to some of his shipmates, who then
killed him, thinking he had all his papers and maps with him. But
they found nothing. Blake was then traveling to New England
(Brunner would not tell me exactly where) to visit his friend and
confidant to whom he'd been sending all his notes, maps, and
writings about the Llanganati treasure. The man (whose name
Brunner would also not reveal to me) was a trustworthy friend
whom Blake had apparently thought would be the perfect companion for the journey back to Ecuador to get the gold. Blake had
written the New Englander in 1888:

> If something should happen to me, and you decide to go
> and search for that hidden cave on my map, look for the
> *Reclining Woman* and all your problems are solved. . . .

Years passed and no one remembered the officers of the Royal
Navy. But one day in the 1930's the grandchildren of Blake's
friend in New England, while restoring their colonial house
situated above the sea overlooking a small island just offshore
[Maine?], were moving furniture and found in their attic, inside a
book, a faded piece of paper that said: "All about the Inca
treasure in Ecuador in the hollow tree on the island."

The boys quickly took a boat to the island on which they all
knew well the old worm-eaten oak where they used to play. One
of the boys climbed it and found in one of the upper branches a
copper wire, which he pulled until a large two-gallon whiskey

bottle appeared. It was sealed. Inside they found all the letters, maps, and papers which Barth Blake had sent from Ecuador to his friend.

They showed it to their parents, and the boys' father remembered that his father had indeed talked from time to time about a treasure and had even planned an expedition which, he remembered now, had never come off.

That was when the family decided to write the British Navy to find out if Blake and Chapman were listed in their archives. After receiving word that the two men were not fictitious and had really been in the service, they wrote the Royal Geographical Society in London asking for information about Spruce's translation of Valverde and the treasure. They also wrote the Explorer's Club to see if it might be interested enough to investigate the Llanganati region based on this new material.

The club wrote back that, by chance, one of England's finest explorers lived in Ecuador, and the retired Air Force Commander George Dyott's address was sent along. Highly recommended, the man had made numerous investigations in India and South America. He was more than qualified for such a job.

The family wrote Dyott in Ecuador, sending along the Blake material, hoping the explorer would undertake an exploration for the gold. Dyott was interested, but World War Two broke out and he had to leave Ecuador on numerous occasions, so he put the treasure problem aside for the time. But later, after a few years of research, Dyott became convinced the treasure was real and that it existed somewhere in the Llanganatis. He himself made a few expeditions into those bewitched mountains.

Leaving from Píllaro (outfitted by none other than Villacresis), the commander entered the strange region in 1947, 1948, and 1949. With him he had both Spruce's translation of Valverde and Blake's maps. On one trip he broke a leg and some ribs. His last trip he came out with a stomach malady. While recovering from his illnesses in Quito he had a lot of time to think about the

treasure which, after these many years, had grown to be an
obsession. But he told Brunner and Andy in the hospital that he
would abandon the search. Yet, in the same breath, he also
affirmed that he was a hundred percent sure the treasure existed.
His opinion, however, that a man would be happier without
looking for it didn't sit well with Andy and Brunner, who wanted
to keep looking until it was found. By this time Dyott was already
in his sixties.

Brunner explained to me, "It was in the late 1940's when I first
met him in the mountains, no? He used to come to my camp and I
went to his. We weren't working together then, we didn't tell any of
what we knew to each other, though each of us tried to coax out the
other's clues. I knew nothing about the Blake material until the early
1960's, at which time Dyott, Andy, and I made a contract."

I broke in to ask, "You and Andy were friends then. Why
can't you be friends now?"

Brunner gazed out the window at the brightening mountains
along the highway and replied, "Time changes people. That is the
only reason, Pete." He seemed sad. Perhaps he missed his old
friendship with Andy. (I know that for the last two years I too
had yearned for those early exuberant days of my indoctrination in
Guayaquil, and I also longed for Diego's swashbuckling company
in late-night discos. Talking of treasure with someone creates
invisible bonds not unlike the bond I have with my twin brother
whom I see so rarely and yet whose closeness never wanes, no
matter how many years and miles intercede.)

"One time," Brunner continued, "in 1947, I believe it was, in
Dyott's camp on the Zunchu Urcu (what the Indians call *Pan de
Azúcar*), talking by the heat of the bonfire, the very heat that
allowed us to forget for only a little while the howl of the hailing
tempest outside, he said to me, 'If ever on your journeys in these
mountains you should come across a rock formation that resem-
bles a reclining woman, tell me at once and I will tell you some
things I've learned recently . . .'

"Naturally I didn't know anything about Blake or Chapman or the family in New England at that time. Not for another sixteen years was it until Dyott finally told me the whole story and I made a contract with him. More about that later. But I can tell you that in the past twenty-five years I have *found* the reclining woman! I can tell you: It is a rock formation. But that is all I can say.

"In November 1947 an American friend of mine in Quito asked me to accompany another American to the Llanganatis; Mendel was his name, from Oregon. He had come to Ecuador quite a while before I met him and he had gone to Píllaro where he met *Señorita* Rosita Alvarez, the sister of the mayor of Píllaro. Lucky for Mendel, who spoke no Spanish, that Rosita was fluent in English and she helped him make preparations for his trek. She hired porters for him and watched out that these men didn't overcharge for supplies and salaries. She was enchanted by the gringo.

"Ready to go, Mendel set out but only to Soguillas, a four-day walk from Píllaro, no? Why the Indians abandoned him there, I don't know. But they did, all right. Just packed up and left. Perhaps it was because he didn't speak Spanish, or maybe because the food he fed them they didn't like, God knows, but they went back to Píllaro under cover of night. They are the same Indians and mestizos, by the way, that I've used many times and I never once had any trouble with them. Oh, well.

"Anyway, this was Mendel's first trip, and when he finally got back to Quito my friend introduced him to me. I liked the man okay and agreed to accompany him if he financed the expedition. Didn't have much money then. You know how it is . . .

"When we got to Soguillas, we found all the equipment that Mendel had hidden there when the Indians had deserted. But before we got to the place, we stopped at Commander Dyott's camp up on Zunchu Urcu. Dyott received us cordially. But after greeting Mendel and hearing his name, something in the commander, my friend, changed radically and he grew dour.

"After dinner he did a thing that disturbed me greatly. I knew him fairly well by then, of course, and we had a custom of sitting by the fire and gossiping after meals. This time, however, there was no gathering. Dyott merely got into his sleeping bag, said a curt good night and went to sleep. Very unusual, very, I thought. I was upset.

"Next morning early, Mendel and a few Indians went off to hunt deer, that is what they said. As Dyott and I drank coffee alone, he turned to me and scolded, 'How could you bring this man to the Llanganatis?' I was shocked. He went on, 'Why, Gino, he is a descendant of one of the mariners who threw Barth Blake into the sea because they thought he had the maps on him leading to the gold.'

"I replied to Dyott, 'Pardon me, but who is Barth Blake anyway, and what does he have to do with the Llanganatis, and what papers did he have, what maps?'

" 'Oh, I'm sorry, Gene, I forgot that you don't know the story of the Englishman, and I've never even told you why I'm in these mountains. We are such competitors, you and I, I suppose. Someday soon I will tell you all the information I have, but before I can, I have to consult some friends in New England.' He meant the family, of course. 'But, Gene, watch out for this fellow Mendel. Keep an open eye on him.'

"That is all he said at the time. It was just confusing enough to pique my curiosity, though. Dyott was a very thorough and credible man, so I watched Mendel for the rest of the trip.

"From time to time this Mendel would take out a notebook from his rucksack, open it, and check the mountaintops around us, no? I am sure now, although I never saw it, that it was a sketch of the three peaks of the Llanganatis. But I knew so little then. It wasn't important to me; I was watching out for my life.

Mendel never achieved anything, nor did he crack me over the skull.

"On our next trip, he and I went in a completely different direction and Mendel had a bad time.

"West of the Cordillera of Las Torres, the Towers, he went off alone with his secret notebook and got lost in snow. My men and I looked for him two days but couldn't find him. On the third morning Mendel came crawling into camp, cut to pieces and soaking wet, freezing to death. He'd fallen down a cliff and it was a miracle he hadn't been killed.

He finally returned to Oregon after that. Whatever it was that he kept so secret didn't help him in the long run, I know that much. The expeditions were futile and the only thing he got out of his journeys in Ecuador was *Señorita* Alvarez, whom he married."

In 1962 Andy Fernández-Salvador told Brunner only a portion of the Blake story which Andy had already heard from Dyott before Brunner did.

"Then in 1965, Andy flew into the Llanganatis by helicopter, only to survey, he thought, and to take photos. But it crashed, as you know, and he landed behind the Cerro on an island in a river.

"But by chance, near where they crashed, he had discovered the 'socabón,' the tunnel of Valverde. A real breakthrough for us all.

"So I went back to where Andy had crashed, climbed the slope of the Cerro, and found the tunnel, too. Higher up, almost at the edge where the vegetation ends, I found the zigzag of an ancient Indian path, cut in rock, and from there I first saw 'the reclining woman' which Dyott had mentioned eighteen years before but had never himself located. I had found it, Pete! But it wasn't as Dyott had thought. Not just a formation of rocks, no. It was the whole mountain, the Cerro Hermoso in which, from this angle, I could see a reclining woman, no?

"I took the photos immediately to Commander Dyott along with the drawings I made of the place. He was eighty-three by then and dying of cancer. What I showed him amazed the old fellow and for many days on that jungle farm of his, he showed me all the Blake material—at last, all of it! That was the first time I got the whole story and now the pieces of the puzzle finally were fitting together. We talked all night long, and the roosters crowed many times before I knew it was dawn.

"Then Andy, Dyott, and I made the famous contract. I would make the expeditions into the mountains for them. I had the most time. Dyott had the maps, and Andy had the money. Since then, Pete, my research has really paid off. Within a few years I had discovered Lake Brunner, my treasure lake, no?

"But I can say no more, Pete. You understand. Do not be offended. There are simply some things I can tell no one."

Brunner's talking on our trip from Quito to El Triunfo had made the trip pass rapidly. But the story of Blake only began to register in my mind when I'd reached Brunner's camp on the *páramo*, in the middle of nowhere.

One of the things Brunner could tell no one was what it really feels like to wake up to an altitude headache at fourteen thousand feet, helplessly throwing aspirin and Alka-Seltzer down my gullet, Juan making a fire that crackled so loudly it snapped against my fragile brain like breaking bones. The heavy smoke penetrated my nostrils and I could not move one inch. It was always Juan who rose from bed first, his energy flawless.

The others collected wood and began cooking while I pretended to be asleep, wishing I were back in Quito.

After an hour of coaxing my body to life, I put on my army-green rain gear and said to the others after breakfast, "I hope there is a store up on Cerro Hermoso that sells Coca-Cola."

Segundo replied, "Yes, of course. Gino Brunner's country store." And we all laughed.

The day was gun-metal grey and much colder than yesterday. Segundo was in high spirits.

"So many times," he said, "I have twisted my leg, or hovered in the fog for days on end, or been soaked cold to the bone for a week up here on this *páramo*. After each trip I resolve never to come back, no, no more. But here I am, I always do come back. Strange, is it not?" Years ago Blomberg had told me the same thing.

"Not just for salary," Segundo continued, "but for the mountains themselves. Perhaps, *Don* Pedro, if you are lucky today you will see the Sacred Mountain and you will discover what I mean."

CHAPTER 16

◆◆◆◆

The next day walking through *páramo* at 13,500 and 14,000 feet was like pushing your way through Satan's greenhouse of gnarled, twisted cat's paws of plants, hostile marmoset nails of vegetation. The *páramo*. That boggy desert, barren, wet, muddy, region of thorns—lovely too in some deceivingly insidious way. Like the delicate lace of the blue-purple-red flower that grew from the crack in an ugly rock. And the occasional cricket-like chirp of a few small energetic birds above, furious little birds you only glimpsed out of the corner of your eye. And the sky open but grey like an oozing wound above you, the sky that any moment could pour out buckets of freezing rain, then close up again, threatening drizzle for hours. Yet in all the strange harshness of the land, there were lagoons and little innocuous-looking streams, places for phantoms and treasures and legends to flourish, and secrets that could never be known. Drizzle and sleet and even hail, one or two times that day, hailstones the size of nickels, and always the fog that rolled over the hills like titanic elephants grazing. Low clouds with great density that conquered distant peaks and ridges as fast as they could move, clouds that filled and emptied valleys, everything in the sky in a frenetic flux.

We crossed certain umber valleys that seemed like the same exact valleys we'd crossed an hour before. Crossed and seemed like we never crossed at all. The *páramo* of the Llanganatis, this is why I had come. To feel the monotony of what seemed like weeks at sea, no ships in sight, no life other than what we carried with us. And always the cold of the sky like novocaine. I pushed on in spite of the body wanting to go on strike.

I didn't even know I was walking anymore, my throat as dry as papyrus, so we'd stop to drink from tiny streams which were the real headwaters of the Amazon. In five minutes, I'd be parched again. That's why I came, I thought, to feel the strange paradox of a dry mouth in a wet land.

The path was steep, up and down and up, and two times I fell ten feet, down a little canyon wall, but caught myself just in time, coming so close to breaking my leg again, an old fracture from boyhood.

Segundo stopped to show me a thorny, dark green plant which, he said, I could eat if I was starving. With his machete he cut away the pointed leaves and exposed the sinuous insides. So there was food here to survive if one knew how to find it.

Juan lit one of the larger furry spider-like trees with a match and it sprung up billowy smoke. A platinum haze filled the sky, a man-made cloud that swelled and swelled until I felt an inexplicable panic, as if that smoke could swallow us all.

But it was too wet out there for fire to spread. The pewter smoke rose until it merged with clouds, eaten by the sky.

Copying Juan, Washington also lit a tree and then another and another, both men smiling and giggling, kid-crazy with pyromania. Perhaps, I thought, in such a peopleless terrain of hostile bog and thorn, this was a sign that humans had come to dominate. This was our challenge to Satan's greenhouse. Fire cut the loneliness of the terrain and made us smile, a Promethean symbol of our arrival.

We found puma, bear, and tapir tracks in the mud of the little-worn path. Segundo told me that three times before he had come upon mountain lions in his trail and both animal and man had jumped back, the cat always running first into the brush. Each time it gave him a shock, he said, that he thought would arrest his heart.

Drizzle, drizzle, and mud. No wonder Captain Loch brought twelve hundred bottles of scotch, I thought. More bear track. Two kinds of bears up here, Segundo said, a small gentle black and a huge hostile brown.

My rain suit was torn in many places.

Juan, it so happened, had become my guardian. Last night he had dried my clothes. And now he opened the path just in front of me whenever he decided it was too overgrown for this lanky gringo. He made me a walking stick, too, which I used so much I got blisters on both hands. When he gave it to me he said, "Here is a poor man's horse."

As we passed through a deep swamp he pointed out tapir track to follow because the animals knew where to place their feet in the quaking bogs. A few times I missed the solid areas and sank hip-deep into the slop, but Juan dragged me out.

Juan was so short I couldn't see how he carried that load on his tiny back. A high-spirited man. Even Segundo had told me he was one of the best men to have out here, a hard worker who never slacked off, as Washington would do any chance he got.

When Juan worked he whistled through his few good teeth. There were times when his gaiety under pressure and my pain did not exactly jibe, but I liked the man more and more. He had a flame inside him I envied.

An hour later after a silent trudge, Segundo pointed to the north and east, "The path to Píllaro." The mist covered it up and we were forced to stand still for a few minutes until the fog lifted enough to see the trail.

◆◆◆

And then, a surprise: Our group had walked a matter of yards along the path to Píllaro when we came across an abandoned camp in the fog. There were candy wrappers lying fresh on the ground, and the camp seemed recently abandoned. I half expected someone to yell at us to keep away. Segundo thought the site had been left only a week or two ago.

Scattered over the frosted mountain grass were the broken shards of empty bottles, tin cans, and boxes. On the edge of where the tents had pressed the grass down leaving their impression, I found two empty Fundador brandy bottles. Of course it could have been someone else, but I felt certain that this had been Diego's camp. So he had made it this year, I thought. He was the only one I knew who drank Fundador in these mountains.

Segundo and I walked around that campsite as if in a sleepwalk, like two boys stunned by an unexpected archaeological discovery. Segundo said quietly, "These treasure hunters drink a lot," and the fact that Diego was still drinking made me sad all over again because I recalled how he had disappointed me.

But seeing his camp (had he come with Francisco, after all?) made me glad in a way, too. For at least now when he bragged about his Llanganati exploits, he could really say he had gone again. Diego was, in spite of his drinking and hyperbole, a treasure hunter.

Segundo said we should move onward. I was sorry to leave Diego's campsite, and wondered if perhaps we might even run into each other up at Lake Brunner. What would I say to him? We passed a large body of water that Segundo said was full of trout.

Segundo spoke (and I was glad to hear his voice out there in the desolation and sadness of my past association with Diego): "I am a practical man. No school education, but all this out here is my university." And, "*Don* Pedro, I see you making notes. Maybe you are a poet. To me this is good. Poets sing songs about what they feel and I hope you are writing how it feels to be up here."

I was surprised when I looked up and saw the sun trying to come through the clouds. Segundo talked as we marched, "I can

read eyes, *Don* Pedro. Your eyes have respect in them. I think
you know what to say about Ecuador's future. Eyes never lie."

When we pushed through high grass, swarms of no-see-ums
rose to our faces.

When we came to another river, which ran through the earth
and over large rocks like a strong rush of wind, I drank greedily,
but Segundo said: "The body is like a car and the stomach is the
carburator. Be careful, *señor,* to drink this cold water more slowly.
Let it warm in your mouth before you swallow. Human life is like
a hot bath. One has always to watch the thermometer."

Sun broke cloud. We walked in eerie-bright sunshine, like a
dream. Segundo on the subject of Brunner again: "He is not a
bad man. He is poor like us. But he shares everything. He
provides for us. Why, once he gave us rain gear, free! Can you
believe that? It is hard to believe until you know what kind of
man Brunner really is. He attends to his sick ones. He has never
found gold up here, *señor.* And I do not think he really wishes to
find it, though I would never say this to his face. I know how
much the man loves to come here alone and wander through the
secrets of the *páramo.*"

Segundo knew about a man's true quest.

As we topped what I thought would be just another ridge, I
suddenly saw the base of the mountain. Cerro Hermoso, at last!

Dark patches of fog roved around the treasure mountain like
bodyguards. The upper half of Beautiful Mountain was encased in
evil-grey storm clouds only a mile from me now. I could reach out
and stroke it. I'd never been so close to such dark slick rock
ascending into the unknown.

But even as we four were gazing at Cerro Hermoso, the mist
moved in to shut down our view and we could see only the earth
in front of us. My heart sank to lose such a vista. Ice pelted out
of the sky. Segundo and I and the others slipped bits of bright
blue and red plastic over our backs and huddled near the ground
until the freezing rain eased.

Then we crossed a large valley that took us hours.

◆◆◆

The lake was not visible from the approach, but a dark line in the rock above marked its presence. Below that line, two or three hundred feet, plunged a loud cascade of white spume. Valverde mentioned the waterfall in his *Guide*, but he never described its roar.

Long ago we had passed the path from Píllaro, so now we had to be on the trail that Rumiñahui took when he hid the gold from Pizarro.

We still had an hour at least to climb, so I tried to relax, take it easy. Too close now to ever give up, I thought. After nearly two and a half years of thinking of this moment, I'd reached the mountain, and was ready to stand at the edge of the lake.

I stopped and started and stopped again as I crawled up the bottom of my mountain. The others were far ahead and I was alone. It was very steep. As I climbed near the cascade it seemed to shout at me, and I thought I heard the distinct sound of men's voices, but they could not have been the voices of my guides, who were so far ahead of me I could see them as dark specks moving slowly along the rock above, near the dark line that marked Lake Brunner.

Last night Segundo told me that when he was alone out here he heard voices. Not Spanish voices, but many different people talking, as in a market or a fiesta in a big city. He said he thought it was the winds of the world gathering here, depositing the voices of all the planet's languages. The winds acted like a tape recorder, he said, picking up words and syllables and dumping them here where all the winds of the world converged.

Brunner had a different theory about the voices. He'd told me about the Sabelas:

"There's a story of a lost tribe in these mountains, Pete. I know they exist but have never seen them myself, no? I've seen their footprints. They've checked all my camps over the years and I've heard them talking.

"One day I asked my companion, an old Indian from Píllaro. We heard them talk and I asked, 'What do you think, could this just be Indians from Leyto who've seen the smoke from our camp?' And he replied, 'Well, the Indians there speak Spanish or Quechua, but these voices are speaking another language, *Don Gino*, some tongue I do not know. And our Indians wear shoes and sandals but these are barefoot. Look!' And he pointed to the mud where, by God, a huge print of a man's bare foot had sunk deep into the muck.

"The average size of the Sabelas is about six and a half feet. And they have big feet, very large, like the Yeti. We've also found wads of bark lying in the trail, bark they chew. It's a kind of drug that gives them the strength to keep moving in that terrible climate."

But they never stole anything at all from Brunner, he said. Outside their territory they were not harmful. The Sabelas might walk the whole day on the other side of the thick jungle that Brunner and his men were cutting, following them, but always out of sight. You could hear how they broke through the jungle without machetes, but, Brunner said, "You'll never see them, never. It's very strange. Captain Loch heard them too on his near-fatal trip to the Napo. He thought he was going crazy.

"But I know an Indian who was washing gold near the black Llanganati, the Yana Llanganati which is behind the White Mountain, Cerro Hermoso. He was washing gold when he looked up and saw twenty of them standing very tall and absolutely silent like stone statues up on a cliff looking down. The Indian and his companion took off, leaving everything behind, all their supplies, their equipment.

"And once I found, behind the Cerro Negro, thousands of wild cattle, but my Indians told me they were Jívaro cattle. 'Jívaro' for them means wild Indians, savages. They live, I was told, on the eastern slope of the Eastern Cordillera, these Sabelas, in a region where it slopes down into the Amazon. Some say they use golden jewelry, I don't know.

"But I wouldn't ever go to their valley, never. If someone wants to go there I wouldn't show my writings and maps to him because I don't want it on my conscience, the disappearance of these Indians, the last tribe in the world. Maybe it's one of the only untouchable tribes left. I don't want them to die off like they do in the new Amazon of Brazil, no?

"I'm almost sure that some of the tribe have even come out into civilization to live for short periods, then gone back. But there is no contact, no concrete knowledge of the tribe anywhere, no one who can say unequivocally, 'I have seen the Sabelas.' "

For years they had checked Brunner's camps, but they never stole much and never harmed Brunner or his men. "They kill no one," Brunner told me, "but, if you should come into their valley, well, they won't let you out."

Brunner had a bold way of speaking, rarely fearful, never terrified, but this was one of the few times his voice quavered. Had he had some contact with those Indians? I wondered.

"They have no salt, some say. So they are like drug addicts for the stuff. Once I lost two pounds of salt to the Sabelas."

"But, Gino," I said, "you just told me they steal nothing."

"Well, perhaps only what they need to survive, no?"

I walked ten paces, stopped, caught my breath, kneaded my calves, worked my thighs with my hands, moved another ten or twelve paces, stopped, caught my breath, moved . . . on and on like this for an hour, right up that mountain wall. I could smell wood smoke, an unbelievable pungency in the nostrils which sent warm human messages to the muscles. The others were already in camp.

Only a few hundred feet were left when I spotted three red

flags on a radio antenna Brunner must have set up behind his hut. For helicopters, he'd told me.

Near to being sick without actually vomiting, I topped the ridge and there I was, by God, not two feet from Brunner's huts, which stood around the little inky water of Lake Brunner like igloos. Valverde's Lake! Seven hundred and fifty tons of worked gold and silver under mountains of mud deposited over the years. 14,500 feet above the sea, one thousand feet below the highest of the Cerro's peaks, the four huts all roofed with plastic sheets and pinto grass sat in the gloom like a mirage. Around the huts, the ground was scattered with straw to help absorb the mud, and Brunner had also built trenches so the rains would not wash them away.

Segundo came out of the first hut and said, *"Buenas tardes,* Welcome, *Don* Pedro, to Hotel Brunner."

This was the southwest flank of the mountain, the area I'd studied years ago on topographic maps. The lake seemed far smaller than Brunner's pictures had shown it. And it didn't have the look of a "lake made by hand"; in fact it appeared quite natural and irregular. Of course, it might have changed over the centuries. Below and behind it, in an awesome, black-walled canyon, was a much bigger lake into which a huge cascade fell, also mentioned by Valverde.

When Segundo and the others were out searching for firewood, I secretly pulled out my copy of Spruce's translation of the *Guide* and read again: "Having come through the cañon and gone a good distance beyond, thou wilt perceive a cascade which descends from an offshoot of the Cerro Llanganati and runs into a quaking-bog on the right hand; and without passing the stream in the said bog there is much gold, so that putting in thy hand what thou shalt gather at the bottom is grains of gold."

I had a sudden impulse to begin looking everywhere, but I also did not really know where to start because the *Guide* seemed vague. It said, for instance, that the cascade ran into a quaking bog, but I could see that this cascade fell into a lake; and I wondered if the geology had changed in the four hundred years since Valverde was here.

To dwell in your mind on a place you have never been, to move it over and over in your imagination for years, then to come upon it in the lightheadedness of that altitude, was to make it all unreal. The whole scene looked fake. And I too felt like an imposter, just one of the stage props in this Hollywood movie set. The unreality made me dizzy. The man at the edge of Rumiñahui's lake was not I, but rather only some two-dimensional forgery.

Inside one hut there was a bed of straw, floors of straw, a tiny fireplace already smoking from Juan's industry. It was so dark inside I didn't see Washington, whose hand I almost stepped on. Juan was already cooking tea. I lay down, exhausted, knowing exactly what it meant to be "soaked to the bone."

The doors of the hut faced east, toward the mountain itself. The valley we'd crossed was behind us. After taking three tablets of Alka-Seltzer, changing my clothes and drinking a little tea, I walked with Segundo to the ridge between the lakes. Here was Brunner's "helicopter landing site."

Segundo said, "This is where Hanz was flown out when he broke his legs."

"So, he really did get a helicopter in here!"

"A near impossible feat," said Segundo.

Flaubert once described a misty day as tears in the air. When I looked at the mist rolling over the two lakes, I saw what Flaubert had meant. There was an overwhelming sadness here. The Cerro's peaks were hidden in lugubrious fog.

Segundo said, "So here, *Don* Pedro, is Brunner's very special place on earth. It changed his life, this place we stand on. When I last came up to get him, he had been alone here for a month. He likes it alone. I told him, 'Gino, I have come back up here to take you out for the Christmas holidays.' We spent three Christmases here, you know, but now I thought the old man should be with his friends or family for the holidays. Then he said to me, 'Okay. You're right Segundo. I am sixty-seven years old and yes there is nothing much I can do here now. Too old. And nothing I can accomplish without the help of the Air Force. So I will go back to Quito to get the armed forces behind me, damn it.' And he came down the next day, fifteen hours it took us from here to Camp Two. He is getting old, he can no longer wander these hills anymore. But he comes here for the memories, to get out of that city and to read and think alone."

As Segundo spoke, I could hear the radio antenna which blew in the steady arctic wind: An empty can of sardines and an old can of beans tied to a post clanged together. It was a lonely sound, but it was a man-made noise. Brunner had put those cans there, I thought, to talk to him when he was alone, to remind him of the outside world.

Brunner's fog-infested camp made me feel suddenly very alive as Brunner's head guide and I stood in the gathering sepulchral darkness, the treasure lake fading in twilight at our feet. Gene Brunner would never again go exploring every inch of these mountains, vivaciously making maps and photographs and doing the research of a younger man. He wouldn't have to do it again for he'd already done it. And by this same token I too would not have to come again to this lake, for I was here now.

We drank more tea in the main hut as the weather closed in over us. I lay back on Brunner's comfortable straw bed. Shelves above were lined with canned goods. A table in the center of the hut held books and maps and a storm lantern that Juan lit, and pots and spoons and gas stoves and all the necessary gear for exploration of the White Llanganati Mountain. The hut was cluttered and it made me feel safe. Hotel Brunner indeed!

Segundo said, "There were more huts but they were ransacked and burned by a few men from Píllaro."

Out back, Brunner had built a latrine with a roof over it. On a wood post near the last hut there was a sign with the letters WC and an arrow pointing to a tiny shack where you could relieve yourself in the rain or the snow and stay warm.

That night Washington groaned like a little child. He couldn't sleep, so he found a flashlight and with one of Brunner's magic markers he quietly drew faces on everything he could, his skin, his Marlboro cigarette pack, his hat, his pants, his coins, his boots. Kindergarten crazy.

Outside, the clanging of sardine and bean cans on the post grew cacophonous in the wind that picked up and swept into the hut. The polar loneliness of the place deepened and I felt a chill that clamped down hard on my bones and wouldn't let go. In the light of Washington's flashlight I saw the roof was charred black from smoke. Dark and dank and so smoky in there, it made you cough all night long.

The men from El Triunfo slept on the floor under a few blankets.

I heard that little-bird sound from the night before, and then I knew it wasn't a bird but something inside my head. It chirped all night long and gave me a terrible headache. But at last, I'd made it to the mountain.

CHAPTER 17

◆◆◆◆◆

The following day the rain was heavy. The storm lantern hissed on the table. For breakfast and lunch: tuna and rice. For dinner: rice and beans.

We couldn't go outside because the fog was too thick. Juan and Segundo broke into Quechua, talking about women, I thought, or perhaps about me. Washington was still marking up his clothes with magic marker. Segundo kept going to the door of the hut to peer out, looking up to where the peak of the mountain should have been.

"No, I told you," he would say again, "it will be very hard to see the Cerro in February."

Segundo wondered why Brunner was the only treasure hunter who bothered to build himself a camp. "Gino does not have any whiskey on the table, *señor*, but he does have a good safe warm camp up here. That says something, does it not?" I might have disagreed with Segundo's idea that this camp was warm. Certainly it felt snug and safe, but it was below freezing, day and night.

Our eyes stung from smoke like tear gas, there was such poor ventilation. At one point I couldn't bear it any longer; I ran outside for air. And was immediately swallowed by fog. I stepped only a few paces away from the hut. Finding my way back wasn't so easy. I stumbled near the lake; I grew frightened.

When I found the right hut five minutes later I was breathing hard. Juan had made *máchica*, a candy-like peanut butter. As he handed me the first plate he smiled and said, "Here, have some powdered beer." Everyone laughed.

The bad weather continued but spirits remained high.

Last week in Quito, Brunner had shown me an old photo of Luis Andrade, the man who led Blomberg to the mountains. I still wanted to meet this expert who, some said, was crazy but who had been into the Llanganatis maybe even more times than Brunner himself. I studied the photo and went to the Plaza de la Independencia looking for the old-timer, as I had done many times two years before. I didn't think I'd find him.

I followed the cement paths of the plaza, past little green plots with well-trimmed flowers and bright bushes shaped into hearts. The old men of Quito's past strolled away their afternoons with their hands behind their backs, some limping, some bent over short walking sticks.

Then I saw an old crooked man with a nose like the nose of the man in the photo Brunner showed me. He was limping, his head down. It could have been Andrade, so I followed him. At first I didn't have the courage to ask if he was the treasure hunter. I followed him for ten minutes through the plaza and down a small back street.

Finally I caught up with him and asked meekly, "Excuse me, *señor*, but are you Luis Andrade, the treasure hunter?" I felt stupid.

The old man stiffened. He struggled to turn to face me. When he grinned I thought I'd hit my mark. His head wobbled with palsy, his face florid, his smile expansive. His unshaven bristles were two shades of grey.

He said, "*No, hijo*. I am only Vaca. *Señor* Vaca, who certainly is no treasure hunter."

I told him I was sorry to disturb him. I'd mistaken him for someone else. As I walked away I felt his eyes watching me and I heard the man laugh such a crazy spooky laugh, a tiny, high-pitched little laugh in the parched afternoon, which made me walk a lot faster.

An hour later, back at Brunner's studio, I was told that Andrade's nickname might be Vaca. He was, after all, as strong and stubborn as a cow.

We did not go out at all that second day. The weather got worse and worse. Rain turned to snow, which turned to sleet and back to rain. It wasn't until the next day at three that all precipitation stopped. But the fog remained.

I took my bottle of cane liquor out of my pack and in celebration I offered Juan and Segundo and Washington a drink. Neither of the older men took any, but Washington wanted some. Later, as we all played cards together at a makeshift table on the floor in the close smoky darkness of the little hut (the cards were damp and thick), Washington took huge eager swigs from that strong *aguardiente* bottle. He attacked the liquor with the fury of a man who could not quite reach orgasm.

Segundo looked silently at his nephew, a slightly sardonic expression on his face. We all knew that Washington would be very drunk. Segundo ignored Washington's more and more garrulous comments. The boy who had been so taciturn was now a talker. Segundo pretended not to listen. Segundo said, "Gino Brunner, unlike many rich Ecuadorians who will not eat off the same plate as us poor Indians, is different. He always eats our *máchica* and *pinol* and he tells us, 'Come here, men, you are hungry and I have food for you.' You, too, *Don* Pedro, you also eat with us. This is good, very good."

I went outside and it struck me that I'd completely forgotten about the gold. Somewhere very near was where Blake may have killed Chapman. The whole story was so close now, but I'd let it slip by. In some ways the story felt distant and secondary to the weather. There was a wonderful sense of lost time and extreme loneliness at the lake. For two days I'd been in a trance. Andy had described the feeling well: a bewitching silence. No linear time here. Even Brunner's stories seemed outside the experience itself, as if the stories and the months of my delays and all the people I'd met during my quest, these were nothing compared to the fourteen-thousand-foot silence of time standing still.

Hours passed like lifetimes; hours passed like seconds.

All of a sudden the fog lifted, and the main peak of Cerro Hermoso stood out in the setting sun like an orange tower. Then the other two peaks emerged from the mist. I ran like crazy to fetch Segundo in the hut.

Segundo came running outside and stood by me and said, "Yes yes yes, you are very fortunate today, *Don* Pedro. She is out in all her splendor."

So here they were, the three peaks of Valverde, "on whose declivity there is a lake, made by hand." All three guides and I stood beside Lake Brunner, that drop of ink, with the blazing peaks way up in the sun, pyramids of basalt.

Somewhere up on that mountain was an offering. In the 1960's, after he'd perused the Blake material, when Brunner finally had discovered this lake, he had climbed to the summit and left an offering of onyx to the Sacred Mountain.

CHAPTER 18

◆◆◆◆◆

Blomberg had said, "You never find anything if you don't look for it." But what was I going to do? Look in the bushes for the treasure? No. With all the material I'd collected, I still had no clear idea where it was. Besides, the stories themselves and the people I'd met, these had been my gold and silver.

I was looking for something else. And I wanted to take advantage of my good fortune, as Segundo called it: this fine fine weather we were having all of a sudden.

Segundo and I climbed the mountain together. The sun was brilliant on the peaks. Rumiñahui was favoring me. It was a two-hour difficult climb, lots of loose rock. Way out to the west from the direction of El Triunfo, soared a solitary speck in the sky, a condor, about a mile above the *páramo* we had climbed through. And there, clear to the east, round and smooth was the black Llanganati, a kilometer from us. Behind it was the area of the lost tribe whose giant footprints had been spotted, and whose cattle Brunner had come close to.

Way below us was the rushing Río Topo where Andrés Fernández-Salvador had crashed in 1965, his helicopter plummeting out of the sky onto a little island. The *"socabón"*—Valverde's tunnel—had been discovered when he climbed the slope below Segundo and me. God, how you could see for miles back down into the rolling mountains diminishing far away into the Amazon basin where Loch finally arrived, starving and half mad, his dreams broken.

Segundo told me someday he'd like to walk behind the Black Llanganati, to see if the Sabelas really did exist. Segundo was fearless and I felt an urge to go with him if he made such a trip. No one had ever entered that valley and come back to tell his story.

"And I will go with you, Segundo," I said. He looked surprised and content.

Later, when we got back down to the huts, Washington developed a bad toothache, so Segundo, who said, No no no, to my offering aspirin, packed a large wad of dark wet mud on the tooth and then wrapped it tightly with a cloth so the mud would stay in place. "Earth medicine." Segundo smiled. Remarkably, the ache disappeared. "Aspirin works," Segundo told me later, "only for a few hours. Mud is good for longer." Segundo used mud on all kinds of ailments.

Not for colds, however. My altitude sickness had vanished, but during these few days I'd developed a bad cough. I was thankful that Segundo asked constantly about my health. Segundo himself had been very sick up here four years ago, with pneumonia and a broken arm, he told me. He knew how it felt, so he brought me cups of tea.

My ballpoint pens froze at that altitude, so I had nothing to write with, which was just as well. We'd been on the mountain for three days, but it might have been a century. Segundo continued to open his heart with his philosophy about the future of Ecuador and the corruption of government officials. Juan would roam around the mountain in the fog alone; he also did most of the cooking. Washington, who had had one hell of a hangover the day after his drunk, retreated into complete silence. Only three of us played cards at night by candle. Segundo taught me new games.

Sometimes Segundo and Juan joked about the men they'd

brought here: another German named Moerner (whom Andy had mentioned too) who was a scam artist and who had blown up a large chunk of the mountain in order to find gold he never found; Hanz who died but was liked by all; and a Canadian who had shot off his foot when his shotgun accidentally went off. This last story put Juan in hysterics: to think a man could shoot his foot off with a gun!

But at no time did these men from El Triunfo talk about the treasure. For them it simply did not exist. What mattered was people and work and marriage and stories about people, all kinds of small-town gossip, not some invisible gold. Showing his disappointment in his son-in-law's obsession with treasure hunts, Andy had said, "You see, Peter, there are practical things to attend to in this life of ours. Family, for one, and making money, too. It's not only a life made of some fantastic search for gold."

◆◆◆

Brunner had popcorn in his camp, so one afternoon we cooked it and had a little party on the Cerro, sitting by the ink-black treasure lake.

The weather had turned better than anyone expected. Each day the Cerro came out of hiding. Segundo was very surprised. He even thought I might be special in some way or other. It was the first time he'd seen the summit so many days and so many hours consecutively.

At night the wind drove the tin cans wild. One night, Washington, in an uncharacteristic bravura, rearranged the cans on the post so they created a kind of very human music, a studied percussion of different pitches. He even added a few cans. The three men from El Triunfo huddled together on the floor of the hut, happy in the cold black night, and I in Brunner's bed; all together we laughed hysterically, thinking of the treasure hunter's music-making helicopter antennae. Then sleep quieted the guides and I lay awake thinking how you work hard getting somewhere and you can get so tired doing it that the little commonplace things become big and good, like a cup of tea, a joke, a game of cards. This was a very simple existence out here. Nothing beyond the slopes of the mountain made any difference to us. No El Salvador, no Nicaragua, no arms race, nothing. All things peripheral faded into fog. Mist became central and the warmth of a card game was central. A good joke was the main thing. Laughter in another language was crucial.

Every morning a layer of snow covered the peaks and a delicate patina of sugary frost lay on the ground outside the huts.

When the fog was not too thick, I went alone over the hills in back of camp. With no one around for many many miles, there was such a savage feeling out there.

One day Juan called us from the hut and we raced up the hill. Way below he pointed at two tapir drinking from a small water hole in the mist. The size of small horses, from a distance they looked like giant phantom rodents. On the south side of the ridge above the lake we stood watching that primordial scene. It was the first sign of real wildlife we'd experienced in days.

Clouds moved up the valley very fast and swallowed the little pond, which was like a fleck of mica, and swallowed also the two dark shapes at its edge. Segundo whispered that he used to hunt tapir with a machete, but only when there was no other food.

The fog, as if it knew we had come to watch two of its secret creations, rolled in to cover the scene and then two minutes later rolled back, but the forms had vanished, stolen; apparitions. The cloud had jealously eaten the animals, engulfed them the way a wave takes back starfish on a beach.

Juan was excited he'd found these animals and shown them to me. It was as if he'd been searching for just this scene for me to witness, as if he had looked and looked for some picture to illustrate Segundo's philosophy. He wondered why I hadn't brought a camera. He was as gleeful as a little kid.

◆◆◆

On the fifth night with the storm lantern hissing kerosene on a
nail in the roof and the fireplace smoldering, I sat up in bed and
turned to the others and said, "Do you realize that we all could be
sitting right now only a few yards from the greatest treasure the
world might ever see?"

The men were silent. Then Segundo the spokesman said, "For
me I don't want any part of it. I suffer. I am poor. I am honest. I
live well. I have already told you this, *Señor* Pedro." There was a
father's reprimand in Segundo's tone, as if his son had not learned
his lesson well.

But the next day he told me that I was one of a very few he'd
met in his life who had come to the mountain with confidence in
him and in the others. Often a barrier, especially with gringos, he
said, came between outsiders and his men. But I had not come with
that barrier.

Partly, I had given myself over to their trust for practical
reasons of protection. They were the experts and my safety was
completely in their hands. Also, I'd come to them with a good
recommendation: Brunner was well-liked, so they liked me. But
more than this, I had come unassumingly to them and to the
Cerro. Two years before I would not have come so vulnerably. By
not preparing for this trip, by not plotting it out, this spontaneity
had allowed me to come to them more genuinely, and more
openly perhaps. And that was what they saw.

◆◆◆

Segundo thought a week here sufficient since I wasn't really
looking for anything in particular. "It is safer not to stay too
long," he said. So by the last afternoon, the little snow on the
ground had melted and left us plenty of mud. The clouds had
cleared and the peaks stood out. I wandered around the hills in
back, through the *caspivela,* the candle brush plant which was

everywhere, that famous survival plant that lights even when it's wet. As I walked in the amber late afternoon light, I felt as if I'd never been in such a magic place. It was a painter's paradise. The clouds moved through the horizon, the wind through my hair like the fingers of a soft but moody woman. A distinct clarity existed in this twilight. I was enchanted, I was convinced.

I grew more excited. The energy mounted, wordless, because words refused to describe this new feeling. The peaks all came out at once, a music of mountains. All the gloom of the place melted in the setting sun, and the freezing rain of last night seemed foreign.

And I knew, yes, I had had to come after all. There was nothing particularly courageous about what I had done. I had lived up to an old commitment, which is a sometimes difficult but a very natural thing to do.

I thought, revelations come to us so roundabout, as if through a twisted mirror. Because I did not want to disturb the Inca's gold or because of Diego's and Brunner's initial disappointments, I had been wrong in deciding the trip was unnecessary. There had been one link missing, and I'd come here to discover that link. There had also been my own self-accusation of cowardice, so I had set myself a test.

Here was a place where everything altered. Segundo said that up here each lake was like another, that pieces of *páramo* were so similar to others you could not differentiate between them. He was right, but everything out here was also just a little different from everything else, and if you opened yourself to the changes, to the tiny alterations of mood in the air, you could see all your moments on the mountain as unique as snowflakes; not one could be duplicated. Each second up here was a slightly different combination and mixture of fog, mist, sun, and gloom. Each moment a sharply etched Vermeer, a Turner of bleeding light, a Munch of sexual gloom: gloom and blindness, suddenly followed by glee and vision.

I'd been wrong. No camera would capture this exactly. It was not to be written, either, not imprisoned on a canvas. It was only to be plunged into as I had finally come to commit myself to the mountain after almost three years of thinking about it. And now I knew something even more important. I knew that the wait had been good. If I had made the trek two years ago before Brunner broke his leg, this gift Atahualpa and the Incas were now giving me would not be nearly so monumental.

I went to the ridge where we had spotted the tapir. There on the horizon to the west and the south were four huge, snow-capped volcanoes, Chimborazo at 22,000 feet the highest, with the sun on its broad shoulder sinking directly behind, primordial Tungurahua, and El Altar like a tooth, and then way to the south was Sangay, still active and smoking as in a nightmare.

Yes, a spell had come over me, but it was not evil, not the evil that some men bring with them to the Llanganatis. I had come for the magic and the beauty of the place, nothing more. That was the fruition of three years' work.

The Incas knew the magic was here, and Brunner came here for it.

I tried to write all this in my notebook, but couldn't. I tried to draw the mountains on the skyline, a bleeding orange sunset, but could not.

When I turned, I saw the peak of the Cerro breathing out a new layer of mist. Within minutes it had blotted itself out and I hurried back to the huts before the fog shut down the *páramo*.

The hut was an oven of smoke. I didn't tell the others what I'd felt outside. How could you translate it? Besides, those men lived with the magic; they knew it just as they knew how to use their machetes. It was an extension of their lives; it was their lives.

Before I went for a short walk that night, I watched Segundo quietly whittling a piece of wood. I wanted to thank him. He was the one who had opened my eyes, for he knew I was a pilgrim. If I had not come alone, if I had come with other gringos, even if I had come with Brunner, would I have talked with Segundo as I had? No, most likely not. Lilian knew: It was good to come alone.

I'd come through the stories of others, through the mud and the pain of cramping legs, through the mist, to the sun. I came through the dreamers and the failures, through waiting and thinking and thinking and doubts. Then came the unexpected. My head was clear, though it was so dark outside not even the lake was visible from the door of the hut.

Tomorrow we were leaving.

I stepped out into the black cold. The capricious weather had cleared. The wind was brisk and the cans on the antennae posts banged out Brunner's symphony. I could hear Juan inside the hut already snoring.

Outside, so rare for Cerro Hermoso, a crystal-clear night filled my head with the wonder of the stars in that bowl of black silhouetted rock. The three peaks, dark and lovely, stood out like noble gods way above. Standing on the brink of Lake Brunner, I sensed the treasure was that very bowl of stars in the cold wind ringed by the magic of the Incas who had come here to mine the metal that was so much more than money.

Then the moon came up over the ridge and everything was swimming in silver, cool, blue, eerie light. And it occurred to me before I stepped back into the cozy smoke of our hut, about those stars up there and the moon between the peaks, that the stars were all the Incan subjects who ever lived and that the moon was Atahualpa himself come back from his murder by Pizarro, and that all the Incan people were hiding here in the Llanganatis, protected forever by Cerro Hermoso, shielded by cloud forest, earthquakes, freezing rain, misery, *páramo,* and fear.

Next day when we left, the clouds had returned and closed down all vision. All we could hear was the strange invisible roar of the cascade tumbling out of Lake Brunner. We weaved up and down and over valleys and canyons in the heavy cold rain, mist and gloom prevailing. Before I topped the last big ridge, I looked back over my shoulder but the mountain and the lake were hidden in a bodyguard of cloud, as if the Inca god had already granted me enough.

EPILOGUE

◆◆◆◆◆

Four years later the following letter was delivered to my house in Garrison, New York, where I had settled down to write about my travels in South America:

October 10 1986

Dear Mr. Lourie,

I obtained your address from my father-in-law's note-book. He was Eugene Brunner of Quito, Ecuador. Eugene died on June 3rd of 1984 and we are attempting to publish his book, "Ecuador y sus Tesoros."

Any information you might be able to supply regarding your associations with him would be of great help.

Thank you for your attention and reply.

Sincerely,
Steven J. Charbonneau

I read that letter at least three times before I could accept that Brunner was dead. Somewhere in the back of my mind I had always believed if Brunner ever died I would feel his death, like a distant tremor, the way a twin will sometimes know when his sibling is in trouble.

But on that day in June 1984, I remember feeling nothing remarkable. I only thought Brunner was alive in Quito, hard at work, earnestly seeking financial assistance for his next expedition.

Holding Charbonneau's letter in my hand, I remembered coming home in 1982 from my trek: that long dump-truck ride down from El Triunfo, Indians and chickens, dogs and corn sacks, all packed together in the open air on that treacherous windy mountain road with Tungurahua rising out of the land in front of us like some perverse Olympian volcanic mushroom, and then a bus from Patate to Ambato, and a bottle of whiskey I bought and passed around, and finally a van to Quito, where I dropped my gear at a hotel and went straight to Brunner's place. I ran into his office and embraced him. I remember his smile, his deep happiness that I had reached his camp on Cerro Hermoso. "So you have seen Lake Brunner!" "Yes, yes, Gino. Here is your equipment," I said. "I can't thank you enough." I hugged him again. I remember his words were, "Now we can get the Army behind us, Pete. You know the terrain, so we need helicopters and men and ropes." He smiled a big smile, but I did not want to linger, for I had had from Gino the thing I wanted, and so I left him for my hotel to shower, and sleep for a day before flying home to New York. I told him I'd be in touch, but it was the old lie. I knew I'd probably never see him again.

Now I felt guilty for abandoning him. He had given me so much. I had written two letters. He did not respond to the first; he knew I had no money to invest. My second letter reached Quito after he was already dead.

It was impossible to keep in touch, for I'd put Quito behind me and hadn't been out of the U.S.A. since then. I have no great desire to travel much now. I am married and life is very different. Sure, I'd like my wife to see Ecuador one day, but we're thinking about children, which will make travel difficult.

It's strange how I've changed.

But after reading Steve Charbonneau's letter I called him in Florida. I had to know the details about Brunner's death, because there had been that famous Quitenian fortune-teller many years ago who had said that Brunner would have a series of terrible accidents until he was sixty-six, but if he lived through them, he would live to ninety. He was already sixty-seven when I left him in 1982. And Blomberg had said, "Brunner will go on forever."

As I dialed the number, I felt a twisting in my chest.

But Mr. Charbonneau had a kind, gentle voice. He said, "The search is over. We are going to take it out now. My father-in-law has pinpointed the treasure ..."

"But ..." I started to say. But these were Brunner's exact words, I could have told him, but stopped myself.

Charbonneau said that he himself had never met Brunner but that all his papers and books had been passed on to him because his wife's mother, Brunner's second wife, had gotten them when he died.

"Your father-in-law and I were pretty close for a short time, anyway," I said. "I cared for him a great deal."

◆◆◆

I remembered well that first day I met Eugene Brunner. He was holding a manuscript he'd written about Spruce and he said, "All this will go to someone when I die. So my work will not be lost. I will carry on, even when I'm dead." That was six years ago. I'd thought he was going to give those papers to me. But I was wrong. Mr. Charbonneau had gotten Brunner's papers. Not I.

And Charbonneau told me that for two years after he got all Brunner's material he had not taken it seriously, but that recently when he looked at it one more time, he suddenly saw that Brunner had been right. "The old man knew exactly where the gold was. He was no flake." Brunner had done so much work. And now, Charbonneau told me, "I'm throwing in the towel here in Florida and my wife and I are moving to Ecuador. I suppose I'll become another Eugene." Charbonneau laughed. I could tell this idea of assuming another man's persona and inheriting a reputation pleased him.

"I'm ninety percent certain of the gold's position. Thanks to Eugene—I've put it all together."

"Will you live in Quito?" I asked.

"My family will. I'll be living in the same country, but in the Llanganatis most of the time." He laughed again, quietly.

"I'm not so sure they are the same country," I said. "Have you been in yet?"

"No, but we're waiting for an investor to give us money."

"When are you actually leaving?"

"Any day now. As soon as we get the money."

I did not tell Mr. Charbonneau how much like his father-in-law he really did sound.

"How long will your first expedition be for?"

"Thirty to sixty days. And if that doesn't work, I'll try a different strategy."

"Will you look under the lake or in a cave?"

"My father-in-law was involved with so many different treasures, he probably confused a lot of people about that issue." Charbonneau meant me, for one. "From his maps and things I can say that it isn't a lake *or* a cave, but one and the same thing. If you don't look at it in the proper way, it's confusing."

"Do you know Andrés Fernández-Salvador?" I asked.

"No. Who's he?"

For some reason I didn't want to tell him. I merely said, "Just another treasure hunter. I wish you luck."

"After getting Brunner's material, knowing exactly where the gold is, to not go looking for the treasure would be like walking away from a sure bet . . ."

"Yes, of course . . . What kind of investor are you looking for?"

"Well, I don't want ten thousand grandmothers donating ten dollars apiece. I'm looking for one person. And we're doing all this in conjunction with various mining companies because Eugene found the Llanganatis rich in ore . . . Have you met Mike Dyott, the son of Commander George Dyott?"

"Yes. Once, years ago. Why?" I wondered.

"I think he has information, but he won't share it."

After my first trip to Ecuador in 1980, one hot July day I had met Michael Dyott. We had lunch in Shakespeare's, a restaurant in New York's Greenwich Village that no longer exists. It was more than ninety degrees and humid even with the air-conditioning. I remember a quiet man with intent eyes, about forty-five years old. He wore a neatly trimmed beard. His voice, too, was soft and gentle like Charbonneau's—perhaps even timid. We talked for four hours. He explained he was going to make his first trip to the Llanganatis. He never really had known his father. He'd grown up with his mother on Long Island and now he was a chemical engineer in California.

While we talked, Dyott had taken notes. He'd never heard of the Valverde *Guide,* nor Spruce, nor Brunner, nor Andy, nor any of the others. He hardly knew the story at all, but I could tell that from that hot-summer-city day onward he would be hooked, although he told me he only wanted to investigate some information that had come to him by way of his father's papers.

In 1967 he had gone to Ecuador once to see his father, who was very old then, but the commander did not mention the treasure. Perhaps he hadn't wanted to infect his son with the

treasure contagion. Then, after his father died, Mike read his
father's Ecuadorian journals and found a large segment—from
April 1947 to June 1949—missing. That was how he first got
hooked by the story: It was the mystery of those missing pages
that he wanted to solve. Now he was trying to squeeze as much
information out of me as he could.

I asked Mike about those papers. He thought they might be in
Ecuador still. He would find out. Dyott was talking about his
father's accomplishments when suddenly I felt the aura of this
treasure story engulf him like a verbal mist, as if all my words—
all the stories I'd heard and was now relating to him—surrounded and captured him, as if I was now the one who could
infect others.

He paused for a moment, then said, with a curious, naive
self-confidence:

"I don't know. If I find the treasure, I'm worried about getting
my share. The government will want it all. But I've always had
luck in finding things. As a kid I could always find a baseball in
the bushes within seconds. Or in a town, if I knew a person was
living there but didn't have his address, I could just drive in my
car and pretty soon I'd find that person. Luck, maybe. I have a
knack for finding things."

I remember thinking to myself, Baseballs in the bushes?

Then he said, "Tell me what that terrain is like."

And I told him that I hadn't yet been in, a confession that
stung me, for it was a painful reminder that I'd left Ecuador
prematurely.

◆◆◆

Mike Dyott wrote me a few letters after he made it to
Cerro Hermoso a year later. But he was secretive and apparently Brunner's son-in-law had contacted him and found
him even more so. How fast one becomes an expert on treasure.

The more Dyott delved into the subject, the deeper the secrecy, perhaps.

"But," Charbonneau told me on the phone, "Dyott is not free with his information. In fact, before Eugene died, when Mike Dyott first met Brunner in Quito, Dyott just got up in the middle of the conversation. Suddenly he was leaving, and Eugene asked, 'But where are you going?' and Dyott said, 'To the Llanganatis, of course.' 'But,' Eugene asked, 'do you know where they are?' 'No,' said Dyott, but left anyway. It was then that Eugene knew that Mike Dyott had some of his father's 'Llanganati papers' from that 1947–49 journal.

"So Mike Dyott has his own special information, but he's a loner. When he goes to Cerro Hermoso he never even takes guides, but goes all alone. Have you heard of someone named Moerner?"

"People used to talk about him . . ."

"A con is what he is. He was in the mountains again this year."

"Mr. Charbonneau," I asked, "who's going in these days?"

"Well, besides Moerner and Dyott there's Bill Johnson of Grand Rapids, Michigan. You heard about his expedition last year: They lost a man. An American died. But Johnson has formed a company to collect more funds for another expedition. The death of his man in there, however, has made it very difficult now for foreigners to get permission to enter the Llanganatis. He's made it difficult for all of us. The Ecuadorian government doesn't want gringos dying in there. It's no good for public relations. No . . . Not one of the original people is still looking. After Eugene, there are only us, the next generation—Dyott and myself. I've done all the work and now I'm ready to take it out . . . We're going in April or May . . ."

"But those are bad months!"

"That's not the information I have. Eugene used to go any month."

"Yes, but he was Eugene Brunner. He was different."

I had that conversation in April 1987 when Charbonneau was ready to leave for Ecuador, to sell his house and move permanently to a country he did not know. I wished him safety and luck, but I knew better than to get involved myself.

I'm teaching now, and writing and starting a family of my own. Not really thinking so much about that treasure anymore, except, of course, when suddenly on a crisp clear Quito-like spring day like today, I remember Brunner. Or when winter clouds lower onto the Hudson Highlands turning everything into Llanganati grey, then I remember Brunner is dead, which makes me sad, for I loved Brunner and his magic, the magic I want to keep alive for as long as I live.

One last thing Charbonneau told me that must have come as a mystery to him but was no real mystery to me:

"It was very strange how Eugene died," Charbonneau said on the phone. "He was sixty-nine years old and in good health. He was about to make another trip into the mountains, this time to take the gold out. But when he went into the hospital for a routine checkup, he never came out. His secretary, you know, was a Soviet/Peruvian spy. And the State Department has told us she's fled to Austria."

Brunner apparently had married Steven Charbonneau's mother-in-law only two months before he died. When he died mysteriously in the hospital only a few days before his final expedition, all Brunner's boxes were delivered to his new wife's house, and so into the hands of Steve Charbonneau.

But looking carefully into those notes, maps, photos, and manuscripts, it was discovered that some important pages were missing. Charbonneau believes they were stolen by Brunner's secretary before she fled the country. Portions of two chapters from Brunner's book were also missing, and certain stories stopped mid-sentence.

But for me those stories will go on living in full because I heard them from the source once upon a time long ago.

APPENDIX

◆◆◆◆◆

Guide of Valverde as translated by Richard Spruce in *Notes of a Botanist on the Amazon and Andes:*

Placed in the town of Pillaro, ask for the farm of Moya, and sleep (the first night) a good distance above it; and ask there for the mountain of Guapa, from whose top, if the day be fine, look to the east, so that thy back be towards the town of Ambato, and from thence thou shalt perceive the three Cerros Llanganati, in the form of a triangle, on whose declivity there is a lake, made by hand, into which the ancients threw the gold they had prepared for the ransom of the Inca [Atahualpa] when they heard of his death. From the same Cerro Guapa thou mayest see also the forest, and in it a clump of Sangurimas standing out of the said forest, and another clump which they call Flechas (arrows), and these clumps are the principal mark for the which thou shalt aim, leaving them a little on the left hand. Go forward from Guapa in the direction and with the signals indicated, and a good way ahead, having passed some cattle-farms, thou shalt come on a wide morass, over which thou must cross, and coming out on the other side, thou shalt see on the left hand a short way off a jucál on a hill-side, through which thou must pass. Having got through the jucál, thou wilt see two small lakes called "Los Anteojos" (the spectacles), from having between them a point of land like to a nose.

From this place thou mayest again descry the Cerros Llanganati, the same as thou sawest them from the top of Guapa, and I warn thee to leave the said lakes on the left, and that in front of the point or "nose" there is a plain, which is the sleeping-place. There thou must leave thy horses, for they can go no farther. Following now on foot in the same direction, thou shalt come on a great black lake [Yanacocha], the which leave on thy left hand, and beyond it seek to descend along the hill-side in such a way that thou mayest reach a ravine, down which comes a waterfall: and here thou shalt find a bridge of three poles, or if it do not still exist thou shalt put another in the most convenient place and pass over it. And having gone on a little way in the forest, seek out the hut which served to sleep in or the remains of it. Having passed the night there, go on thy way the following day through the forest in the same direction, till thou reach another deep dry ravine, across which thou must throw a bridge and pass over it slowly and cautiously, for the ravine is very deep; that is, if thou succeed not in finding the pass which exists. Go forward and look for the signs of another sleeping-place, which I assure thee, thou canst not fail to see in the fragments of pottery and other marks, because the Indians are continually passing along there. Go on thy way, and thou shalt see a mountain which is all of margasitas (pyrites), the which leave on thy left hand, and I warn thee that thou must go round it in this fashion ⌒. On this side thou wilt find a pajonál (pasture) in a small plain, which having crossed thou wilt come on a cañon between two hills, which is the Way of the Inca. From thence as thou goest along thou shalt see the entrance of the socabón (tunnel), which is in the form of a church porch. Having come through the cañon and gone a good distance beyond, thou wilt perceive a cascade which descends from an offshoot of the Cerro Llanganati and runs into a quaking-bog on the right hand; and without passing the stream in the said bog there is much gold, so that putting in thy hand what thou shalt gather at the bottom is grains of gold. To ascend the mountain, leave the bog and go along to the right, and pass above the cascade, going round the offshoot of the mountain. And if by chance the mouth of the socabón be closed with certain herbs which they call "Salvaje," remove them, and thou wilt find the entrance. And on the left-hand side of the mountain thou mayest see the "Guayra" (for thus the ancients called the furnace where they founded metals), which is nailed with golden nails. And to reach the third mountain, if thou canst not pass in front of the socabón, it is the same thing to pass behind it, for the water of the lake falls into it.

If thou lose thyself in the forest, seek the river, follow it on the right bank; lower down take to the beach, and thou wilt reach the cañon in such sort that, although thou seek to pass it, thou wilt not find where; climb, therefore, the mountain on the right hand, and in this manner thou canst by no means miss thy way.